For Elizabeth Gould in
honor of her achievement,
with my best wishes,
Walter Harding

THE SAMUEL ROWSE CRAYON PORTRAIT OF THOREAU, 1854.
See Eben J. Loomis' comments, pp. 179-180.

THOREAU
as Seen by His Contemporaries

edited by
Walter Harding
State University College
Geneseo, New York

DOVER PUBLICATIONS, INC., NEW YORK

Published in Canada by General Publishing Company, Ltd.,
30 Lesmill Road, Don Mills, Toronto, Ontario.
Published in the United Kingdom by Constable and Company, Ltd.,
10 Orange Street, London WC2H 7EG.

This Dover edition, first published in 1989, is a revised republication of the work originally published by Holt, Rinehart and Winston, New York, 1960, under the title *Thoreau: Man of Concord*. The following changes have been made for the Dover edition. Twenty-six documents, a new Preface, several new Biographical Notes, and an Index to the entire volume have been added. The table of Contents, List of Documents, and Bibliography have been revised. "A Word to the Student," now retitled "Preface to the First Edition," has had its last three paragraphs deleted. A few typographical errors have been corrected. And two Appendixes, "Selections from Thoreau's Writings" and "Suggested Topics for Papers," have been deleted.

Manufactured in the United States of America
Dover Publications, Inc., 31 East 2nd Street, Mineola, N.Y. 11501

Library of Congress Cataloging-in-Publication Data

Thoreau as seen by his contemporaries / edited by Walter Harding.
  p.   cm.
Rev. ed. of: Thoreau, man of Concord. 1960.
Includes bibliographical references.
ISBN 0-486-26160-3
1. Thoreau, Henry David, 1817–1862—Biography—Sources. 2. Thoreau, Henry David, 1817–1862—Contemporaries. 3. Authors, American—19th century—Biography. I. Harding, Walter Roy, 1917– . II. Thoreau, man of Concord.
PS3053.T49   1989
818'.309—dc20
  [B]   89-37221
                                                                   CIP

TO THE MEMBERS OF
The Thoreau Society

Preface to the Dover Edition

THIS VOLUME, first published in 1960 (under the title *Thoreau: Man of Concord*), when the popularity of the "casebook" method of teaching research composition in our college classes was at its height, has been for many years out of print. But there has been a growing demand for it, not as a casebook, but for its portrait of Thoreau as seen by his contemporaries. Well-worn paperback copies of the first edition have been regularly bringing twenty-five dollars on the second-hand-book market on those rare occasions when they can be found at all. It therefore has seemed worthwhile to bring the volume back into print and to bring it up to date by adding appropriate material that has come to light since 1960.

The major new discovery has been the notes that Dr. Edward Waldo Emerson, Ralph Waldo Emerson's son, gathered, just before and just after the turn of the century, in interviewing those people in Concord and neighboring towns who could still remember Thoreau personally. Some of this material he presented in his *Henry Thoreau as Remembered by a Young Friend* (1917), excerpts from which were included in the 1960 edition of the present book. But in working on my biography of Thoreau, *The Days of Henry Thoreau* (Knopf, 1965; Dover, 1982), I was impelled to ask Raymond Emerson, Edward Waldo's son, if by any chance there were among the vast Emerson family papers any of Dr. Emerson's notes for his book. After a long search in the attic of their Concord home, Mrs. Emerson found not only her father-in-law's Thoreau notes, but also the diaries of her own father, John Shepard Keyes, which also included further reminiscences of Thoreau. With their typical generosity, the Emersons gave me complete access to all these manuscripts. And so, more than a hundred years after Thoreau's death, I was able to include in the *Days* and in my *Henry David Thoreau: A Profile* (Hill & Wang, 1971) an astonishing amount of new material. Appropriate sections from these two books are thus reprinted here and to them are added further Edward Emerson notes that have not hitherto seen print. To the Edward Emerson and Keyes material I have added other miscellaneous writings that have turned up in various places.

One may very well ask, Has all such material about Thoreau hidden in attics, on library shelves, and in historical-society files now been located? I am certain it has not. New material keeps turning up, often in the most unexpected places, and I am certain it will continue to do so. I therefore urge all students of Thoreau to continue the search for new material about him that will add to our knowledge of that challenging and enigmatic man.

I would also like to call to the attention of my readers the existence of The Thoreau Society, of which I have for nearly fifty years had the privilege of being secretary. It publishes its *Thoreau Society Bulletin* quarterly and annually holds a meeting in Concord on the Saturday nearest to Thoreau's birthday (July 12). All Thoreau enthusiasts are cordially invited to join. They may learn further details by writing either to the society at 156 Belknap Street, Concord, MA 01742, or directly to me at the State University College, Geneseo, NY 14454.

In bringing out this new updated edition of this book, I have dropped out as no longer appropriate the selections from Thoreau's writings and the suggested topics for student papers included in the original edition. In their place I have added the new material spoken of above, I have expanded the biographical notes on the authors to cover the new authors included, and I have added a comprehensive index.

For permission to reprint the new material in this edition, I am indebted to The Thoreau Society, Hill & Wang, *American Heritage*, the University of Illinois Press, and the late Mr. and Mrs. Raymond Emerson. I wish also to express my appreciation to Thomas Blanding, Kenneth Cameron, Bradley Dean, Kent Ljungquist, and Richard O'Connor for calling to my attention new material for this volume.

WALTER HARDING

State University College
Geneseo, New York

Preface to the First Edition

PEOPLE SELDOM REACT TO Henry David Thoreau mildly. For a century his writings have been a center of controversy, with his partisans ardently hailing him as *the* major American writer and their opponents vehemently denouncing him as a second-rate imitator of Emerson. To some, his philosophy of simplicity offers the only antidote to the evils of modern civilization; to others, his ideas seem nothing more than a reversion to primitivism and a negation of the hard-won victories of man in his battle against his environment.

Here, however, we are going to deal only in part with Thoreau's ideas. We will concentrate chiefly on Thoreau the man. And here again we find him a center of controversy. His contemporaries reacted no less violently to Thoreau as a person than our contemporaries do today to his ideas. In fact, so violently did they react that their descendants in Concord, Massachusetts, his home town, today—a century later—are still debating his personality as though he were still alive. I know of one dear old lady who once each year makes a pilgrimage to Sleepy Hollow Cemetery in Concord where Thoreau is buried, and there, after laying wreaths of flowers on the nearby graves of Emerson and Hawthorne, turns to Thoreau's grave, and shaking her fist, says, "None for you, you dirty little atheist." In direct contrast is the Concord librarian who each day, as soon as the library is opened, sets out on a pedestal Thoreau's journal opened to the entry for a century ago that day for all the patrons of the library to read.

Because his contemporaries reacted so violently to Thoreau, they often took particular pains to write down their opinions. Thus, despite the fact that Thoreau never in his lifetime achieved anything approaching national or international prominence, as did for example his neighbors and friends Ralph Waldo Emerson and Nathaniel Hawthorne, nonetheless, upon searching the records—the journals, diaries, letters, autobiographies, memoirs, and even the newspapers of Thoreau's day—we are able to find a large body of contemporary opinion on Thoreau's personality. I use the word "opinion" advisedly, for most of the comment is highly opinionated either for or against Thoreau, depending of course upon the reactions of the writer. Although at times we might be tempted to dismiss opinionated statements as invalid, it is well to remember what Thoreau himself once said of such statements about one of his own heroes, Sir Walter Raleigh: "The enthusiastic and often extravagant, but always hearty and emphatic, tone in which he is spoken of by his contemporaries is not the least remarkable fact about him, and it does not matter much whether the current stories are true or not, since they at least prove his reputation." (*Sir Walter Raleigh* [Boston: Bibliophile Society, 1905], p. 18)

Thus Thoreau offers a unique opportunity to face in exaggerated form a problem that all biographers, all historians, in fact all who would call themselves scholars, have to face in one form or another whenever they try to re-create accurately a portrait of the past—or, indeed, of the present—namely, where in the center of controversy does the truth lie? When we have violently differing reports by eyewitnesses, how do we decide who is telling the truth? Or, to speak more accurately, because we do not wish to accuse anyone of deliberately falsifying the record, how do we achieve anything approaching an accurate portrait in the welter of controversial confusion?

Therefore, taking advantage of this unique opportunity, I have gathered together into this volume a selection from the multitude of eyewitness reports on Thoreau by his contemporaries. To include all that are available would produce both unnecessary repetition and a volume far too unwieldy in size. In making a selection I have tried to choose representative pieces that give the student a fairly accurate picture of the whole body of material through which I have searched. (It should be noted that in a *few* cases, since the material was not otherwise available, I have had to use a secondary source, but these are still always based on eyewitness reports.)

To simulate as closely as possible in this volume the problem the student would face in the library were he to begin original research on the subject, I have arranged the material in chronological order according to its date of publication. Thus a letter written, for example, in 1837, but not published until 1860, will be found under the latter date.

I have taken the selections verbatim from the sources, occasionally inserting a *sic,* always within brackets, to point out an error, typographical or otherwise, in the source. A bracketed identification or correction is occasionally inserted to clear up an obscure pronoun reference or factual error. I have also taken the liberty of abridging many of the selections to eliminate irrelevant or repetitious material; in each such instance I have inserted the customary ellipsis (. . .). Aside from these minor exceptions, the transcriptions are verbatim.

Each item is followed by a standard bibliographical note (based on Kate L. Turabian, *A Manual for Writers of Term Papers, Theses and Dissertations* [Chicago: University of Chicago Press, 1955]) giving the publication data. In those cases where the material has been taken from more than one page of the source, the page breaks are indicated by bracketed insertions—for example, [p. 62]—within the text, the page numeral referring to the material *above* the insertion.

Acknowledgments

IT IS IMPOSSIBLE TO ACKNOWLEDGE fully all my indebtedness for help in compiling the material in this volume. For the nineteen years that I have been secretary of the Thoreau Society, the members of that society have kept a constant stream of Thoreauviana flowing over my desk, and many of the selections in this book have been chosen from that stream. But I am particularly indebted to two vice presidents of the society, Mrs. Herbert Hosmer and Mrs. Caleb Wheeler, both of Concord, for aid in identifying some of the more obscure authors I have used. For permission to use unpublished manuscript materials, I am indebted to the Concord Free Public Library, Miss Edith Guerrier, Mr. and Mrs. Herbert Hosmer, and Mrs. Henry J. Wheelwright. For permission to reprint copyrighted materials, I am indebted to Professor Raymond Adams, *The Atlantic Monthly*, Beacon Press, Boston Public Library, Bruce Humphries, Inc., Professor Kenneth W. Cameron, Columbia University Library, Columbia University Press, Thomas Y. Crowell Company, the Ralph Waldo Emerson Memorial Association, Professor Wendell Glick, Miss Edith Guerrier, Harper & Brothers, Harvard University Press, Houghton Mifflin Company, Macmillan Company, the *New England Quarterly*, Oxford University Press, G. P. Putnam's Sons, the late Mr. Francis Sanborn, Mrs. Eleanor Conway Sawyer, Professor Odell Shepard, the Social Circle in Concord, the Thoreau Society, and Miss Gertrude Traubel.

Contents

List of Documents

[The following documents have been added to the Dover edition.]

And such I knew, a forest seer,
A minstrel of the natural year,
Foreteller of the vernal ides,
Wise harbinger of spheres and tides,
A lover true, who knew by heart
Each joy the mountain dales impart;
It seemed that Nature could not raise
A plant in any secret place,
In quaking bog, on snowy hill,
Beneath the grass that shades the rill,
Under the snow, between the rocks,
In damp fields known to bird and fox.
But he would come in the very hour
It opened in its virgin bower,
As if a sunbeam showed the place,
And tell its long-descended race.
It seemed as if the breezes brought him,
It seemed as if the sparrows taught him;
As if by secret sight he knew
Where, in far fields, the orchis grew.
Many haps fall in the field
Seldom seen by wishful eyes,
But all her shows did Nature yield,
To please and win this pilgrim wise.
He saw the partridge drum in the woods;
He heard the woodcock's evening hymn;
He found the tawny thrushes' broods;
And the shy hawk did wait for him;
What others did at distance hear,
And guessed within the thicket's gloom,
Was shown to this philosopher,
And at his bidding seemed to come.

—Ralph Waldo Emerson, "Woodnotes," *Poems* (Boston: Munroe, 1847), p. 44.

We are continually receiving letters from young gentlemen who deem themselves born to enlighten the world in some way—to "strike the sounding lyre," or from the Editorial tripod dispense wisdom and guidance to an instructed and admiring world. These generally want to know why they cannot be employed in our establishment, or find a publisher for their poems, or a chance in some shape to astonish mankind and earn a livelihood by letters.—To this large and increasing class, we wish to propound one question: "Suppose all who desire to live by Literature or Trade could find places, who would hoe the needful corn or dig the indispensable potatoes?"— But we purposed in beginning to ask their attention to the following extract from a private letter we have just received from a very different sort of literary youth [Thoreau]—a thorough classical scholar true poet (though he rarely or never wrote verses,) and never sought to make a livelihood by his writings, though there are not six men in America who can surpass them. We feel indeed honored by his friendship; and in the course of a private letter we have just received from him he casually says:

"For the last five years, I have supported myself solely by the labor of my hands. I have not received one cent from any other source, and this has cost me so little time—say, a month in the Spring and another in the Autumn—doing the coarsest work of all kinds, that I have probably enjoyed more leisure for literary pursuits than any contemporary. For more than two years past, I have lived alone in the woods, in a good plastered and shingled house entirely of my own building, earning only what I wanted, and sticking to my proper work. The fact is, Man need not live by the sweat of his brow —unless he sweats easier than I do—he needs so little. For two years and two months, all my expenses have amounted to but 27 cents a week, and I have fared gloriously in all respects. If a man must have money—and he needs but the smallest amount—the true and independent way to earn it is by day-labor with his hands at a dollar a day. I have tried many ways and can speak from experience.

"Scholars are apt to think themselves privileged to complain as if their lot were a peculiarly hard one. How much have we heard about the attainment of knowledge under difficulties—of poets starving in garrets—of literary men depending on the patronage of the wealthy, and finally dying mad! It is time that men sang another song.—There is no reason why the scholar, who professes to be a little wiser than the mass of men, should not do his work in the ditch occasionally, and, by means of his superior wisdom, make much less suffice for him. A wise man will not be unfortunate. How otherwise would you know that he was not a fool?"

—We trust our friend will pardon the liberty we have taken in printing the foregoing, since we are sure of effecting signal good thereby. We have no idea of making a hero of him. Our object is simply to shame the herd of pusillanimous creatures who whine out their laziness in bad verses, and execrate the stupidity of publishers and readers who will not buy these maudlin effusions at the paternal estimate of their value, and thus spare them the dire necessity of doing something useful for a living. It is only *their* paltriness that elevates our independent friend above the level of ordinary manhood, and whenever they shall rise to the level of true self-respect, his course will be no longer remarkable.

"What!" says one of them, "Do you mean that every one must hoe corn or swing the sledge?—that no life is useful or honorable but one of rude manual toil?"—No, Sir; we say no such thing.—If any one is sought out, required, demanded, for some vocation specially intellectual, let him embrace it and live by it. But the general rule is that Labor—that labor which produces food and clothes and shelter —is every man's duty and destiny, for which he should be fitted, in which he should be willing to do his part manfully. But let him study, and meditate, and cultivate his nobler faculties as he shall find opportunity; and whenever a career of intellectual exertion shall open before him, let him embrace it if he be inclined and qualified. But to coin his thoughts into some marketable semblance, disdain useful labor of the hands because he has a facility of writing, and go crying his mental wares in the market, seeking to exchange them for bread and clothes—this is most degrading and despicable. Shall not the world outgrow such shabbiness?

—[Horace Greeley], "A Lesson for Young Poets," *New York Tribune,* May 25, 1848.

∞ ∝

> There comes [Thoreau], for instance; to see him's rare sport,
> Tread in Emerson's tracks with legs painfully short;
> How he jumps, how he strains, and gets red in the face,
> To keep step with the mystagogue's natural pace!
> He follows as close as a stick to a rocket,
> His fingers exploring the prophet's each pocket.
> Fie, for shame, brother bard; with good fruit of your own,
> Can't you let Neighbor Emerson's orchards alone?

—James Russell Lowell, *A Fable for Critics* (New York: Putnam, 1848), p. 21.

Mr. Thoreau, of Concord, gave his auditors a lecture on Wednesday evening, sufficiently *Emersonian* to have come from the great philosopher himself. We were reminded of Emerson continually. In thought, style and delivery, the similarity was equally obvious. There was the same keen philosophy running through him, the same jutting forth of "brilliant edges of meaning" as Gilfillan has it. Even in tone of voice, Emerson was brought strikingly to the ear; and, in personal appearance also, we fancied some little resemblance. The close likeness between the two would almost justify a charge of plagiarism, were it not that Mr. Thoreau's lecture furnished ample proof of being a native product, by affording all the charm of an original. Rather than an imitation of Emerson, it was the unfolding of a like mind with his; as if the two men had grown in the same soil and under the same culture.

The reader may remember having recently seen an article from the N. Y. Tribune, describing the recluse life led by a scholar, who supported himself by manual labor, and on a regime which cost only *twenty-seven cents a week,* making it necessary to labor but six weeks to provide sufficient of the necessaries of life to serve the balance of the year. Mr. Thoreau is the hero of that story—although he claims no heroism, considering himself simply an economist.

The subject of this lecture was Economy, illustrated by the experiment mentioned.—This was done in an admirable manner, in a strain of exquisite humor, with a strong under current of delicate satire against the follies of the times. Then there were interspersed observations, speculations, and suggestions upon dress, fashions, food, dwellings, furniture, etc., etc., sufficiently queer to keep the audience in almost constant mirth, and sufficiently wise and new to afford many good practical hints and precepts.

The performance has created "quite a sensation" amongst the Lyceum goers.

—*The Salem Observer*, November 25, 1848.

⤺ ⤻

Mr. Thoreau, of Concord, delivered a second lecture on Wednesday evening upon his life in the woods. The first lecture was upon the economy of that life; this was upon its object and some of its enjoyments. Judging from the remarks which we have heard concerning it, Mr. Thoreau was even less successful this time in suiting all, than on the former occasion. The diversity of opinion is quite amusing. Some persons are unwilling to speak of his lecture as any better than "tom-foolery and nonsense," while others think they perceived, beneath the outward sense of his remarks, something wise and valuable. It is undoubtedly true that Mr. Thoreau's style is rather too allegorical for a popular audience. He "peoples the solitudes" of the woods too profusely, and gives voices to their "dim aisles" not recognized by the larger part of common ears.

Some parts of this lecture—which on the whole we thought less successful than the former one—were generally admitted to be excellent. He gave a well-considered defence of classical literature, in connection with some common sense remarks upon books; and also some ingenious speculations suggested by the inroads of railroad enterprise upon the quiet and seclusion of Walden Pond; and told how he found nature a counsellor and companion, furnishing

> Tongues in the trees, books in running brooks
> Sermons in stones, and good in everything.

We take the purpose of Mr. T's lecture to have been, the elucidation of the poetical view of life—showing how life may be made poetical, the apprehensive imagination clothing all things with divine forms, and getting from them a divine language.

> He went to the gods of the wood
> To bring their word to man.

—*The Salem Observer*, March 3, 1849.

∽ ⌒

A sylvan philosopher (Mr. Thoreau of Concord) delivered a lecture at the City Hall Friday evening. His discourse was intended as an autobiography of two years of life in the woods;—an experiment by the lecturer to illustrate, not perhaps so much the absurdity of the present organization and customs of society, as the ease with which a man of resolution and stern expedients may have ample leisure for the cultivation of his intellectual powers and the acquisition of knowledge. This sylvan philosopher, after leaving college (perhaps a little charmed by some "representative" man) betook himself to the woods, where they slope down to the margin of a lakelet of clear water resting upon a fine gravelly bottom. There with a little aid from a brawny Emeralder, the young man Thoreau erected a house of ample accommodation for himself. Around his house he planted corn, beans, and other esculents, which at a trifling cost furnished him the means of living. At the end of the time he found that he had lived at the expense of about $27 a year, and that his income exceeded his outgoes $13 a year; and that most of his time had been given to study, to reading, and to reflection. His lecture was a history of his experience; and is said to have been witty, sarcastic, and amusing.

Such philosophers illustrate the absurdities the human mind is capable of. What would a forest of them be good for? Nothing but curiosities for people to look after, as they pay their shilling to see a menagerie. They are watches without any pointers; their springs and wheels are well adjusted, and perform good service; but nobody is the wiser for it, as they do not tell the time of day. They are a train of carwheels; they run well, and in good time, but can carry no passengers or luggage. A wheel-barrow, with an Irishman for its vitals, renders the world a far better service.

—*The Worcester Palladium*, April 25, 1849.

                          ∽ ∾

Once Emerson and Thoreau arrived to pay a call on Hawthorne at the Old Manse. They were shown into the little parlor upon the avenue, and Hawthorne presently entered. Each of the guests sat upright in his chair like a Roman Senator. "To them," Hawthorne, like a Dacian King. The call went on, but in a most melancholy manner. The host sat perfectly still, or occasionally propounded a question which Thoreau answered accurately, and there the thread broke short off. Emerson delivered sentences that only needed the setting of an essay, to charm the world; but the whole visit was a vague ghost of the Monday evening club at Mr. Emerson's,—it was a great failure. Had they all been lying idly upon the river bank, or strolling in Thoreau's blackberry pastures, the result would have been utterly different. But imprisoned in the proprieties of a parlor, each a wild man in his way, with a necessity of talking inherent in the nature of the occasion, there was only a waste of treasure. This was the only "call" in which I ever knew Hawthorne to be involved.

—George William Curtis, *Homes of American Authors* (New York: Putnam, 1853), p. 302.

                          ∽ ∾

Henry D. Thoreau of Concord . . . took for his subject one in whom all mankind are now interested, 'Captain John Brown of Ossawattomie.' This exciting theme seemed to have awakened 'the hermit of Concord' from his usual state of philosophic indifference, and he spoke with real enthusiasm for an hour and a half, giving much information respecting Captain Brown's earlier life, and bestowing hearty praise upon the enterprise at Harper's Ferry, and as hearty dispraise upon the apathy and reserve shown in regard to it by those portions of the periodical press which did not take the equally shameful ground of direct censure.

Mr. Thoreau took special pains to include the *Liberator* in the censure which he had at first bestowed upon the press generally. In doing this, he ignored the fact that Mr. Garrison has bestowed high and hearty eulogy upon Captain Brown, representing him as not only (judged from the ordinary stand-point of patriotism) superior in nobleness to the heroes of the American Revolution, but entitled to the higher praise of faithfully practising towards the most oppressed people of our country the lessons of the Golden Rule; and, moreover, he distorted Mr. Garrison's first statement, (made on receipt of the first day's telegraphic reports,) that the *attempt* was apparently an insane one, into a charge that he had represented Captain Brown as insane.

A very large audience listened to this lecture, crowding the hall half an hour before the time of its commencement, and giving hearty applause to some of the most energetic expressions of the speaker.

—C[harles] K[ing] W[hipple], "Fifth Fraternity Lecture," *Liberator*, November 4, 1859.

ᔰ ᔱ

The Funeral of Thoreau, which took place in Concord yesterday, drawing together a large company of his townspeople, with some votive pilgrims from parts beyond, was an occasion more impressive and memorable, by much, than is the wont of such scenes. It derived uncommon interest from the remarkable character of the man whose earthly life was ended, and from the weight and worth of the tributary words so fitly, so tenderly spoken there by friendly and illustrious lips. As that fading image of pathetic clay, strewn with wild flowers and forest sprigs, lay awaiting interment, thoughts of its former occupant seemed blent with all the local landscapes. And though the church bell—after the affecting old custom—tolled the forty-four years he had numbered, we could not deem that *he* was dead whose ideas and sentiments were so vividly alive in our souls.

Selections from the Bible were read by the minister. A brief ode, written for the purpose by William Ellery Channing, was plaintively sung. Mr. Emerson read an address of considerable length, marked by all his felicity of conception and diction—an exquisite appreciation of the salient and subtle traits of his friend's genius—a high strain of sanative thoughts, full of beauty and cheerfulness, chastened by the gentle sorrow of the hour. Referring to the Alpine flower *edelweiss,* or noble purity, which the young Switzers sometimes lose their lives in plucking from its perilous heights, Mr. Emerson said, "Could we pierce to where he is we should see him wearing profuse chaplets of it; for it belonged to him. Where there is knowledge, where there is virtue, where there is beauty, where there is progress, there is now his home."

Mr. Alcot [*sic*] read some very appropriate passages from the writings of the deceased, and the service closed with a prayer by the Rev. Mr. Reynolds. A long procession was then formed to follow the body to the grave. The hands of friends reverently lowered it into the bosom of the earth, on the pleasant hillside of his native village, whose prospects will long wait to unfurl themselves to another observer so competent to discriminate their features, and so attuned to their moods. And now that it is too late for any further boon amidst his darling haunts below,

> There will yet his mother yield
> A pillow in her greenest field,
> Nor the June flowers scorn to cover
> The clay of their departed lover.

—[William Rounseville Alger?], "The Funeral of Thoreau," *Boston Transcript,* May 10, 1862.

➤◦ ◦◄

Henry D. Thoreau, the genial writer on the natural scenery of New England, died at Concord, Mass., on Tuesday, May 6, after a protracted illness of more than eighteen months. He was a native of Boston [no, Concord], but removed with his family at the age of five years to Concord, where he has since resided. He graduated at Harvard College in 1837, and was nearly forty-five years old at the time of his death. His writings include *A Week on the Concord and Merrimack Rivers; Walden, or Life in the Woods;* and various contributions to the periodical literature of the day. They are remarkable for their freedom and originality of thought, their quaint humor, and their warm sympathy with all the manifold aspects of nature. His disease was consumption, and, as we are informed, "his humor and cheerful courage did not forsake him during his sickness, and he met death as gayly [*sic*] as Theramenes in Xenophon's story." Mr. Thoreau, in spite of the racy individuality of his character, was much beloved and respected by his townsmen, and his writings have numerous admirers. He was honored with a public funeral from the Town Hall [no, First Parish Church] of Concord, on Friday, the 9*th* inst.

—*New York Tribune,* May 10, 1862.

It was during the year 1857, while revelling in our school-life at Concord, that we first became attracted by a singular person [Thoreau] who might be seen each day pacing through the long village street, with sturdy step and honest mien, now pausing to listen to some rich warble from the elms high overhead, or stooping to examine some creeping thing, of interest only to him who knew its ways. A casual observer might have passed him in the street without noticing in him anything peculiar or interesting, for his dress was plain, befitting the man, and consistent with his stoical principles respecting matters of this description; yet whoever penetrated deeper, could not fail to mark in him the "honest man," nor in his countenance, half hidden by a generous beard, his nut-brown complexion and soft blue eye, help discerning beneath them only a warm heart, and a nature keenly alive to what was most impressive in the world around him. Spite of the faded corduroy, this salient trait in his character shone forth with unmistakable sincerity. He seemed like some sturdy mountaineer or hardy lumberman, in whom a rugged life has left only yet sturdier strength, with finer traits awakened by a daily contemplation of stupendous mountains or primeval forests. This love for man formed his passport to the favor of all whom he chanced to meet. It procured for him respect among his townsmen, and a welcome greeting from every schoolboy, for he "carried his heart in his hand," as it were, always willing to offer it to him who might justly claim a share of it.

Our curiosity, once excited, increased daily. In the ramble

[p. 313] after school, we often met him, sometimes far from the town, deep in the thickest of the wood, searching untiringly among the brambles or underbrush, as though he had yet something to find, for which his search had hitherto been vain; or oftener we passed him on the river, paddling in his strange craft, built long ago for visiting the Merrimack, gliding silently along so as hardly to ruffle the surface of the water, the prow, sturdy forerunner of himself, parting the lilypads with gentle touch, quietly cleaving a way among them, or thrusting them impatiently beneath. As he glided on, the ripple at the bow appeared to herald unto each denizen of the stream the coming of a friend. All seemed to know him, and hail his approach with increased song. The "red-wing" kept his perch beside his mate, the little "yellow-throat" moved listlessly about, chasing his reflection in the water, or sang his kind welcome, "Don't you wish it? don't you wish it? don't you wish it?" Even the staid turtle thought twice before dropping from his seat, finally deciding with wonted judgment, after the boat had passed. Every living thing, every leaf and flower, were known to him, nor did the smallest objects of interest escape the glance of his observing eye. There was no corner of the way but it contained something for him, though others might look in vain to find it. No barren twig but it held in its grasp some new chrysalis, or the ova of some strange insect. Thus did Nature [p. 314] reveal to him the richest treasures of her store, as if sure of finding in this disciple a worthy advocate.

It was with joy that we hailed our first approach to this man, and gradually came to know more in regard to his private life. As our acquaintance grew, we found him to be one of the rarest companions, beneath whose rugged exterior there lay a lively appreciation of all that is vivifying in nature, and a natural yearning toward his fellow-men, together with a kindly sympathy, which was but the basis of his simple philosophy. In place of affected eccentricity, we discovered in him only originality, every thought and action revealing to us a mind singularly individual, acknowledging no model save that fashioned by the dictates of conscience, and by the inferences drawn from a thoughtful contemplation of the natural world. He appeared to us more than all men to enjoy life, not for its hypocrisies, its conventional shams and barbarisms, but for its intrinsic worth, taking great interest in everything connected with the welfare of the town, no less than delight in each changing aspect of Nature, with an instinctive love for every creature of her realm.

In this he may have found the philosopher's-stone, or at least the pebble adjoining it, which all the world aspire to reach, yet few attain. This feature, which, as I have said, formed the predominating element in his character, was contagious. No one could approach without feeling himself irresistibly drawn yet nearer to him, for he bore his credentials for our esteem in his bronzed and honest countenance. [p. 315] Thus we could not fear, though we had great reverence for him, and must needs deem it the greatest privilege to associate with him. In the wood, his spirits were always most elastic and buoyant. At such times he evinced the liveliest interest in our conversation, entering into our feelings with an earnestness and warmth of sentiment which only bound us still closer to him, and taught us to look upon him rather as a glorious boy, than one who had arrived at full maturity; one whose healthy life and vigorous thought had put to flight all morbidness, leaving his mind yet unclouded by the sorrows which too often tinge the years of riper manhood. He climbed and leaped as though he knew every "rope" of the wood, and quite shamed our efforts, the results of bars, racks, and wooden contrivances unknown to him.

But he was to be to us more than a charming companion; he became our instructor, full of wisdom and consideration, patiently listening to our crude ideas of Nature's laws and to our juvenile philosophy, not without a smile, yet in a moment ready to correct and set us right again. And so in the afternoon walk, or the long holiday jaunt, he first opened to our unconscious eyes a thousand beauties of earth and air, and taught us to admire and appreciate all that was impressive and beautiful in the natural world around us. When with him, objects before so tame acquired new life and interest. We saw no beauty in the note of veery or wood-thrush until he pointed out to us their sad yet fascinating melancholy. He taught us the rich variety of the thrasher's song, bidding us compare with it the shrieks of the modern *prima donna*. The weary peep of Hyla had for us no charm until he showed us how well it consorted with the surrounding objects,—the dark pool with the andromeda weeping over it, as if in fear of the little "sea-monster." Nor did we fancy the flaming red-wing, with his anxious cry, the Perseus of the story, who makes his home near by, to keep the maiden company, until by his very love he caused us too to like him. Then we sought to know more of the young gallant, and saw how wonderfully well he built his home, and laughed at the grotesque markings upon the eggs. He turned our hearts toward every flower, revealing to us the haunts of [p. 316] of rhodora and arethusa, or in the fragrant wood, half hidden by the withered leaves,

> "He saw beneath dim aisles, in odorous beds,
> The sweet Linnea hang its twin-born heads."

His ear was keenly alive to musical sounds, discriminating with astonishing accuracy between the notes of various songsters. This discernment enabled him to distinguish at once the songs of many birds singing together, selecting each one with great nicety of perception. A single strain was enough for him to recall the note at once, and he always had some English translation, or carefully marked paraphrase of it, singularly expressive and unique.

His love of nature was unbounded. No subject of the animate creation was beneath his notice; no uncouth reptile, no blade of grass nor wayside weed, but it might confidently claim a share in his esteem. To him Nature seemed to speak a language clear, intelligible. He never wearied of her; but from whatever he found uncongenial and prosaic in daily life,—from the cares which must come home to him, from bereavement and sorrows,—he always returned again, with renewed devotion unto her sweet embrace.

His philosophy contained little that could be called visionary, but every tenet of it was made subservient to some practical end. He had a passion for Oriental literature, especially admiring, as he tells us, the "Bhagvat Geeta," full of sublimity and divine thought. From these heathen writings his keen discernment enabled him to gather much practical good, gleaning from them maxims which to-day may help to shape the perfect mind and character.

It seemed part of his generous heart, that in all his researches, he rarely [p. 317] injured the smallest insect, never indulging in wanton slaughter, that he might stock cabinets, but respecting the life of every creature. Life, with its gushing melody and happy enjoyment, was to him far dearer than death with its "pickled victims," designed to show every little dimension, to the extent of a barleycorn.

> *"Hast thou named all the birds without a gun,*
> Loved the wood-rose, and left it on its stalk,—
> O be my friend, and teach me to be thine!"

Nothing seems to me more touching in the life of this man than his veneration for every little songster of the wood, which appeared to minister to him, and answer the inmost cravings of his nature. These were his pets, for whom he ever had a ready sympathy, regarding them with an affection almost paternal.

Thus the good man seemed to be Nature's child, rather than ours. By her was he fostered, under her willing guidance he grew up, and now within her bosom he sleeps the long sleep. From her he learned the lesson of forbearance, of sympathy for his fellowmen, of pity for the needy, nay, more, of godlike trust and holy reverence. His life was moulded from a serious contemplation of her laws, and a careful study of the world in which he lived. For him Nature donned her costliest dress, that he might view her in her fairest attire. Nor did he ever desert her, but passively yielded to her charms, and suffered no rude hand to tear him away. The freshness of spring, the long monotony of the dreamy summer, the changing glories of autumn, and the crisp and merry winter,—all had for him a significance deeper than we could conceive, and lent their influence to quicken and intensify his life.

But Nature needed him, and with firm but gentle hand broke down his mighty strength, and with the fair May morning lifted him away within herself. As was his life, so was his lingering decline, and death the same beautiful dream, as it were, in which he clung yet closer to the haunts be loved, though unable longer to revisit them.

—[Samuel Storrow Higginson], "Henry D. Thoreau," *Harvard Magazine,* VIII (May, 1862), 313-318.

∽ ∾

Henry David Thoreau was the last male descendant of a French ancestor who came to this country from the Isle of Guernsey. His character exhibited occasional traits drawn from this blood, in singular combination with a very strong Saxon genius.

He was born in Concord, Massachusetts, on the 12th of July, 1817. He was graduated at Harvard College in 1837, but without any literary distinction. An iconoclast in literature, he seldom thanked colleges for their service to him, holding them in small esteem, whilst yet his debt to them was important. After leaving the University, he joined his brother in teaching a private school, which he soon renounced. His father was a manufacturer of lead-pencils, and Henry applied himself for a time to this craft, believing he could make a better pencil than was then in use. After completing his experiments, he exhibited his work to chemists and artists in Boston, and having obtained their certificates to its excellence and to its equality with the best London manufacture, he returned home contented. His friends congratulated him that he had now opened his way to fortune. But he replied, that he should never make another pencil. "Why should I? I would not do again what I have done once." He resumed his endless walks and miscellaneous studies, making every day some new acquaintance with Nature, though as yet never speaking of zoölogy or botany, since, though very studious of natural facts, he was incurious of technical and textual science.

At this time, a strong, healthy youth, fresh from college, whilst all his companions were choosing their profession, or eager to begin some lucrative employment, it was inevitable that his thoughts should be exercised on the same question, and it required rare decision to refuse all the accustomed paths, and keep his solitary freedom at the cost of disappointing the natural expectations of his family and friends: all the more difficult that he had a perfect probity, was exact in securing his own independence, and in holding every man to the like duty. But Thoreau never faltered. He was a born protestant. He declined to give up his large ambition of knowledge and action for any narrow craft or profession, aiming at a much more comprehensive calling, the art of living well. If he slighted and defied the opinions of others, it was only that he was more intent to reconcile his practice with his own belief. Never idle or self-indulgent, he preferred, when he wanted money, earning it by some piece of manual labor agreeable to him, as building a boat or a fence, planting, grafting, surveying, or other short work, to any long engagements. With his hardy habits and few wants, his skill in wood-craft, and his powerful arithmetic, he was very competent to live in any part of the world. It would cost him less time to supply his wants than another. He was therefore secure of his leisure.

A natural skill for mensuration, growing out of his mathematical knowledge and his habit of ascertaining the measures and distances of objects which interested him, the size of trees, the depth and extent of ponds and rivers, the height of mountains, and the air-line distance of his favorite summits,—this, and his intimate knowledge of the territory about Concord, made him drift into the profession of land-surveyor. It had the advantage for him that it led him continually into new and secluded grounds, and helped his studies of Nature. His accuracy and skill in this work were readily appreciated, and he found all the employment he wanted.

He could easily solve the problems of the surveyor, but he was daily beset with graver questions, which he manfully confronted. He interrogated every custom, and wished to settle all his practice on an ideal foundation. He was a protes[p. 239]tant à l'outrance, and few lives contain so many renunciations. He was bred to no profession; he never married; he lived alone; he never went to church; he never voted; he refused to pay a tax to the State; he ate no flesh, he drank no wine, he never knew the use of tobacco; and, though a naturalist, he used neither trap nor gun. He chose, wisely, no doubt, for himself, to be the bachelor of thought and Nature. He had no talent for wealth, and knew how to be poor without the least hint of squalor or inelegance. Perhaps he fell into his way of living without forecasting it much, but approved it with later wisdom. "I am often reminded," he wrote in his journal, "that if I had bestowed on me the wealth of Croesus, my aims must be still the same, and my means essentially the same." He had no temptations to fight against,—no appetites, no passions, no taste for elegant trifles. A fine house, dress, the manners and talk of highly cultivated people were all thrown away on him. He much preferred a good Indian, and considered these refinements as impediments to conversation, wishing to meet his companion on the simplest terms. He declined invitations to dinner-parties, because there each was in every one's way, and he could not meet the individuals to any purpose. "They make their pride," he said, "in making their dinner cost much; I make my pride in making my dinner cost little." When asked at table what dish he preferred, he answered, "The nearest." He did not like the taste of wine, and never had a vice in his life. He said,—"I have a faint recollection of pleasure derived from smoking dried lily-stems, before I was a man. I had commonly a supply of these. I have never smoked anything more noxious."

He chose to be rich by making his wants few, and supplying them himself. In his travels, he used the railroad only to get over so much country as was unimportant to the present purpose, walking hundreds of miles, avoiding taverns, buying a lodging in farmers' and fishermen's houses, as cheaper, and more agreeable to him, and because there he could better find the men and the information he wanted.

There was somewhat military in his nature not to be subdued, always manly and able, but rarely tender, as if he did not feel himself except in opposition. He wanted a fallacy to expose, a blunder to pillory, I may say required a little sense of victory, a roll of the drum, to call his powers into full exercise. It cost him nothing to say No; indeed he found it much easier than to say Yes. It seemed as if his first instinct on hearing a proposition was to controvert it, so impatient was he of the limitations of our daily thought. This habit, of course, is a little chilling to the social affections; and though the companion would in the end acquit him of any malice or untruth, yet it mars conversation. Hence, no equal companion stood in affectionate relations with one so pure and guileless. "I love Henry," said one of his friends, "but I cannot like him; and as for taking his arm, I should as soon think of taking the arm of an elm-tree."

Yet, hermit and stoic as he was, he was really fond of sympathy, and threw himself heartily and childlike into the company of young people whom he loved, and whom he delighted to entertain, as he only could, with the varied and endless anecdotes of his experiences by field and river. And he was always ready to lead a huckleberry-party or a search for chestnuts or grapes. Talking, one day, of a public discourse, Henry remarked, that whatever succeeded with the audience was bad. I said, "Who would not like to write something

which all can read, like 'Robinson Crusoe'? and who does not see
with regret that his page is not solid with a right materialistic treatment, which delights everybody?" Henry objected, of course, and
vaunted the better lectures which reached only a few persons. But,
at supper, a young girl, understanding that he was to lecture at the
Lyceum, sharply asked him, "whether his lecture would be a nice,
interesting story, such as she wished to hear, or [p. 240] whether it
was one of those old philosophical things that she did not care
about." Henry turned to her, and bethought himself, and, I saw, was
trying to believe that he had matter that might fit her and her
brother, who were to sit up and go to the lecture, if it was a good
one for them.

He was a speaker and actor of the truth,—born such,—and was
ever running into dramatic situations from this cause. In any circumstance it interested all bystanders to know what part Henry would
take, and what he would say; and he did not disappoint expectation,
but used an original judgment on each emergency. In 1845 he built
himself a small framed house on the shores of Walden Pond, and
lived there two years alone, a life of labor and study. This action
was quite native and fit for him. No one who knew him would tax
him with affectation. He was more unlike his neighbors in his thought
than in his action. As soon as he had exhausted the advantages of
that solitude, he abandoned it. In 1847 [correctly, 1846], not ap-
proving some uses to which the public expenditure was applied, he
refused to pay his town tax, and was put in jail. A friend paid the
tax for him, and he was released. The like annoyance was threatened
the next year. But, as his friends paid the tax, nothwithstanding his
protest, I believe he ceased to resist. No opposition or ridicule had
any weight with him. He coldly and fully stated his opinion of the
company. It was of no consequence if every one present held the
opposite opinion. On one occasion he went to the [Harvard] University Library to procure some books. The librarian refused to lend
them. Mr. Thoreau repaired to the President, who stated to him the
rules and usages, which permitted the loan of books to resident graduates, to clergymen who were alumni, and to some others resident within
a circle of ten miles' radius from the College. Mr. Thoreau explained
to the President that the railroad had destroyed the old scale of
distances,—that the library was useless, yes, and President and Col-

lege useless, on the terms of his rules,—that the one benefit he owed
to the College was its library,—that, at this moment, not only his
want of books was imperative but he wanted a large number of
books, and assured him that he, Thoreau, and not the librarian, was
the proper custodian of these. In short, the President found the peti-
tioner so formidable, and the rules getting to look so ridiculous, that
he ended by giving him a privilege which in his hands proved unlimited thereafter.

No truer American existed than Thoreau. His preference of his
country and condition was genuine, and his aversation from English
and European manners and tastes almost reached contempt. He
listened impatiently to news or *bon mots* gleaned from London cir-
cles; and though he tried to be civil, these anecdotes fatigued him.
The men were all imitating each other, and on a small mould. Why
can they not live as far apart as possible, and each be a man by himself? What he sought was the most energetic nature; and he wished
to go to Oregon, not to London. "In every part of Great Britain,"
he wrote in his diary, "are discovered traces of the Romans, their
funereal urns, their camps, their dwellings. But New England, at
least, is not based on any Roman ruins. We have not to lay the foun-
dations of our houses on the ashes of a former civilization."

But, idealist as he was, standing for abolition of slavery, abolition of tariffs, almost for abolition of government, it is needless to
say he found himself not only unrepresented in actual politics, but
almost equally opposed to every class of reformers. Yet he paid the
tribute of his uniform respect to the Anti-Slavery party. One man,
whose personal acquaintance he had formed, he honored with exceptional regard. Before the first friendly word had been spoken for
Captain John Brown, he sent notices to most houses in Concord that
he would speak [p. 241] in a public hall on the condition and character of John Brown, on Sunday evening, and invited all people to
come. The Republican Committee, the Abolitionist Committee, sent
him word that it was premature and not advisable. He replied,—"I
did not send to you for advice, but to announce that I am to speak."
The hall was filled at an early hour by people of all parties, and his
earnest eulogy of the hero was heard by all respectfully, by many
with a sympathy that surprised themselves.

It was said of Plotinus that he was ashamed of his body, and 'tis very likely he had good reason for it,—that his body was a bad servant, and he had not skill in dealing with the material world, as happens often to men of abstract intellect. But Mr. Thoreau was equipped with a most adapted and serviceable body. He was of short stature, firmly built, of light complexion, with strong, serious blue eyes, and a grave aspect,—his face covered in the late years with a becoming beard. His senses were acute, his frame well-knit and hardy, his hands strong and skillful in the use of tools. And there was a wonderful fitness of body and mind. He could pace sixteen rods more accurately than another man could measure them with rod and chain. He could find his path in the woods at night, he said, better by his feet than his eyes. He could estimate the measure of a tree very well by his eyes; he could estimate the weight of a calf or a pig, like a dealer. From a box containing a bushel or more of loose pencils, he could take up with his hands fast enough just a dozen pencils at every grasp. He was a good swimmer, runner, skater, boatman, and would probably outwalk most countrymen in a day's journey. And the relation of body to mind was still finer than we have indicated. He said he wanted every stride his legs made. The length of his walk uniformly made the length of his writings. If shut up in the house, he did not write at all.

He had a strong common sense, like that which Rose Flammock, the weaver's daughter in Scott's romance, commends in her father, as resembling a yardstick, which, whilst it measures dowlas and diaper, can equally well measure tapestry and cloth of gold. He had always a new resource. When I was planting forest-trees, and had procured half a peck of acorns, he said that only a small portion of them would be sound, and proceeded to examine them and select the sound ones. But finding this took time, he said, "I think, if you put them all into water, the good ones will sink"; which experiment we tried with success. He could plan a garden, or a house, or a barn; would have been competent to lead a "Pacific Exploring Expedition"; could give judicious counsel in the gravest private or public affairs.

He lived for the day, not cumbered and mortified by his memory. If he brought you yesterday a new proposition, he would bring you to-day another not less revolutionary. A very industrious man, and settling, like all highly organized men, a high value on his time, he seemed the only man of leisure in town, always ready for any excursion that promised well, or for conversation prolonged into late hours. His trenchant sense was never stopped by his rules of daily prudence, but was always up to the new occasion. He liked and used the simplest food, yet, when some one urged a vegetable diet, Thoreau thought all diets a very small matter, saying that "the man who shoots the buffalo lives better than the man who boards at the Graham House." He said,—"You can sleep near the railroad, and never be disturbed: Nature knows very well what sounds are worth attending to, and has made up her mind not to hear the rail-road-whistle. But things respect the devout mind, and a mental ecstasy was never interrupted." He noted, what repeatedly befell him, that, after receiving from a distance a rare plant, he would presently find the same in his own haunts. And those pieces of luck which happen only to good players happened to him. One day, walking with a stranger, who in[p. 242]quired where Indian arrow-heads could be found, he replied, "Everywhere," and, stooping forward, picked one on the instant from the ground. At Mount Washington, in Tuckerman's Ravine, Thoreau had a bad fall, and sprained his foot. As he was in the act of getting up from his fall, he saw for the first time the leaves of the *Arnica mollis.*

His robust common sense, armed with stout hands, keen perceptions and strong will, cannot yet account for the superiority which shone in his simple and hidden life. I must add the cardinal fact, that there was an excellent wisdom in him, proper to a rare class of men, which showed him the material world as a means and symbol. This discovery, which sometimes yields to poets a certain casual and inter-rupted light, serving for the ornament of their writing, was in him an unsleeping insight; and whatever faults or obstructions of tempera-ment might cloud it, he was not disobedient to the heavenly vision. In his youth, he said, one day, "The other world is all my art; my pen-cils will draw no other; my jack-knife will cut nothing else; I do not use it as a means." This was the muse and genius that ruled his opin-ions, conversation, studies, work and course of life. This made him a searching judge of men. At first glance he measured his companion, and, though insensible to some fine traits of culture, could very well report his weight and calibre. And this made the impression of genius which his conversation sometimes gave.

He understood the matter in hand at a glance, and saw the limitations and poverty of those he talked with, so that nothing seemed concealed from such terrible eyes. I have repeatedly known young men of sensibility converted in a moment to the belief that this was the man they were in search of, the man of men, who could tell them all they should do. His own dealing with them was never affectionate, but superior, didactic, scorning their petty ways,—very slowly conceding, or not conceding at all, the promise of his society at their houses, or even at his own. "Would he not walk with them?" "He did not know. There was nothing so important to him as his walk; he had no walks to throw away on company." Visits were offered him from respectful parties, but he declined them. Admiring friends offered to carry him at their own cost to the Yellow-Stone River,—to the West Indies,—to South America. But though nothing could be more grave or considered than his refusals, they remind one, in quite new relations, of that fop Brummel's reply to the gentleman who offered him his carriage in a shower, "But where will *you* ride, then?"—and what accusing silences, and what searching and irresistible speeches, battering down all defenses, his companions can remember!

Mr. Thoreau dedicated his genius with such entire love to the fields, hills, and waters of his native town, that he made them known and interesting to all reading Americans, and to people over the sea. The river on whose banks he was born and died he knew from its springs to its confluence with the Merrimack. He had made summer and winter observations on it for many years, and at every hour of the day and night. The result of the recent survey of the Water Commissioners appointed by the State of Massachusetts he had reached by his private experiments, several years earlier. Every fact which occurs in the bed, on the banks, or in the air over it; the fishes, and their spawning and nests, their manners, their food; the shad-flies which fill the air on a certain evening once a year, and which are snapped at by the fishes so ravenously that many of these die of repletion; the conical heaps of small stones on the river-shallows, one of which heaps will sometimes overfill a cart,—these heaps the huge nests of small fishes; the birds which frequent the stream, heron, duck, sheldrake, loon, osprey; the snake, muskrat, otter, woodchuck and fox, on the banks; the turtle, frog, hyla, and cricket which make the banks vocal,—were all known to him, and, as it were, towns[p. 243]-men and fellow-creatures; so that he felt an absurdity or violence in any narrative of one of these by itself apart, and still more of its dimensions on an inch-rule, or in the exhibition of its skeleton, or the specimen of a squirrel or a bird in brandy. He liked to speak of the manners of the river, as itself a lawful creature, yet with exactness, and always to an observed fact. As he knew the river, so the ponds in this region.

One of the weapons he used, more important to him than microscope or alcohol-receiver to other investigators, was a whim which grew on him by indulgence, yet appeared in gravest statement, namely, of extolling his own town and neighborhood as the most favored centre for natural observation. He remarked that the Flora of Massachusetts embraced almost all the important plants of America,—most of the oaks, most of the willows, the best pines, the ash, the maple, the beech, the nuts. He returned Kane's "Arctic Voyage" to a friend of whom he had borrowed it, with the remark, that "most of the phenomena noted might be observed in Concord." He seemed a little envious of the Pole, for the coincident sunrise and sunset, or five minutes' day after six months: a splendid fact, which Annursnuc had never afforded him. He found red snow in one of his walks, and told me that he expected to find yet the *Victoria regia* in Concord. He was the attorney of the indigenous plants, and owned to a preference of the weeds to the imported plants, as of the Indian to the civilized man,—and noticed, with pleasure, that the willow bean-poles of his neighbor had grown more than his beans. "See these weeds," he said, "which have been hoed at by a million farmers all spring and summer, and yet have prevailed, and just now come out triumphant over all lanes, pastures, fields and gardens, such is their vigor. We have insulted them with low names, too,—as Pigweed, Wormwood, Chickweed, Shad-Blossom." He says, "They have brave names, too,— Ambrosia, Stellaria, Amelanchia, Amaranth, etc."

I think his fancy for referring everything to the meridian of Concord did not grow out of any ignorance or depreciation of other longitudes or latitudes, but was rather a playful expression of his conviction of the indifferency of all places, and that the best place for each is where he stands. He expressed it once in this wise:—"I think nothing is to be hoped from you, if this bit of mould under your feet is not sweeter to you to eat than any other in this world, or in any world."

The other weapon with which he conquered all obstacles in science was patience. He knew how to sit immovable, a part of the rock he rested on, until the bird, the reptile, the fish, which had retired from him, should come back, and resume its habits, nay, moved by curiosity, should come to him and watch him.

It was a pleasure and a privilege to walk with him. He knew the country like a fox or a bird, and passed through it as freely by paths of his own. He knew every track in the snow or on the ground, and what creature had taken this path before him. One must submit abjectly to such a guide, and the reward was great. Under his arm he carried an old music-book to press plants; in his pocket, his diary and pencil, a spy-glass for birds, microscope, jack-knife, and twine. He wore straw hat, stout shoes, strong gray trousers, to brave shrub-oaks and smilax, and to climb a tree for a hawk's or a squirrel's nest. He waded into the pool for the water-plants, and his strong legs were no insignificant part of his armor. On the day I speak of he looked for the Menyanthes, detected it across the wide pool, and, on examination of the florets, decided that it had been in flower five days. He drew out of his breast-pocket his diary, and read the names of all the plants that should bloom on this day, whereof he kept account as a banker when his notes fall due. The Cypripedium not due till to-morrow. He thought, that, if waked up from a trance, in this swamp, he could tell by the plants what time of the year it was within two days. The redstart was flying about, and presently the fine gros[p. 244]beaks, whose brilliant scarlet makes the rash gazer wipe his eye, and whose fine clear note Thoreau compared to that of a tanager which has got rid of its hoarseness. Presently he heard a note which he called that of the night-warbler, a bird he had never identified, had been in search of twelve years, which always, when he saw it, was in the act of diving down into a tree or bush, and which it was vain to seek; the only bird that sings indifferently by night and by day. I told him he must beware of finding and booking it, lest life should have nothing more to show him. He said, "What you seek in vain for, half your life, one day you come full upon, all the family at dinner. You seek it like a dream, and as soon as you find it you become its prey."

His interest in the flower or the bird lay very deep in his mind, was connected with Nature,—and the meaning of Nature was never attempted to be defined by him. He would not offer a memoir of his observations to the Natural History Society. "Why should I? To detach the description from its connections in my mind would make it no longer true or valuable to me: and they do not wish what belongs to it." His power of observation seemed to indicate additional senses. He saw as with microscope, heard as with ear-trumpet, and his memory was a photographic register of all he saw and heard. And yet none knew better than he that it is not the fact that imports, but the impression or effect of the fact on your mind. Every fact lay in glory in his mind, a type of the order and beauty of the whole.

His determination on Natural History was organic. He confessed that he sometimes felt like a hound or a panther, and, if born among Indians, would have been a fell hunter. But, restrained by his Massachusetts culture, he played out the game in this mild form of botany and ichthyology. His intimacy with animals suggested what Thomas Fuller records of Butler the apiologist, that "either he had told the bees things or the bees had told him." Snakes coiled around his leg; the fishes swam into his hand, and he took them out of the water; he pulled the woodchuck out of its hole by the tail, and took the foxes under his protection from the hunters. Our naturalist had perfect magnanimity; he had no secrets: he would carry you to the heron's haunt, or even to his most prized botanical swamp,—possibly knowing that you could never find it again, yet willing to take his risks.

No college ever offered him a diploma, or a professor's chair; no academy made him its corresponding secretary, its discoverer, or even its member. Perhaps these learned bodies feared the satire of his presence. Yet so much knowledge of Nature's secret and genius few others possessed, none in a more large and religious synthesis. For not a particle of respect had he to the opinions of any man or body of men, but homage solely to the truth itself; and as he discovered everywhere among doctors some leaning of courtesy, it discredited them. He grew to be revered and admired by his townsmen, who had at first known him only as an oddity. The farmers who employed him as a surveyor soon discovered his rare accuracy and skill, his knowledge of their lands, of trees, of birds, of Indian remains, and the like, which enabled him to tell every farmer more than he knew before of his own farm; so that he began to feel a little as if Mr. Thoreau had better rights in his land than he. They felt, too, the superiority of character which addressed all men with a native authority.

Indian relics abound in Concord,—arrow-heads, stone chisels, pestles, and fragments of pottery; and on the river-bank, large heaps of clam-shells and ashes mark spots which the savages frequented. These, and every circumstance touching the Indian, were important in his eyes. His visits to Maine were chiefly for love of the Indian. He had the satisfaction of seeing the manufacture of the bark-canoe, as well as of trying his hand in its management on the rapids. He was inquisitive about the making of the stone arrow-head, and in his last days charged a [p. 245] youth setting out for the Rocky Mountains to find an Indian who could tell him that: "It was well worth a visit to California to learn it." Occasionally, a small party of Penobscot Indians would visit Concord, and pitch their tents for a few weeks in summer on the river-bank. He failed not to make acquaintance with the best of them; though he well knew that asking questions of Indians is like catechizing beavers and rabbits. In his last visit to Maine he had great satisfaction from Joseph Polis, an intelligent Indian of Oldtown, who was his guide for some weeks.

He was equally interested in every natural fact. The depth of his perception found likeness of law throughout Nature, and I know not any genius who so swiftly inferred universal law from the single fact. He was no pedant of a department. His eye was open to beauty, and his ear to music. He found these, not in rare conditions, but wheresoever he went. He thought the best of music was in single strains; and he found poetic suggestion in the humming of the telegraph-wire.

His poetry might be bad or good; he no doubt wanted a lyric facility and technical skill, but he had the source of poetry in his spiritual perception. He was a good reader and critic, and his judgment on poetry was to the ground of it. He could not be deceived as to the presence or absence of the poetic element in any composition, and his thirst for this made him negligent and perhaps scornful of superficial graces. He would pass by many delicate rhythms, but he would have detected every live stanza or line in a volume, and he knew very well where to find an equal poetic charm in prose. He was so enamored of the spiritual beauty that he held all actual written poems in very light esteem in the comparison. He admired Aeschylus and Pindar; but, when some one was commending them, he said that "Aeschylus and the Greeks, in describing Apollo and Orpheus, had given no song, or no good one. They ought not to have moved trees, but to have chanted to the gods such a hymn as would have sung all their old ideas out of their heads, and new ones in." His own verses are often rude and defective. The gold does not yet run pure, is drossy and crude. The thyme and marjoram are not yet honey. But if he want lyric fineness and technical merits, if he have not the poetic temperament, he never lacks the causal thought, showing that his genius was better than his talent. He knew the worth of the Imagination for the uplifting and consolation of human life, and liked to throw every thought into a symbol. The fact you tell is of no value, but only the impression. For this reason his presence was poetic, always piqued the curiosity to know more deeply the secrets of his mind. He had many reserves, an unwillingness to exhibit to profane eyes what was still sacred in his own, and knew well how to throw a poetic veil over his experience. All readers of "Walden" will remember his mythical record of his disappointments:—"I long ago lost a hound, a bay horse and a turtle-dove, and am still on their trail. Many are the travellers I have spoken concerning them, describing their tracks, and what calls they answered to. I have met one or two who had heard the hound, and the tramp of the horse, and even seen the dove disappear behind a cloud; and they seemed as anxious to recover them as if they had lost them themselves."

His riddles were worth the reading, and I confide that if at any time I do not understand the expression, it is yet just. Such was the wealth of his truth that it was not worth his while to use words in vain. His poem entitled "Sympathy" reveals the tenderness under that triple steel of stoicism, and the intellectual subtility it could animate. His classic poem on "Smoke" suggests Simonides, but is better than any poem of Simonides. His biography is in his verses. His habitual thought makes all his poetry a hymn to the Cause of causes, the Spirit which vivifies and controls his own:—[p. 246]

> "I hearing get, who had but ears,
>   And sight, who had but eyes before;
> I moments live, who lived but years,
>   And truth discern, who knew but learning's lore."

And still more in these religious lines:—

> "Now chiefly is my natal hour
>   And only now my prime of life;
> I will not doubt the love untold,
> Which not my worth nor want hath bought,
> Which wooed me young, and wooes me old,
>   And to this evening hath me brought."

Whilst he used in his writings a certain petulance of remark in reference to churches or churchmen, he was a person of a rare, tender and absolute religion, a person incapable of any profanation, by act or by thought. Of course, the same isolation which belonged to his original thinking and living detached him from the social religious forms. This is neither to be censured nor regretted. Aristotle long ago explained it, when he said, "One who surpasses his fellow-citizens in virtue is no longer a part of the city. Their law is not for him, since he is a law to himself."

Thoreau was sincerity itself, and might fortify the convictions of prophets in the ethical laws by his holy living. It was an affirmative experience which refused to be set aside. A truth-speaker he, capable of the most deep and strict conversation; a physician to the wounds of any soul; a friend, knowing not only the secret of friendship, but almost worshipped by those few persons who resorted to him as their confessor and prophet, and knew the deep value of his mind and great heart. He thought that without religion or devotion of some kind nothing great was ever accomplished: and he thought that the bigoted sectarian had better bear this in mind.

His virtues, of course, sometimes ran into extremes. It was easy to trace to the inexorable demand on all for exact truth that austerity which made this willing hermit more solitary even than he wished. Himself of a perfect probity, he required not less of others. He had a disgust at crime, and no wordly success would cover it. He detected paltering as readily in dignified and prosperous persons as in beggars, and with equal scorn. Such dangerous frankness was in his dealing that his admirers called him "that terrible Thoreau," as if he spoke when silent, and was still present when he had departed. I think the severity of his ideal interfered to deprive him of a healthy sufficiency of human society.

The habit of a realist to find things the reverse of their appearance inclined him to put every statement in a paradox. A certain habit of antagonism defaced his earlier writings,—a trick of rhetoric not quite outgrown in his later, of substituting for the obvious word and thought its diametrical opposite. He praised wild mountains and winter forests for their domestic air, in snow and ice he would find sultriness, and commended the wilderness for resembling Rome and Paris. "It was so dry, that you might call it wet."

The tendency to magnify the moment, to read all the laws of Nature in the one object or one combination under your eye, is of course comic to those who do not share the philosopher's perception of identity. To him there was no such thing as size. The pond was a small ocean; the Atlantic, a large Walden Pond. He referred every minute fact to cosmical laws. Though he meant to be just, he seemed haunted by a certain chronic assumption that the science of the day pretended completeness, and he had just found out that the *savans* had neglected to discriminate a particular botanical variety, had failed to describe the seeds or count the sepals. "That is to say," we replied, "the blockheads were not born in Concord; but who said they were? It was their unspeakable misfortune to be born in London, or Paris, or Rome; but, poor fellows, they did what they could, considering that they never saw Bateman's Pond, or Nine-Acre Corner, or Becky Stow's Swamp; besides, what were you sent into the world for, but to add this observation?" [p. 247]

Had his genius been only contemplative, he had been fitted to his life, but with his energy and practical ability he seemed born for great enterprise and for command; and I so much regret the loss of his rare powers of action, that I cannot help counting it a fault in him that he had no ambition. Wanting this, instead of engineering for all America, he was the captain of a huckleberry-party. Pounding beans is good to the end of pounding empires one of these days; but if, at the end of years, it is still only beans!

But these foibles, real or apparent, were fast vanishing in the incessant growth of a spirit so robust and wise, and which effaced its defeats with new triumphs. His study of Nature was a perpetual ornament to him, and inspired his friends with curiosity to see the world through his eyes, and to hear his adventures. They possessed every kind of interest.

He had many elegances of his own, whilst he scoffed at conventional elegance. Thus, he could not bear to hear the sound of his own steps, the grit of gravel; and therefore never willingly walked in the road, but in the grass, on mountains and in woods. His senses were acute, and he remarked that by night every dwelling-house gives out bad air, like a slaughter-house. He liked the pure fragrance of melilot. He honored certain plants with special regard, and, over all, the pond-lily,—then, the gentian, and the *Mikania scandens,* and "life-everlasting," and a bass-tree which he visited every year when it bloomed, in the middle of July. He thought the scent a more oracular inquisition than the sight,—more oracular and trustworthy. The scent, of course, reveals what is concealed from the other senses. By it he detected earthiness. He delighted in echoes, and said they were almost the only kind of kindred voices that he heard. He loved Nature so well, was so happy in her solitude, that he became very jealous of cities, and the sad work which their refinements and artifices made with man and his dwelling. The axe was always destroying his forest. "Thank God," he said, "they cannot cut down the clouds!" "All kinds of figures are drawn on the blue ground with this fibrous white paint." ... [p. 248]

There is a flower known to botanists, one of the same genus with our summer plant called "Life-Everlasting," a *Gnaphalium* like that, which grows on the most inaccessible cliffs of the Tyrolese mountains, where the chamois dare hardly venture, and which the hunter, tempted by its beauty, and by his love (for it is immensely valued by the Swiss maidens), climbs the cliffs to gather, and is sometimes found dead at the foot, with the flower in his hand. It is called by botanists the *Gnaphalium leontopodium,* but by the Swiss *Edelweisse,* which signifies *Noble Purity.* Thoreau seemed to me living in the hope to gather this plant, which belonged to him of right. The scale on which his studies proceeded was so large as to require longevity, and we were the less prepared for his sudden disappearance. The country knows not yet, or in the least part, how great a son it has lost. It seems an injury that he should leave in the midst his broken task which none else can finish, a kind of indignity to so noble a soul, that he should depart out of Nature before yet he has been really shown to his peers for what he is. But he, at least, is content. His soul was made for the noblest society; he had in a short life exhausted the capabilities of this world; wherever there is knowledge, wherever there is virtue, wherever there is beauty, he will find a home.

—Ralph Waldo Emerson, "Thoreau," *Atlantic Monthly*, X (August, 1862), 239-249.

Henry D. Thoreau, of Concord, Mass., died at the age of 44 years, of pulmonary consumption.

His grandfather was a French emigrant from the island of Guernsey, and settled in Concord. His father was well known as a manufacturer of black-lead pencils, an art which young Thoreau learned, but never practised as a business, his tastes leading him wholly into the field of science, while he abhored trade.

Henry D. Thoreau was distinguished for the great accuracy of his observations, and for the thoroughness with which he executed every research upon which he entered. He was esteemed as an accurate land surveyor, the only business upon which he ever entered for pay. As a botanist he was highly esteemed by those who are the best judges of the subject.

As an observer of the habits of animals he was unrivalled. He would wait all day if it was necessary, for a bird to approach him. He said their curiosity would bring them to examine him if he would remain quiet long enough; and he generally managed to make familiar acquaintance with all living creatures he met with in his rambles through the forest. Thoreau had a genuine love of nature, and pursued natural history for his own gratification, and not with any ambitious views. He was greatly troubled to find that anything had escaped the observation of eminent naturalists, and seemed to be surprised that anything should have been left for him to discover.

Thoreau was a man of original genius, and very peculiar in his views of society and the ways of life. He was conscientiously scrupulous, and was opposed to aiding or abetting, even by a poll-tax, measures which he did not approve of, and therefore got into trouble occasionally with the constituted authorities of the town, who could not indulge him in his opposition to a tax because any part of it might go to support the militia; so they twice [No, only once] shut him up in the jail, from whence his friends took him by paying his tax against his protest.

His published works are full of knowledge of the secrets of nature, and are enlivened by much quaint humor, and warmed with kindness towards all living beings. Those who knew Thoreau best loved and appreciated him most.

—C. T. Jackson, "Henry D. Thoreau," *Proceedings of the Boston Society of Natural History*, IX (1862-1863), 70.

∽ ∾

He [Thoreau] passed for nothing, it is suspected, with most of us [Thoreau's college classmates] ; for he was cold and unimpressible. The touch of his hand was moist and indifferent, as if he had taken up something when he saw your hand coming, and caught your grasp upon it. How the prominent, grey-blue eyes seemed to rove down the path, just in advance of his feet, as his grave Indian stride carried him down to University Hall!

—John Weiss, "Thoreau," *Christian Examiner*, LXXIX (July, 1865), 97.

∽ ∾

He did not care for people; his classmates seemed very remote. This reverie hung always about him, and not so loosely as the odd garments which the pious household care furnished. Thought had not yet awakened his countenance; it was serene, but rather dull, rather plodding. The lips were not yet firm; there was almost a look of smug satisfaction lurking round their corners. It is plain now that he was preparing to hold his future views with great setness, and personal appreciation of their importance. The nose was prominent, but its curve fell forward without firmness over the upper lip; and we remember him as looking very much like some Egyptian sculptures of faces, large-featured, but brooding, immobile, fixed in a mystic egotism. Yet his eyes were sometimes searching, as if he had dropped, or expected to find, something. It was the look of Nature's own child learning to detect her way-side secrets; and those eyes have stocked his books with subtile traits of animate and inanimate creation which had escaped less patient observers. For he saw more upon the ground than anybody suspected to be there. His eyes slipped into every tuft of meadow or beach grass, and went winding in and out of the thickest undergrowth, like some slim, silent, cunning animal. They were amphibious besides, and slid under fishes' eggs and into their nests [p. 98] at the pond's bottom, to rifle all their contents. Mr. Emerson has noticed, that Thoreau could always find an Indian arrow-head in places that had been ploughed over and ransacked for years. "There is one," he would say, kicking it up with his foot. In fact, his eyes seldom left the ground, even in his most earnest conversation with you, if you can call earnest a tone and manner that was very confident, as of an opinion that had formed from granitic sediment, but also very level and unflushed with feeling. The Sphinx might have become passionate and exalted as soon.

In later years his chin and mouth grew firmer as his resolute and audacious opinions developed, the curves of the lips lost their flabbiness, the eyes twinkled with the latent humor of his criticisms of society. Still the countenance was unruffled: it seemed to lie deep, like a mountain tarn, with cool, still nature all around. There was not a line upon it expressive of ambition or discontent: the affectional emotions had never fretted at it. He went about, like a priest of Buddha who expects to arrive soon at the summit of a life of contemplation, where the divine absorbs the human. All his intellectual activity was of the spontaneous, open-air kind, which keeps the forehead smooth. His thoughts grew with all the rest of nature, and passively took their chance of summer and winter, pause and germination: no more forced than pine-cones; fragrant, but not perfumed, owing nothing to special efforts of art. His extremest and most grotesque opinion had never been under glass. It all grew like the bolls on forest-trees, and the deviations from stem-like or sweeping forms. No man was ever such a placid thinker. It was because his thinking was observation isolated from all the temptations of society, from the artificial exigencies of literature, from the conventional sequence. Its truthfulness was not logically attained, but insensibly imbibed, during woodchopping, fishing, and scenting through the woods and fields. So that the smoothness and plumpness of a child were spread over his deepest places.

His simple life, so free from the vexations that belong to the most ordinary provision for the day, and from the wear [p. 99] and tear of habits helped his countenance to preserve this complacency. He had instincts, but no habits; and they wore him no more than they do the beaver and the blue-jay. Among them we include his rare intuitive sensibility for moral truth and for the fitness of things. For, although he lived so closely to the ground, he could still say, "My desire for knowledge is intermittent; but my desire to bathe my head in atmospheres unknown to my feet is perennial and constant. The highest that we can attain to is not knowledge, but sympathy with intelligence." But this intuition came up, like grass in spring, with no effort that is traceable, or that registers itself anywhere except in the things grown. You would look in vain for the age of his thoughts upon his face.

Now, it is no wonder that he kept himself aloof from us in college; for he was already living on some Walden Pond, where he had run up a temporary shanty in the depths of his reserve. He built it better afterwards, but no nearer to men. Did anyone ever tempt him down to Snow's, with the offer of an unlimited molluscous entertainment? The naturalist was not yet enough awakened to lead him to ruin a midnight stomach for the sake of the constitution of an oyster. Who ever saw him sailing out of Willard's long entry upon that airy smack which students not intended for the pulpit launched from portwine sangarees? We are confident that he never discovered the backparlor aperture through which our finite thirst communicated with its spiritual source. So that his observing faculty must, after all, be charged with limitations. We say, *our* thirst, but would not be understood to include those who were destined for the ministry, as no clergyman in the embryonic state was ever known to visit Willard's. But Thoreau was always indisposed to call at the ordinary places for his spiritual refreshment; and he went farther than most persons when apparently he did not go so far. He soon discovered that all sectarian and denominational styles of thinking had their Willard within economical distance; but the respective taps did not suit his country palate. He was in his cups when he was out of doors, where [p. 100] his lips fastened to the far horizon, and he tossed off the whole costly vintage that mantled in the great circumference.

But he had no animal spirits for our sport or mischief. We cannot recollect what became of him during the scenes of the Dunkin Rebellion [a student uprising]. He must have slipped off into some "cool retreat or mossy cell." We are half inclined to suppose that the tumult startled him into some metamorphose, that corresponded to a yearning in him of some natural kind, whereby he secured a temporary evasion till peace was restored. He may also, in this interim of qualified humanity, have established an understanding with the mute cunning of nature, which appeared afterwards in his surprising recognition of the ways of squirrels, birds, and fishes. It is certainly quite as possible that man should take off his mind, and drop into the medium of animal intelligence, as that Swedenborg, Dr. Channing, and other spirits of just men made perfect, should strip off the senses and conditions of their sphere, to come dabbling about in the atmosphere of earth among men's thoughts. However this may be, Thoreau disappeared while our young absurdity held its orgies, stripping shutters from the lower windows of the buildings, dismantling recitation rooms, greeting tutors and professors with a frenzied and groundless indignation which we symbolized by kindling the spoils of sacked premises upon the steps. It probably occurred to him that fools might rush in where angels were not in the habit of going. We recollect that he declined to accompany several fools of this description, who rushed late, all in a fine condition of contempt, with Corybantic gestures, into morning prayers,—a college exercise which we are confident was never attended by the angels.

It is true he says, "Give me for my friends and neighbors wild men, not tame ones;" and a little after, in the same essay, "I rejoice that horses and steers have to be broken before they can be made the slaves of men, and that men themselves have some wild oats still left to sow before they become submissive members of society." But, in fact, there is nothing so conventional as the mischief of a boy who is grown large enough to light bonfires, and run up a bill for [p. 101] "special repairs," and not yet large enough to include in such a bill his own disposition to "haze" his comrades and to have his fits of anarchy. Rebellion is "but a faint symbol of the awful ferity with which good men and lovers meet."

There was no conceit of superior tendencies and exclusive tastes which prevented him from coming into closer contact with individuals. But it was not shyness alone which restrained him, nor the reticence of an extremely modest temperament. For he was complacent; his reserve was always satisfactory to himself. Something in his still latent and brooding genius was sufficiently attractive to make his wit "home-keeping;" and it very early occurred to him, that he should not better his fortunes by familiarity with other minds. This complacency, which lay quite deep over his youthful features, was the key to that defect of sympathy which led to defects of expression, and to unbalanced statements of his thought. It had all the effect of the seclusion that some men inflict upon themselves, when from conceit or disappointment they restrict the compass of their life to islands in the great expanse, and become reduced at last, after nibbling every thing within the reach of their tether, to simple rumination, and incessant returns of the same cud to the tongue. This, and not listlessness, nor indolence, nor absolute incapacity for any professional pursuit, led him to the banks of Walden Pond, where his cottage, sheltering a self-reliant and homely life, seemed like something secreted by a quite natural and inevitable constitution. You might as well quarrel with the self-sufficiency of a perfect day of Nature, which makes no effort to conciliate, as with this primitive disposition of his. The critic need not feel bound to call it a vice of temper because it nourished faults. He should, on the contrary, accept it as he sees that it secured the rare and positive characteristics which make Thoreau's books so full of new life, of charms unborrowed from the resources of society, of suggestions lent by the invisible beauty to a temperate and cleanly soul. A greater deference to his neighborhood would have impaired the peculiar genius which we ought to delight to recognize as fresh from a divine inspiration, filled with [p. 102] possibilities like an untutored America, as it hints at improvement in its very defects, and is fortunately guarded by its own disability. It was perfectly satisfied with its own ungraciousness, because that was essential to its private business. Another genius might need to touch human life at many points, to feel the wholesome shocks; to draw off the subtile nourishment which the great mass generates and comprises; to take in the reward for parting with some effluence: but this would have been fatal to Thoreau. It would have cured his faults and weakened his genius. He would have gained friends within the world, and lost his friends behind it.

—*Ibid.*, LXXIX, 98-103.

‽   ‽

He once asked the writer, with that deliberation from which there seemed as little escape as from the pressure of the atmosphere, "Have you ever yet in preaching been so [p. 105] fortunate as to say anything?" Tenderness for the future barrel, which was then a fine plump keg, betrayed us into declaring confidently that we had. "Then your preaching days are over. Can you bear to say it again? You can never open your mouth again for love or money."

—*Ibid.*, LXXIX, 105-106.

‽   ‽

Toward the close of his life, he was visited by one of those dealers in ready-made clothing, who advertise to get any soul prepared at a moment's notice for a sudden trip. Complete outfits, including "a change," and patent fire-proof, are furnished at the very bedside, or place of embarkation, of the most shiftless spirits. "Henry, have you made your peace with God?" To which our slop-dealer received the somewhat noticeable reply, "I have never quarrelled with him." We [p. 111] fancy the rapid and complete abdication of the cheap-clothing business in the presence of such forethought.

A friend of the family was very anxious to know how he stood affected toward Christ, and he told her that a snow-storm was more to him than Christ. So he got rid of these cankers that came round to infest his soul's blossoming time. Readers ought not to bring a lack of religion to the dealing with his answers.

—*Ibid.*, LXXIX, 111-112.

‽   ‽

On a summer morning about fourteen years ago I went with Mr. Emerson and was introduced to Thoreau. I was then connected with Divinity College at Cambridge, and my new acquaintance was interested to know what we were studying there at the time. "Well, the Scriptures." "But *which?*" he asked, not without a certain quiet humor playing about his serious blue eye. It was evident that, as Morgana in the story marked all the doors so that the one ceased to be a sign, he had marked Persian and Hindu and other ethnical Scriptures with the reverential sign usually found on the Hebrew writings alone. He had the best library of Oriental books in the country, and subsequently Mr. Cholmondeley, an English gentleman to whom he was much attached, sent him from England more than a score of important works of this character. His books show how closely and reverently he had studied them, and indeed are worthy of attention from lovers of Eastern Scriptures apart from their other values. Out of courtesy to my introducer, doubtless, he asked me to go with him on the following day to visit some of the pleasant places around the village (in which I was as yet a stranger), and I gladly accepted the offer. When I went to the house next morning, I found them all (Thoreau was then living in his father's house) in a state of excitement by reason of the arrival of a fugitive negro from the South, who had come fainting to their door about daybreak and thrown himself on their mercy. Thoreau took me in to see the poor wretch, whom I found to be a man with whose face as that of a slave in the South I was familiar. The negro was much terrified at seeing me, supposing that I was one of his pursuers. Having quieted his fears by the assurance that I too, though in a different sense, was a refugee from the bondage he was escaping, and at the same time being able to attest the negro's genuineness, I sat and [p. 191] watched the singularly tender and lowly devotion of the scholar to the slave. He must be fed, his swollen feet bathed, and he must think of nothing but rest. Again and again this coolest and calmest of men drew near to the trembling negro, and bade him feel at home, and have no fear that any power should again wrong him. He could not walk that day, but must mount guard over the fugitive, for slave-hunters were not extinct in those days; and so I went away after a while much impressed by many little traits that I had seen as they had appeared in this emergency, and not much disposed to cavil at their source, whether Bible or Bhaghavat.

A day or two later, however, I enjoyed my first walk with Thoreau which was succeeded by many others. We started westward from the village, in which direction his favorite walks lay, for I then found out the way he had of connecting casual with universal things. He desired to order his morning walk after the movement of the planet. The sun is the grand western pioneer; he sets his gardens of Hesperides on the horizon every evening to lure the race; the race moves westward, as animals migrate by instinct; therefore we are safe in going by Goose pond to Baker's farm. Of every square acre of ground, he contended, the western side was the wildest, and therefore the fittest for the seeker to explore. *Ex oriente lux, ex occidente frux.* I now had leisure to observe carefully this man. He was short of stature, well built, and such a man as I have fancied Julius Caesar to have been. Every movement was full of courage and repose; the tones of his voice were those of Truth herself; and there was in his eye the pure bright blue of the New-England sky, as there was sunshine in his flaxen hair. He had a particularly strong aquiline Roman nose, which somehow reminded me of the prow of a ship. There was in his face and expression, with all its sincerity, a kind of intellectual furtiveness; no wild thing could escape him more than it could be harmed by him. The gray huntsman's suit which he wore enhanced this expression.

> "He took the color of his vest
> From rabbit's coat and grouse's breast;
> For as the wild kinds lurk and hide,
> So walks the huntsman unespied."

The cruellest weapons of attack, however, which this huntsman took with him were a spyglass for birds, a microscope for the game that would hide in smallness, and an old book in which to press plants. His powers of conversation were extraordinary. I remember being surprised and delighted at every step with revelations of laws and significant attributes in common things—as a relation between different kinds of grass, and the geological characters beneath them, the variety and grouping of pine needles, and the effect of these differences on the sounds they yield when struck by the wind, and the shades, so to speak, of taste represented by grasses and common herbs when applied to the tongue. The acuteness of his senses was marvellous: no hound could scent better, and he could hear the most faint and distant sounds without even laying his ear to the ground like an Indian. As we penetrated farther and farther into the woods he seemed to gain a certain transformation, and his face shone with a light that I had not seen in the village. He had a calendar of the plants and flowers of the neighborhood, and would sometimes go around a quarter of a mile to visit some floral friend, whom he had not seen for a year, who would appear for that day only. We were too early for the *hibiscus,* a rare flower in New-England which I desired to see. He pointed out the spot by the river side where alone it could be found, and said it would open about the following Monday and not stay long. I went on Tuesday evening and found myself a day too late—the petals were scattered on the ground.

—Moncure D. Conway, "Thoreau," *Eclectic Magazine,* LXVII (August, 1866), 191-192.

Thoreau, the Concord hermit, who lived by himself in the woods, used to come smiling up to his neighbors, to announce that the bluebirds had arrived, with as much interest in the fact as other men take in messages by the Atlantic cable. On certain days, he made long pilgrimages to find

"The sweet rhodora in the wood,"

welcoming the lonely flower like a long-absent friend. He gravely informed us once, that frogs were much more confiding in the spring, than later in the season; for then, it only took an hour to get well acquainted with one of the speckled swimmers, who liked to be tickled with a blade of grass, and would feed from his hand in the most sociable manner.

—Louisa May Alcott, "Merry's Monthly Chat with His Friends," *Merry's Museum,* March 1869, p. 147.

My friend and neighbor united these qualities of sylvan and human in a more remarkable manner than any whom it has been my happiness to know. Lover of the wild, he lived a borderer on the confines of civilization, jealous of the least encroachment upon his possessions.

> "Society were all but rude
> In his umbrageous solitude." [p. 11]

I had never thought of knowing a man so thoroughly of the country, and so purely a son of nature. I think he had the profoundest passion for it of any one of his time; and had the human sentiment been as tender and pervading, would have given us pastorals of which Virgil and Theocritus might have envied him the authorship had they chanced to be his contemporaries. As it was, he came nearer the antique spirit than any of our native poets, and touched the fields and groves and streams of his native town with a classic interest that shall not fade. Some of his verses are suffused with an elegiac tenderness, as if the woods and brooks bewailed the absence of their Lycidas, and murmured their griefs meanwhile to one another,—responsive like idyls. Living in close companionship with nature, his muse breathed the spirit and voice of poetry. For when the heart is once divorced from the senses and all sympathy with common things, then poetry has fled and the love that sings.

The most welcome of companions was this plain countryman. One seldom meets with thoughts like his, coming so scented of mountain and field breezes and rippling springs, so like a luxuriant clod from under forest leaves, moist and mossy with earth-spirits. His presence was tonic, like ice-water in dog-days to the parched citizen pent in chambers and under brazen ceilings. Welcome as the gurgle of brooks and dipping of pitchers,—then drink and be cool! He seemed one with things, of nature's essence and core, knit of [p. 12] strong timbers,—like a wood and its inhabitants. There was in him sod and shade, wilds and waters manifold,—the mould and mist of earth and sky. Self-poised and sagacious as any denizen of the elements, he had the key to every animal's brain, every plant; and were an Indian to flower forth and reveal the scents hidden in his cranium, it would not be more surprising than the speech of our Sylvanus. He belonged to the Homeric age,—was older than pastures and gardens, as if he were of the race of heroes and one with the elements. He of all men seemed to be the native New-Englander, as much so as the oak, the granite ledge; our best example of an indigenous American, untouched by the old country, unless he came down rather from Thor, the Northman, whose name he bore.

A peripatetic philosopher, and out-of-doors for the best part of his days and nights, he had manifold weather and seasons in him; the manners of an animal of probity and virtue unstained. Of all our moralists, he seemed the wholesomest, the busiest, and the best republican citizen in the world; always at home minding his own affairs. A little over-confident by genius, and stiffly individual, dropping society clean out of his theories, while standing friendly in his strict sense of friendship, there was in him an integrity and love of justice that made possible and actual the virtues of Sparta and the Stoics,—all the more welcome in his time of shuffling and pusillanimity. Plutarch [p. 13] would have made him immortal in his pages had he lived before his day. Nor have we any so modern withal, so entirely his own and ours: too purely so to be appreciated at once. A scholar by birthright, and an author, his fame had not, at his decease, travelled far from the banks of the rivers he described in his books; but one hazards only the truth in affirming of his prose, that in substance and pith, it surpasses that of any naturalist of his time; and he is sure of large reading in the future. There are fairer fishes in his pages than any swimming in our streams; some sleep of his on the banks of the Merrimack by moonlight that Egypt never rivalled; a morning of which Memmon might have envied the music, and a greyhound he once had, meant for Adonis; frogs, better than any of Aristophanes; apples wilder than Adam's. His senses seemed double, giving him access to secrets not easily read by others; in sagacity resembling that of the beaver, the bee, the dog, the deer; an instinct for seeing and judging, as by some other, or seventh sense; dealing with objects as if they were shooting forth from his mind mythologically, thus completing the world all round to his senses; a creation of his at the moment. I am sure he knew the animals one by one, as most else knowable in his town; the plants, the geography, as Adam did in his Paradise, if indeed, he were not that ancestor himself. His works are pieces of exquisite sense, celebrations of Nature's virginity exemplified by rare learning, deli[p. 14]cate art, re-

plete with observations as accurate as original; contributions of the
unique to the natural history of his country, and without which it
were incomplete. Seldom has a head circumscribed so much of the
sense and core of Cosmos as this footed intelligence.

If one would learn the wealth of wit there was in this plain man,
the information, the poetry, the piety, he should have accompanied
him on an afternoon walk to Walden, or elsewhere about the skirts of
his village residence. Pagan as he might outwardly appear, yet he was
the hearty worshipper of whatsoever is sound and wholesome in nature,—a piece of russet probity and strong sense, that nature delighted to own and honor. His talk was suggestive, subtle, sincere,
under as many masks and mimicries as the shows he might pass; as
significant, substantial,—nature choosing to speak through his mouth-
piece,—cynically, perhaps, and searching into the marrows of men
and times he spoke of, to his discomfort mostly and avoidance.

Nature, poetry, life,—not politics, not strict science, not society
as it is,—were his preferred themes. The world was holy, the things
seen symbolizing the things unseen, and thus worthy of worship, calling men out-of-doors and under the firmament for health and whole-
someness to be insinuated into their souls, not as idolators, but as
idealists. His religion was of the most primitive type, inclusive of all
natural creatures and things, even to "the sparrow that falls to the
ground," though never by shot of his, and for whatsoever was [p. 15]
manly in men, his worship was comparable to that of the priests and
heroes of all time. I should say he inspired the sentiment of love, if,
indeed, the sentiment did not seem to partake of something purer,
were that possible, but nameless from its excellency. Certainly he was
better poised and more nearly self-reliant than other men.

> "The happy man who lived content
> With his own town, his continent,
> Whose chiding streams its banks did curb
> As ocean circumscribes its orb,
> Round which, when he his walk did take,
> Thought he performed far more than Drake;
> For other lands he took less thought
> Than this his muse and mother brought."

More primitive and Homeric than any American, his style of
thinking was robust, racy, as if Nature herself had built his sentences

and seasoned the sense of his paragraphs with her own vigor and salubrity. Nothing can be spared from them; there is nothing superfluous; all is compact, concrete, as nature is.

His politics were of a piece with his individualism. We must admit that he found little in political or religious establishments answering to his wants, that his attitude was defiant, if not annihilating, as if he had said to himself:—

"The state is man's pantry at most, and filled at an enormous cost,—a spoliation of the human common-wealth. Let it go. Heroes can live on nuts, and free-men sun themselves in the clefts of rocks, rather than [p. 16] sell their liberty for this pottage of slavery. We, the few honest neighbors, can help one another; and should the state ask any favors of us, we can take the matter into consideration leisurely, and at our convenience give a respectful answer.

"But why require a state to protect one's rights? the man is all. Let him husband himself; needs he other servant or runner? Self-keeping is the best economy. That is a great age when the state is nothing and man is all. He founds himself in freedom, and maintains his uprightness therein; founds an empire and maintains states. Just retire from those concerns, and see how soon they must needs go to pieces, the sooner for the virtue thus withdrawn from them. All the manliness of individuals is sunk in that partnership in trade. Not only must I come out of myself, if I will be free and independent. Shall one be denied the privilege on coming of mature age of choosing whether he will be a citizen of the country he happens to be born in, or another? And what better title to a spot of ground than being a man, and having none? Is not man superior to state or country? I plead exemption from all interference by men or states with my individual prerogatives. That is mine which none can steal from me, nor is that yours which I or any man can take away."

> "I am too high born to be propertied,
>   To be a secondary at control,
>   Or useful serving man and instrument
>   To any sovereign state throughout the world."

—Bronson Alcott, "Thoreau," *Concord Days* (Boston: Roberts Brothers, 1872), pp. 11-17.

Henry retained a peculiar pronunciation of the letter *r*, with a decided French accent. He says, "September is the first month with a *burr* in it;" and his speech always had an emphasis, a *burr* in it."

—Ellery Channing, *Thoreau: the Poet-Naturalist* (Boston: Roberts Brothers, 1873), p. 2.

∞ ∞

Once when a follower was done up with a headache and incapable of motion, hoping his associate would comfort him and perhaps afford him a sip of tea, he said, "There are people who are sick in that way every morning, and go about their affairs," and then marched off about his.

—*Ibid.*, p. 3.

∞ ∞

He also had the firmness of the Indian, and could repress his pathos; as when he carried (about the age of ten) his pet chickens to an innkeeper for sale in a basket, who thereupon told him "*to stop,*" and for convenience' sake took them out one by one and wrung their several pretty necks before the poor boy's eyes, who did not budge. He had such a seriousness at the same age that he was called "judge."

—*Ibid.*, p. 11.

∞ ∞

A pleasing trait of his warm feeling is remembered, when he asked his mother, before leaving college, what profession to choose, and she replied pleasantly, "You can buckle on your knapsack, and roam abroad to seek your fortune." The tears came in his eyes and rolled down his cheeks, when his sister Helen, who was standing by, tenderly put her arm around him and kissed him, saying, "No, Henry, you shall not go: you shall stay at home and live with us."

—*Ibid.*

∞ ∞

Being complained of for taking a knife belonging to another boy, Henry said, "I did not take it,"—and was believed. In a few days the culprit was found, and Henry then said, "I knew all the time who it was, and the day it was taken I went to Newton with father." "Well, then," of course, was the question, "why did you not say so at the time?" "I did not take it," was his reply.

—*Ibid.*, p. 12.

∾ ∿

A school-fellow complained of him because he would not make him a bow and arrow, his skill at whittling being superior. It seems he refused, but it came out after that he had no knife.

—*Ibid.*

∾ ∿

An early anecdote remains of his being told at three years that he must die, as well as the men in the catechism. He said he did not want to die, but was reconciled; yet, coming in from coasting, he said he "did not want to die and go to heaven, because he could [p. 12] not carry his sled with him; for the boys said, as it was not shod with iron, it was not worth a cent."

—*Ibid.*, pp. 12-13.

∾ ∿

Another school experience was the town school in Concord, which he took after leaving college, announcing that he should not flog, but would talk morals as a punishment instead. A fortnight sped glibly along, when a knowing deacon, one of the School Committee, walked in and told Mr. Thoreau that he must flog and use the ferule, or the school would spoil. So he did, by feruling six of his pupils after school, one of whom was the maid-servant in his own house. But it did not suit well with his conscience, and he reported to the committee that he should no longer keep their school, as they interfered with his arrangements; and they could keep it.

—*Ibid.*, p. 24.

∾ ∿

In height, he was about the average; in his build, spare, with limbs that were rather longer than usual, or of which he made a longer use. His face, once seen, could not be forgotten. The features were quite marked: the nose aquiline or very Roman, like one of the portraits of Caesar (more like a beak, as was said) ; large, overhanging brows above the deepest set blue eyes that could be seen, in certain lights, and in others gray,—eyes expressive of all shades of feeling, but never weak or near-sighted; the forehead not unusually broad or high, full of concentrated energy and purpose; the mouth with prominent lips, pursed up with meaning and thought when silent, and giving out when open a stream of the most varied and unusual and instructive sayings. His hair was a dark brown, exceedingly abundant, fine and soft; and for several years he wore a comely beard. His whole figure had an active earnestness, as if he had no moment to waste. The clenched hand betokened purpose. In walking, he made a short cut if he could, and when sitting in the shade or by the wall-side seemed merely the clearer to look forward into the next piece of activity. Even in the boat he had a wary, transitory air, his eyes on the outlook,—perhaps there might be ducks, or the Blondin turtle, or an otter, or sparrow.

—*Ibid.*, p. 25.

>⚮ ⚮

Once walking in old Dunstable, he much desired the town history by C. J. Fox; and, knock[p. 26]ing as usual at the best house, went in and asked a young lady who made her appearance whether she had the book in question: she had,—it was produced. After consulting it somewhat, Thoreau in his sincere way inquired very modestly whether she "would not *sell* it to him." I think the plan surprised her, and have heard that she smiled; but he produced his wallet, gave her the pistareen, and went his way rejoicing with the book.

—*Ibid.*, pp. 26-27.

>⚮ ⚮

If he needed a box on his walk, he would strip a piece of birch-bark off the tree, fold it when cut straightly together, and put his tender lichen or [p. 249] brittle creature therein. In those irritable thunderclaps which come, he says, "with tender, graceful violence," he sometimes erected a transistory house by means of his pocket-knife, rapidly paring away the white-pine and oak, taking the lower limbs of a large tree and pitching on the cut brush for a roof. Here he sat, pleased with the minute drops from off the eaves, not questioning the love of electricity for trees. If out on the river, haul up your boat, turn it upside-down, and yourself under it. Once he was thus doubled up, when Jove let drop a pattern thunderbolt in the river in front of his boat, while he whistled a lively air as accompaniment. This is noted, as he was much distressed by storms when young, and used to go whining to his father's room, and say, "I don't feel well," and then take shelter in the paternal arms, when his health improved.

—*Ibid.*, pp. 249-250.

∾ ∾

When Thoreau laughed, like Shelley, the operation was sufficient to split a pitcher.

—*Ibid.*, p. 258.

∾ ∾

As an honorary member, Thoreau appertained to the Boston Society of Natural History, adding to its reports, besides comparing notes with the care-takers or curators of the *mise en scène*. To this body he left his collections of plants, Indian tools, and the like. His latest traffic with it refers to the number of bars or fins upon a pike, which had more or less than was decent. He sat upon his eggs with theirs. His city visit was to their books, and there he made his call, not upon the swift ladies of Spruce Street, and more than once he entered by the window before the janitor had digested his omelet.

—*Ibid.*, p. 263.

∾ ∾

When asked whether he knew a young miss, celebrated for her beauty, he inquired, "Is she the one with the goggles?"

—*Ibid.*, p. 311.

As long [sic] he [Thoreau during his last illness] could possibly sit up, he insisted on his chair at the family-table, and said, "It would not be social to take my meals alone." And on hearing an organ in the streets, playing some old tune of his childhood he should never hear again, the tears fell from his eyes, and he said, "Give him some money! give him some money!"

—*Ibid.*

I knew Thoreau well when we were school-boys together. He was considered by most of us boys as rather stupid, and unsympathetic, though by no means a poor scholar. I suppose we thought him stupid because he did not join heartily in our plays. I cannot recollect that he ever played with us at all. He seemed to have no fun in him. We used to bother him a good deal calling him "the fine scholar with a big nose." His quietness was more noticeable, no doubt, from the contrast between him and his brother John, who was as chock full of fun as an egg is of meat. I remember as if it were but yesterday, his sitting on the fence by the old brick school house, telling stories to the boys, and making our sides ache with laughter, or our eyes flood with tears. He would for hours together pour out a continual stream of anecdotes, so full of wit, humor, and pathos, that it seemed to me a wonder then, as it does even now when I think of it. I liked him better than his brother, though the former did at times invent some most improbable stories.

—A[lfred] M[unroe], "Concord Authors Continued," *Richmond County Gazette* (Stapleton, New York), August 15, 1877.

There were frequent opportunities of seeing Henry Thoreau, as he often came with his father to work on the land belonging to the house in which Mr. Robinson lived, or, as the children said, to "paint the handles of the trees." His meditative figure was often seen walking across the sunny meadows, with some live specimen of a "species" dangling from his hand, while (to use his own expression) "the sun on his back seemed like a gentle herdsman driving him home at evening." He sometimes called on Mr. Robinson. He was a great talker, sitting with his head bent over, and carrying on the "conversation" all by himself. On one occasion we had a visitor who had written several town histories, and was learned in Indian matters. Thoreau called while he was there; and, the conversation soon turning to [p. 67] Indian affairs, Thoreau talked our friend dumb in a very short time.

—Mrs. W. S. Robinson, *"Warrington" Pen-Portraits* (Boston: Robinson, 1877), pp. 67-68.

ᔓ ᔑ

When a boy he manifested peculiar traits of character. He perfectly hated street parades and shows, with their band accompaniment, that so generally excites the youthful mind. Nothing could induce him to engage in any game or sport,—he preferred to be an indifferent spectator.

—Joseph Hosmer, "Henry D. Thoreau," *Concord Freeman: Thoreau Annex*, 1880, p. 1.

ᔓ ᔑ

Early in September, 1845, (can it be so long,) on his invitation I spent a Sunday at his lake side retreat, as pure and delightful as with my mother.

The building was not then finished, the chimney had no beginning—the sides were not battened, or the walls plastered. It stood in the open field, some thirty rods from the lake, and the "Devil's Bar" and in full view of it.

Upon its construction he had evidently bestowed much care, and the proportions of it, together with the work, were very much better than would have been expected of a novice, and he seemed well pleased with his effort.

The entrance to the cellar was thro' a trap door in the center of the room. The king-post was an entire tree, extending from the bottom of the cellar to the ridge-pole, upon which we descended, as the sailors do into the hold of a vessel.

His hospitality and manner of entertainment were unique, and peculiar to the time and place.

The cooking apparatus was primitive and consisted of a hole made in the earth and inlaid with stones, upon which the fire was made, after the manner at the sea-shore, when they have a clam-bake.

When sufficiently hot remove the smoking embers and place on the fish, frog, etc. Our bill of fare included roasted horn pout, corn, beans, bread, salt, etc. Our viands were nature's own, "sparkling and bright."

I gave the bill of fare in English and Henry rendered it in French, Latin and Greek.

The beans had been previously cooked. The meal for our bread was mixed with lake water only, and when prepared it was spread upon the surface of a thin stone used for that purpose and baked. It was according to the old Jewish law and custom of unleavened bread, and of course it was very, very primitive.

When the bread had been sufficiently baked the stone was removed, then the fish placed over the hot stones and roasted—some in wet paper and some without—and when seasoned with salt, were delicious.

He was very much disappointed in not being able to present to me one of [p. 1] his little companions—a mouse.

He described it to me by saying that it had come upon his back as he leaned against the wall of the building, ran down his arm to his hand, and ate the cheese while holding it in his fingers; also, when he played upon the flute, it would come and listen from its hiding place, and remain there while he continued to play the same tune, but when he changed the tune, the little visitor would immediately disappear.

Owing perhaps to some extra noise, and a stranger present, it did not put in an appearance, and I lost that interesting part of the show—but I had enough else to remember all my life.

The land where he raised his beans and other vegetables had been so continuously cropped with rye in the years preceding that the weeds had a stunted and sickly look: this however was favorable, as the crops needed but little cultivation.

Perhaps it was in this "field of glory," strewn with the bones and fur of the wood-chucks and rabbits, that he took his first lessons in combativeness: as he had to contend with the woodchucks by day, and the owls (his faithful allies,) stood sentry by night to keep away the rabbits, (literal fact,) otherwise he would not have harvested a bean.

One of the axioms of his philosophy had been to take the life of nothing that breathed, if he could avoid it: but, it had now become a serious question with him, whether to allow the wood-chucks and rabbits to destroy his beans, or fight.

Having determined on the latter, he procured a steel trap, and soon caught a venerable old fellow to the "manor born," and one who had held undisputed possession there for all time.

After retaining the enemy of all beans in "durance vile" for a few hours, he pressed his foot on the spring of the trap and let him go—expecting and hoping never to see him more. Vain delusion!

In a few days after, on returning from the village post-office, on looking in the direction of the bean field, to his disgust and apprehension he saw the same old grey-back disappear behind some brush just outside the field.

On a reconnoisance he discovered that the enemy had taken up a strategic position covered by some brush near his beans, and had entrenched himself by digging a "rifle pit," and otherwise made preparations for a determined siege. Accordingly he again set the trap and again caught the thief.

Now it so happened that those old knights of the shot gun, hook and line, Wesson, Pratt and Co., were on a piscatorial visit to the "devil's bar," equipped with all the necessary appliances to allure the finny tribe to destruction. A council of war was held at the "Bar," to determine what should be done with the wood-chuck.

A decision was rendered immediately by that old and popular

landlord of the Middlesex, in his terse and laconic manner "knock his brains out."

This however was altogether too severe on the woodchuck, thought Henry; even woodchucks had some rights that "Squatter Sovereigns" should respect. Was he not the original occupant there? and had he not "jumped" the "wood-chucks claim" destroyed his home, and built his "hut" upon the ruins? After considering the question carefully he took the woodchuck in his arms and carried him some two miles away; and then with a severe admonition at the end of a good stick, he opened the trap, and again let him "depart in peace"; and he never saw him more.

—*Ibid.*, pp. 1-2.

∾ ∾

I like to see him come in, he always smells of the pine woods.

—James T. Fields, in Annie Fields, *James T. Fields* (Boston: Houghton Mifflin, 1881), p. 102.

∾ ∾

Just after the tragedy in Virginia [Harpers Ferry], and before the companions of Brown had been executed, I received a message from Dr. David Thayer, of Boston, implying, as I thought, that John Brown, Jr. was at his house, and I went in haste to meet him there. I found, instead, young Francis Jackson Merriam, of Boston, who had joined Brown's band in Maryland a few weeks before, had escaped with Owen Brown, and, after a little rest in Canada, had come back to Boston to raise another expedition against the slave-holders. He was quite unfit to lead or even join in such an affair, being weak in body and almost distracted in mind; and I insisted that he should return at once to Canada. Wendell Phillips and Dr. Thayer had given him the same advice, and he finally, before I left him, agreed to go back that night, by a train on the Fitchburg Railroad. But by accident he took another train which ran no farther than Concord, and early in the evening repaired to my house there, and was received by my sister in my absence. A reward of several thousand dollars had been offered for his arrest, and it was unsafe, even in Massachusetts, for him to be seen. Nor did I think it well to see him again, lest I should be questioned about him. I therefore obtained from Mr. Emerson the loan of his horse and covered wagon, to be ready at sunrise next morning; then went to Mr. Thoreau who lived near me, and asked him to drive the wagon from Mr. Emerson's to my house, take in a Mr. Lockwood (the name by which Merriam was then called,) and see that he was put on board the next train for Canada, at the South Acton station, four miles away. Thoreau readily consented, and early the next morning walked to Mr. Emerson's, found the horse harnessed, drove him to my door, and took in Merriam, under the name of "Lockwood," neither of them knowing who the other really was. Merriam was in a flighty state of mind, and though he had agreed to go [p. 215] back to Canada, and knew his own life depended on it, could not keep to that purpose. He insisted to Mr. Thoreau that he must see Mr. Emerson before he left Concord, must lay before him the plan of invading the South, and must consult him also about certain moral and religious questions that troubled his mind. Mr. Thoreau gravely listened, and drove the horse along toward Acton. Merriam grew more positive and suspicious. He had never seen Mr. Emerson; perhaps he might have no other chance. "Perhaps *you* are Mr. Emerson; you look like the portraits of him." "No," said Thoreau, "I am not,"—and drove steadily on toward Acton. Whereupon the unfortunate youth cried, "Well, then I am going back to Concord," and flung himself out of the wagon. What measures my friend took to get his passenger in again he never told me, but I suspect some judicious force was used, accompanied by the grave, persuasive speech which was natural to Thoreau. At any rate, he drove on, brought his man in due season to South Acton, saw him on board the Canada train, returned the wagon to Mr. Emerson, (who knew nothing of its use, though suspecting it, and glad to promote such escapes,) and reported to me that "Mr. Lockwood had taken passage for Montreal," where he safely arrived the next day.

The matter was then dismissed, and nothing was said of it by Thoreau to his own family or to me, until more than two years afterward, in his last illness, when he one day inquired who my friend Lockwood was. Merriam at that time was out of all danger on the old score, and had been for some time a soldier in the Union army of 1861-2. I therefore told Thoreau the story,—that "Lockwood" was the grandson of his mother's old friend, Francis Jackson, the abolitionist, and was the person whose escape from Harper's Ferry he well remembered. Thoreau then related, with much amusement, the incidents of his brief acquaintance with Merriam, and some of the odd sayings of the young fugitive, whose true history he had suspected at the time. Thoreau died on May 6, 1862, and Merriam not long after, in the military service, though not in battle.

—F. B. Sanborn, "Henry David Thoreau," *Harvard Register*, III (April, 1881), 215-216.

∽ ∾

Who nearer Nature's life would truly come
Must nearest come to him [Thoreau] of whom I speak;
He all kinds knew,—the vocal and the dumb;
Masterful in genius was he, and unique,
Patient, sagacious, tender, frolicsome.
This Concord Pan would oft his whistle take,
And forth from wood and fen, field, hill, and lake,
Trooping around him, in their several guise,
The shy inhabitants their haunts forsake:
Then he, like Esop, man would satirize,
Hold up the image wild to clearest view
Of undiscerning manhood's puzzled eyes,
And mocking say, "Lo! mirrors here for you:
Be true as these, if ye would be more wise."

—Amos Bronson Alcott, Sonnet XIII, in *Sonnets and Canzonets* (Boston: Roberts, 1882), p. 119.

∽ ∾

Much do they wrong our Henry, wise and kind,
Morose who name thee, cynical to men,
Forsaking manners civil and refined
To build thyself in Walden woods a den,—
Then flout society, flatter the rude hind.

We better knew thee, loyal citizen!
Thou, friendship's all-adventuring pioneer,
Civility itself didst civilize:
Whilst braggart boors, wavering twixt rage and fear,
Slave hearths lay waste, and Indian huts surprise,
And swift the Martyr's gibbet would uprear:
Thou hail'dst him great whose valorous emprise
Orion's blazing belt dimmed in the sky,—
Then bowed thy unrepining head to die.

—Amos Bronson Alcott, Sonnet XIV, in *ibid.*, p. 121.

Some times I have gone with Thoreau and his young comrades
for an expedition on the river. Upon such excursions his resources
for our entertainment was inexhaustible. He would tell stories of the
Indians who once dwelt thereabout, until the children almost looked
to see a red man skulking with his arrow on shore; and every plant
or flower on the bank or in the water, and every fish, turtle, frog,
lizard about us was transformed by the wand of his knowledge from
the low form into which the spell of our ignorance had [p. 286] reduced its princely beauty. One of his surprises was to thrust his
hand softly into the water, and raise up before our astonished eyes a
bright fish which lay in his hand as if they were old acquaintances!
If the fish had also dropped a penny from its mouth, it could not
have been a more miraculous proceeding to us. The entire crew bared
their arms and tried to get hold of a fish, but only our captain succeeded. We could not get his secret from him then, for it was to surprise and delight many another merry boat-full; but later I have read
in his account of the bream or ruff (*Pomotis vulgaris*) of that river,
that it is a simple and inoffensive fish, whose nests are visible all
along the shore, hollowed in the sand, over which it is steadily poised
through the summer hours on waving fin. "The breams are so careful
of their charge, that you may stand close by in the water and examine
them at your leisure. I have thus stood over them half an hour at a
time, and stroked them familiarly without frightening them: suffering them to nibble my fingers harmlessly; and seen them erect their

dorsal fins in anger when my hand approached their ova; and have even taken them gently out of the water with my hand."

—Moncure Daniel Conway, *Emerson at Home and Abroad* (Boston: Osgood, 1882), pp. 286-287.

∽ ∾

April 11, 1855.

To-night we had a call from Mr. Thoreau, who came at eight and stayed till ten. He talked about Latin and Greek—which he thought ought to be studied—and about other things. In his tones and gestures he seemed to me to imitate Emerson, so that it was annoying to listen to him, though he said many good things. He looks like Emerson, too,—coarser, but with something of that serenity and sagacity which E. has. Thoreau looks eminently *sagacious*—like a sort of wise, wild beast. He dresses plainly, wears a beard in his throat, and has a brown complexion.

—F. B. Sanborn, *Henry D. Thoreau* (Boston: Houghton Mifflin, 1882), p. 198.

∽ ∾

Your view concerning Thoreau is entirely in consent with that which I entertain. His general conduct has been very satisfactory and I was willing and desirous that whatever falling off there had been in his scholarship should be attributable to his sickness.

He had, however, imbibed some notions concerning emulation & College rank, which had a natural tendency to diminish his zeal, if not his exertions.

His instructors were impressed with the conviction that he was indifferent, even to a degree that was faulty and that they could not recommend him consistent with the rule, by which they are usually governed in relation to beneficiaries. I [p. 53] have, always, entertained a respect for, and interest in, him, and was willing to attribute any apparent neglect, or indifference to his ill-health rather than to wilfulness. I obtained from the instructors the authority to state all the facts to the Corporation, and submit the result to their discretion.

This I did, and that body granted *Twenty-five dollars*, which was within *ten*, or at most *fifteen* dollars of any sum, he would have received had no objection been made.

There is no doubt that from some cause an unfavorable opinion has been entertained, since his return, after his sickness, of his disposition to exert himself. To what it has been owing, may be doubtful. I appreciate very fully the goodness of his heart and the strictness of his moral principle; and have done as much for him, as under the circumstances was possible.

—Josiah Quincy, Letter to Ralph Waldo Emerson, June 25, 1837, in *ibid.*, pp. 53-54. [Written in reply to a request from Emerson that Thoreau be granted a larger scholarship at Harvard.]

The undersigned very cheerfully hereby introduces to public notice, the bearer, Mr. David Henry Thoreau, as a Teacher in the higher branches of useful literature. He is a native of this town, [p. 57] & a graduate of Harvard University. He is well disposed & well qualified to instruct the rising generation. His scholarship & moral character will bear the strictest scrutiny. He is modest & mild in his disposition & government, but not wanting in energy of character & fidelity in the duties of his profession. It is presumed, his character & usefulness will be appreciated more highly as an acquaintance with him shall be cultivated. Cordial wishes for his success, reputation, & usefulness attend him, as an instructor & gentleman.

—Ezra Ripley, Letter "To the Friends of Education," May 1, 1838, in *ibid.*, pp. 57-58. [Written as a letter of recommendation for Thoreau when he was looking for a teaching position.]

I cordially recommend Mr. Henry D. Thoreau, a graduate of Harvard University in August, 1837, to the confidence of such parents or guardians as may propose to employ him as an instructor. I have the highest confidence in Mr. Thoreau's moral character and in his intellectual ability. He is an excellent Scholar, a man of energy

& kindness, & I shall esteem the town fortunate that secures his Services.

—Ralph Waldo Emerson, Letter of recommendation, May 2, 1838, in *ibid.*, p. 59.

≈ ≈

I certify that Henry D. Thoreau, of Concord, in this State of Massachusetts, graduated at this seminary [Harvard College] in August, 1837; that his rank was high as a scholar in all the branches, and his morals and general conduct unexceptionable and exemplary. He is recommended as well qualified as an instructor, for employment in any public or private school or private family.

—Josiah Quincy, Letter "To whom it may concern," March 26, 1838, in *ibid.*, p. 61. [Written as a letter of recommendation for Thoreau when he was looking for a teaching position.]

≈ ≈

Henry talks about Nature just as if she'd been born and brought up in Concord.

—Mrs. Samuel Hoar, in *ibid.*, p. 96.

≈ ≈

The time when Mr. Thoreau was our more intimate playfellow must have been in the years from 1850 to 1855. He used to come in, at dusk, as my brother and I sat on the rug before the dining-room fire, and, taking the great green rocking-chair, he would tell us stories. Those I remember were his own adventures, as a child. He began with telling us of the different houses he had lived in, and what he could remember about each. The house where he was born was on the Virginia road, near the old Bedford road. The only thing he remembered about that house was that from its windows he saw a flock of geese walking along in a row on the other side of the road; but to show what a long memory he had, when he told his mother of this, she said the only [p. 270] time he could have seen that sight was, when he was about eight months old, for they left that house then. Soon after, he lived in the old house on the Lexington road, nearly opposite Mr. Emerson's. There he was tossed by a cow as he played near the door, in his red flannel dress,—and so on, with a story for every house. He used to delight us with the adventures of a brood of fall chickens, which slept at night in a tall old fashioned fig-drum in the kitchen, and as their bed was not changed when they grew larger, they packed themselves every night each in its own place, and grew up, not shapely, but shaped to each other and the drum, like figs!

Sometimes he would play juggler tricks for us, and swallow his knife and produce it again from our ears or noses. We usually ran to bring some apples for him as soon as he came in, and often he would cut one in halves in fine points that scarcely showed on close examination, and then the joke was to ask Father to break it for us and see it fall to pieces in his hands. But perhaps the evenings most charming were those when he brought some ears of pop-corn in his pocket and headed an expedition to the garret to hunt out the old brass warming-pan; in which he would put the corn, and hold it out and shake it over the fire till it was heated through, and at last, as we listened, the rattling changed to pop[p. 271]ping. When this became very brisk, he would hold the pan over the rug and lift the lid, and a beautiful fountain of the white corn flew all over us. It required both strength and patience to hold out the heavy warming-pan at arm's length so long, and no one else ever gave us that pleasure.

I remember his singing 'Tom Bowline' to us, and also playing on his flute, but that was earlier. In the summer he used to make willow whistles, and trumpets out of the stems of squash leaves, and onion leaves. When he found fine berries during his walks, he always remembered us, and came to arrange a huckleberrying for us. He took charge of the 'hay rigging' with the load of children, who sat on the floor which was spread with hay, covered with a buffalo-robe; he sat on a board placed across the front and drove, and led the frolic with his jokes and laughter as we jolted along, while the elders of the family accompanied us in a 'carryall.' Either he had great tact and skill in managing us and keeping our spirits and play within bounds, or else he became a child in sympathy with us, for I do not remember a check or reproof from him, no matter how noisy we were. He always was most kind to me and made it his especial care to establish me in the 'thickest places,' as we used to call them. Those sunny afternoons are bright memories, and the lamb-kill flowers and sweet [p. 272] 'everlasting,' always recall them and his kind care. Once in a while he took us on the river in his boat, a rare pleasure then; and I remember one brilliant autumn afternoon, when he took us to gather the wild grapes overhanging the river, and we brought home a load of crimson and golden boughs as well. He never took us to walk with him, but sometimes joined us for a little way, if he met us in the woods on Sunday afternoons. He made those few steps memorable by showing us many wonders in so short a space: perhaps the only chincapin oak in Concord, so hidden that no one but himself could have discovered it—or some remarkable bird, or nest, or flower. He took great interest in my garden of wild flowers, and used to bring me seeds, or roots, of rare plants. In his last illness it did not occur to us that he would care to see us, but his sister told my mother that he watched us from the window as we passed, and said: 'Why don't they come to see me? I love them as if they were my own.' After that we went often, and he always made us so welcome that we liked to go. I remember our last meetings with as much pleasure as the old play-days.

—Anonymous ("a lady who knew him when she was a child, from the age of six to that of fifteen"), in *ibid.*, pp. 270-273.

∽ ∾

I always think of Thoreau when I look at a sunset [p. 306]. . . . He said to me in his last illness, 'I shall leave the world without regret,'—that was the saying either of a grand egotist or of a deeply religious soul.

—Bronson Alcott, in *ibid.*, pp. 306-307.

∽ ∾

One reader and friend of yours dwells now in my house, and, as I hope, for a twelvemonth to come,—Henry Thoreau,—a poet whom you may one day be proud of;—a noble, manly youth, full of melodies and inventions. We work together day by day in my garden, and I grow well and strong.

—Ralph Waldo Emerson, Letter to Thomas Carlyle, May 30, 1841, in *The Correspondence of Thomas Carlyle and Ralph Waldo Emerson* (Boston: Osgood, 1883), I, 335.

∞ ∞

It happened, one day, that Mr. Emerson was passing the house of Dr. Robbins, dentist, just as I was leaving it; and, while on the top of the steps, closing the door behind me, he hailed me from the sidewalk with the greeting, "Pray, what have you been doing there?"

"I have been getting a mutilated mouth repaired," was my reply.

"Indeed; have you come to that already? When Thoreau reached that stage of experience, and the operation had been ended, he exclaimed, 'What a pity that I could not have known betimes how much Art outdoes Nature in this kind of outfit for life, so that I might have spoken for such a set to start with!' "

—William Hague, *Life Notes or Fifty Years' Outlook* (Boston: Lee & Shepard, 1887), p. 187.

∞ ∞

I happened to meet Thoreau in Mr. Emerson's study at Concord. I think it was the first time we had come together after leaving college. I was quite startled by the transformation that had taken place in him. His short figure and general cast of countenance were, of course, unchanged; but in his manners, in the tones and inflections of his voice, in his modes of expression, even in the hesitations and pauses of his speech, he had become the counterpart of Mr. Emerson. Mr. Thoreau's college voice bore no resemblance to Mr. Emer[p. 121]son's, and was so familiar to my ear that I could readily have identified him by it in the dark. I was so much struck with the change, and with the resemblance in the respects referred to between Mr. Emerson and Mr. Thoreau, that I remember to have taken the opportunity as they sat near together, talking, of listening to their conversation with closed eyes, and to have been unable to determine with certainty which was speaking. It was a notable instance of unconscious imitation. Nevertheless it did not surpass my comprehension. I do not know to what subtle influence to ascribe it, but, after conversing with Mr. Emerson for even a brief time, I always found myself able and inclined to adopt his voice and manner of speaking.

—David Greene Haskins, *Ralph Waldo Emerson: His Maternal Ancestors* (Boston: Cupples, Upham, 1887), pp. 121-122.

જ઼ ભ

I liked Thoreau though he was morbid. I do not think it was so much a love of woods, streams, and hills that made him live in the country, as from a morbid dislike of humanity. I remember Thoreau saying once, when walking with him in my favorite Brooklyn— "What is there in the people? Pshaw! what do you (a man who sees as well as anybody) see in all this cheating political corruption?" I did not like my Brooklyn spoken of in this way.

—Walt Whitman, in Herbert H. Gilchrist, ed., *Anne Gilchrist: Her Life and Writings* (London: Unwin, 1887), p. 237.

જ઼ ભ

From my first introduction, Thoreau seemed to me a man who had experienced Nature as other men are said to have experienced religion. An unmistakable courage, sincerity, and manliness breathed in every word he uttered.

—Edwin P. Whipple, *Recollections of Eminent Men* (Boston: Ticknor & Co., 1887), p. 134.

જ઼ ભ

Mr. Alcott, in 1847, fashioned from gnarled limbs of pine, oak with knotty excrescences and straight trunks of cedar, a fantastic but pleasing structure, some hundred steps from the [Emerson] house, for a retired study for his friend.

In this work he was helped by Mr. Thoreau, whose practical

mind was chafed at seeing a building, with no plan, feeling its way up, as it were, dictated at each step by the suggestion of the crooked bough that was used and necessarily often altered. He said, "I feel as if I were nowhere doing nothing." When it was nearly done some [p. 127] one said, "It looks like a church." The idea was not to be tolerated by the transcendental architect, so the porch had to come down for its look of untimely sanctimony.

Thoreau drove the nails, and drove them well, but as Mr. Alcott made the eaves curve upward for beauty, and lined the roof with velvet moss and sphagnum, Nature soon reclaimed it. Indeed Madam Emerson naively called it "The Ruin" when it was fresh from the hand of the builder. In spite of its real beauty, which drew many people to see it, the draughts (for it was full of apertures for doors and windows) and the mosquitoes from the meadow close by made it untenable, and my father never used it as a study.

—Edward Waldo Emerson, *Emerson in Concord* (Boston: Houghton Mifflin, 1888), pp. 127-128.

∾ ∾

If he had any affectation in his sincere and aspiring nature, it was a sort of inherited petulance, that covered a sensitive and affectionate nature, easily wounded by the scornful criticism which his new departure sometimes brought upon him.

—Edward Hoar, in H. S. Salt, *The Life of Henry David Thoreau* (London: Bentley, 1890), p. 118.

∾ ∾

I was introduced to him first by Mr. Emerson more than forty years ago, though I had known him by sight before at college. I recall nothing of that first interview unless it be some remarks upon astronomy, and his want of interest in the study [p. 144] as compared with studies relating more directly to this world—remarks such as he made here and there in his writings. My first real introduction was from the reading of an article of his in the *Dial* on "Aulus Persius Flaccus," which appears now in the *Week*. That led to my first writing to him, and to his reply, which is published in the volume of letters. Our correspondence continued for more than twelve years, and we visited each other at times, he coming here to Worcester, commonly to read something in public, or being on his way to read somewhere else.

As to the outward incidents of our intercourse, I think of little or nothing that it seems worth while to write. Our conversation, or rather his talking, when we were together, was in the strain of his letters and of his books. Our relation, as I look back on it, seems almost an impersonal one, and illustrates well his remark that "our thoughts are the epochs in our lives: all else is but as a journal of the winds that blew while we were here." His personal appearance did not interest me particularly, except as the associate of his spirit, though I felt no discord between them. When together, we had little inclination to talk of personal matters. His aim was directed so steadily and earnestly towards what is essential in our experience, that beyond all others of whom I have known, he made but a single impression on me. Geniality, versatility, personal familiarity are, of course, agreeable in those about us, and seem necessary in human intercourse, but I did not miss them in Thoreau, who was, while living, and is still in my recollection and in what he has left to us, such an effectual witness to what is highest and most precious in life. As I re-read his letters from time to time, which I never tire of doing, I am apt to find new significance in them, am still warned and instructed by them, with more force occasionally than ever before; so that in a sense they are still in the mail, have not [p. 145] altogether reached me yet, and will not probably before I die. They may well be regarded as addressed to those who can read them best.

—H. G. O. Blake, in *ibid.*, pp. 144-146.

But of Thoreau, that hypethral and separated man, I cannot say enough. Of no one did Mr. Emerson talk so often and tenderly. The relation between the two needs a clearer understanding. Emerson made Thoreau; he was the child of Emerson, as if of his own flesh. The elder took the younger fresh from college (rather drowsy; and

he dozed after his return, but the woods and rivers of Concord were
his college). Emerson woke him, gave him his start, and immediately
and astonishingly nourished him. He lived much at Emerson's house,
kept the garden and the home while their master [p. 76] was absent
in Europe, and instructed him in the mysteries of grafting and
parsley.

Emerson called him "My Spartan-Buddhist, Henry," "My Henry
Thoreau." With no one was he so intimate, until the disciple became
as his master, adopting his accent and form, realizing his attractions
and antipathies, and knowing his good and evil. The development of
this sturdy bud into its sturdier flower was a perpetual delight to the
philosopher. In Thoreau, he lived himself over again. He said he liked
Thoreau because "he had the courage of his convictions," but I
think he meant his own convictions. In both we mark the same features: as a severe and *outre* way of looking at events, and a searching
for lessons in them; avoidance of association; determination toward
the expression of their ideals in their life; choice of straitened ways
over broad ones, [p. 77] and refusal to turn aside for livings, re-
wards, and comforts; jealousy of domestic and local intellectual re-
straints, even to discontent with the pressure of the average public
sentiment; intolerance of make-shifts; keeping away from court
rooms, newspapers, and presidents' messages; "reading, not the
Times, but the Eternities," as one said; "Standing every man alone
on his own peak," as the other said. But the similarity does not go
much beyond these limitations. Though Emerson was larger, Thoreau
was the more concentrated and sinewy of the two; and, once beginning to carry out the parent's discipline and thought into his own
life, he was uncompromising; and the end was not seen, nor to be
anticipated. He ceased to be illustrator and personifier, or in any
sense derived. His movements, which had been projectile, a recognition of the elder's thorough and wholesome methods, now went far
beyond them; and, thenceforward, this resolute man advanced his
own kinetic principles, and went his own way to his own life. As of
himself he said—

"But after manned him for *his own* stronghold."

And, thereafter, though dwelling in Con[p. 78]cord, he lived in
a far country, and was differentiated to almost a distinct species.

The variations began soon, and his loyalty plunged him occasionally into dramatic situations. I shall never forget with what gusto Mr. Emerson related to me the story of Thoreau's constancy to his political resolutions created by John Brown's execution, and his amusing week [*sic*] of incarceration:—

"He was served with the writ of arrest on his way to the shoeshop; but he kept on, his shoe in his pail, to have them both mended."

"Henry was," continued Mr. Emerson, "homely in appearance, a rugged stone hewn from the cliff. I believe it is accorded to all men to be moderately homely; but he surpassed sex. He had a beautiful smile and an earnest look. His character reminds me of Massillon. One could jeopard anything on him. A limpid man, a realist with caustic eyes that looked through all words and shows and bearing with terrible perception! He was a greater Stoic than Zeno or Scaevola or Xenophanes—greater, because nothing of impurity clung to him, a man whose core and whose breath was conscience; and not one of those giants, not one of [p. 79] Europe's best, not Pitt or Burke or Grattan, but could come to him and say, *Peccavi*. His fault was that he brought nothing near to his heart; he kept all influences toward his extremities. Exaggerated moods we all have to suppress; for some amiability, or at least reciprocity, are necessary to make society possible. But he thought and said that society is always diseased, and the best most so. Men of note would come to talk with him.

" 'I don't know,' he would say; 'perhaps a minute would be enough for both of us.'

" 'But I come to walk with you when you take your exercise.'

" 'Ah, walking—that is my holy time.'

"And yet he was not a grave or austere man. I remember he made us all laugh with his accounts of what he sometimes saw in his walks. What was that he told me of the young Irishman whom he found kneeling before his mother in the attitude of prayer? But, drawing nearer, he discovered that the posture of the worshipper was merely in order that his mother might remove a dust particle from his eye with her tongue!

"His energy was exhausted in projecting a new path. He could not follow an old one, [p. 80] even when it was better for him. He believed things are lies because words are.

"He was an out of doors man. He would stand in the snow for hours measuring the increments in the growth of trees. These and other similar excesses brought on an affection of the throat which caused his end. He suffered with a stoicism beyond the race, and died in great pain, nobly, refusing opiates, yielding himself to death during sleepless nights and days.

"His ideas of living have been condemned, but let us remember he lived them out. A Mr. Cholmondeley, an English gentleman and graduate of Oxford, boarded while here with his mother; and, becoming much attached to him, wished him to accompany himself to the mountains of the Yellowstone, and afterwards to South America, engaging to defray all expenses. But not only to [p. 81] those invitations, but also to another of a trip across the States, Thoreau returned the unvarying response—

" 'I think I had better stay in Concord.'

"On one of these occasions, Cholmondeley enlarged fancifully upon the Hamadryads that would be found lurking among the Druidical forests about New Orleans, and the gorgeousness of the flora they would find on the Amazon River, mentioning particularly the Victoria Regia.

" 'And I am expecting to find some day the Victoria Regia on Concord River,' he said."

The Victoria Regia for every man, he may have meant, is to be found in the duty at his own doorway—a habit of thought characteristically Emerson's.

"He refused on graduating from Harvard to take his degree; 'It isn't worth five dollars,' he said. [p. 82. This legend has been proven apochryphal; his college diploma is still in existence.]

"I have always thought that he did not do justice to the influence of his college in forming him.

"Though living in civilization, he was the keenest observer of external nature I have ever seen. He had the trained sense of the Indian, eyes that saw in the night, his own way of threading the woods and fields, so that he felt his path through them in the densest night, without delay or interruption. He would hear a partridge fly into a bush in the dark of dawn, and guide you to the spot after day unerringly. The tread and trail of wild creatures were apparent to him by sight, hearing, and, I believe, smell; for he said that the mud-turtle obtained its peculiar odour after spring has come, *like other flowers.*" [p. 83] ...

"He was wont to assert that even in the oldest woods one could see foreign phenomena, if always on the watch with direct eyes and the right perception. And so he insisted that he found revolutionary army cans and the red Polar snow near the ponds of Fair Haven; and the *Labrador Ledium, Kalmia Glauca,* Canadian Lynx, a stormy petrel, and the little auk with the tanager, in the meadow of Sudbury." [p. 84] ...

"The fibre of nature was all through his joints and marrow, and through life he wore her livery. I don't know how long ago, far away in his ancestry (he said he was descended from the Northman, Thorer the dog-footed), she planned him, measured him for his suit.

"He will be blamed for his shortcomings in natural science, of which he made a profession; but his early death should be remembered.

"He understood the flora and the birds, but not the rocks. Out of doors he used instead of a gun a spy-glass. 'A gun,' he said, 'gives you the body, not the bird.' He would trace a fish-hawk to her nest; and then, examining the *débris* at the bottom, he would find out more about the nature of the fish-hawk than the veriest sportsman of them all. He was a naturalist, but also a poet, and would have penetrated from all external aspects of nature to the secrets of her heart. She always gave him a quick home and shelter—always just the tree at hand, with its low sloping branches ready for the poles and roof, and the boughs and foliage of spruce for a bed on which to cast his blanket. No sweeter sleeps than those! He saturated himself with the growing wheat until he came himself to be a bearded blade. [p. 86]

"His out of doors life made him sensitive within doors, so that he could endure the atmosphere of few houses. He used to say, by night every dwelling gives out bad air like a slaughter-house.

"Things happened to him, came to him as they will to lovers of the woods and fields.

"I remember once a friend accosted him while they were walking with a request for an arrow-head, if he should ever find one, lamenting how fruitlessly he had searched for one.

" 'They *are* rare,' said Thoreau, stooping and picking up a fragment of earth-covered substance he saw in the sod; 'and now that you have an opportunity, you had better examine this!' And he presented a fine specimen from which he finished disengaging the earthrust. An accident? I do not know. Sometimes I have thought the entire woods were a *cache* for him; he had such secrets of hiding things and finding them again. His invention of a new lead pencil was quite characteristical. He could buy none that would suit him, so he determined to make some. After close study and experiment, he produced the most excellent pencil I have ever seen, and manufactured [p. 87] some hundreds of them, which he distributed among his friends. A few found their way to a neighbouring city, and he was approached by capitalists with liberal offers to manufacture them in quantities for commercial purposes. But he refused, with the remark that he merely wished to make a good pencil for his own use; and the secret died with him. He overflowed with ridicule for household utensils, etc., such as the store-keepers offer, and the few such things he used he provided for himself, and they were much superior and more convenient. Did he want a portmanteau or box? Forthwith he produced it, stripping the bark off a tree, joining by dovetail without tack or nail, and chamfering the edges and bottom.

"He was a close student of a few books. He liked the ethnic scriptures. Cholmondeley had given him some rare and costly copies of the Bhagavad-Gita and other bibles. His style had been sometimes criticized as opaque, but that is a quality frequently found in the reader. It was a style that refused compromise as did the man. 'If the spirit of poetry,' he said, 'chooses to descend upon me as I stand still, it is well; if not, I will not go in search of her. Here, on this rugged [p. 88] soil of Massachusetts, I take my stand, baring my brow to the breeze of my own country and invoking the genius of my own words.'

"It is better to translate him than Epictetus or Marcus Antoninus. He looked inward, inward at the soul of things. Conscientious, earnest, he talked in plain words to the superstitious, and commanded his publishers not to change a line. Thus his pages seem profane and sometimes blasphemous. He did not hesitate at shocking any weather-worn creed or belief. Men called him sceptic; but he was too conscientious to go to church. It was curious how much his opinion was sought, considering how much it was derided. No sooner did any extraordinary news arrive than every one must know what Thoreau thought about the last happening. His poetry is of a new order. [p. 89] . . .

"He was penetrated with the elder classical influence; he breathed the antique. Yet it was impossible for him to copy words or anything.

"There was during his literary life between himself and Mr. Ticknor an inequality of temperament and taste, by which the publishing house of that gentleman was always prevented from doing Thoreau justice. Consequently, the *Atlantic* has published for Thoreau, but not his best work. Mr. Greeley was his most influential publishing friend. Thoreau has an always increasing number of readers, and the selectest class of any American in all Christendom. The 'Week on the Concord River' is his noblest work, pervaded with delightful ideas. And you must have the 'Letters and Select Poems' of his I have lately edited. I will give them to you.

"He had a great contempt for those who made no effort to gauge accurately their own powers and weaknesses, and by no means spared himself, of whom he said that a man [p. 90] gathers materials to erect a palace, and finally concludes to build a shantee with them."

—Charles J. Woodbury, *Talks with Ralph Waldo Emerson* (New York: Baker & Taylor, 1890), pp. 76-91. [An account of visits with Emerson from 1865 to 1870.]

～ ～

An old Concordian has favored me with some of the village impressions of Julian Hawthorne and others of that semi-Pagan annex to the Hub. "Did you know Thoreau?" I asked.

"I should say I did. We used to go, at his invitation, on huckleberrying excursions with him. We used to call him 'Henery.' Some of the town's people didn't like him at all, and thought him a sort of hermit boor, but he was very kind to children. He loved birds and the woods, and hated to see birds shot or rabbits trapped. He would not have harmed a fly. His rustication out on the shore of Walden

Pond was a good deal of an affectation. He would have starved, if it had not been that his sisters and mother cooked up pies and dough-nuts and sent them to him in a basket. The trouble with Thoreau was that he tried to live on an intellectual east wind. He died young, but would have lived on for years had his diet been roast beef and mutton chops. Thoreau was a good deal of a wag in a quiet humorous way. He once put cloth bandages on the claws of Mrs. Emerson's hens, that good lady having been sorely tried by her fowls invading the family flower patch. I guess Mrs. Emerson invented the notion of gloving her hens, and Thoreau carried out her instructions to the letter, and then went off and had his laugh out."

—Anonymous, "Thoreau Gloving Mrs. Emerson's Hens," *The Minneapolis Tribune,* undated clipping [c.1890].

All his life he kept out of people's way,—you were more apt to see his disappearing coat-tails than his face.

—Julian Hawthorne, *American Literature* (Boston: Heath, 1891), p. 146.

One of my most amusing impressions of Thoreau relates to a time when, in the Quixotism of youthful admiration, I had persuaded him to give a lecture in Boston, at my risk. He wrote (April 3, 1852) in a tone of timidity which may surprise those who did not know him, "I certainly do not feel prepared to offer myself as a lecturer to the Boston public, and hardly know whether more to dread a small audience or a large one. Nevertheless I will repress this squeamish-ness, and propose no alteration in your arrangements." The scene of the lecture was to be a small hall in a court, now vanished, opening from Tremont street, opposite King's Chapel, the hall itself being leased by an association of young mechanics, who had a reading-room opening out of it. The appointed day ushered in a furious snow-storm before which the janitor of the building retreated in despair, leaving the court almost blockaded. When Thoreau and I ploughed through, we found a few young mechanics reading newspapers; and when the appointed hour came, there were assembled only Mr. Alcott, Dr. Walter Channing and at most three or four ticket-holders. No one wished to postpone the affair and Mr. Alcott suggested that the thing to be done was to adjourn to the reading-room, where, he doubted not, the young men would be grateful for the new gospel offered; for which he himself undertook to prepare their minds. I can see him now, going from one to another, or collecting them in little groups and expounding to them, with his lofty Socratic mien, the privileges they were to share. "This is his life; this is his book; he is to print it presently; I think we shall all be glad, shall we not, either to read his book or to hear it?" Some laid down their newspapers, more retained them; the lecture proved to be one of the most introspective chapters from "Walden." A few went to sleep, the rest rustled their papers; and the most vivid impression which I retain from the whole enterprise is the profound gratitude I felt to one auditor (Dr. Walter Channing), who forced upon me a five-dollar bill towards the expenses of the disastrous entertainment.

—Thomas Wentworth Higginson, "Glimpses of Authors," *Brains,* I (December 1, 1891), 105.

ᴂ ᴄ

The last time that the Easy Chair saw that remarkable man, Henry Thoreau, he came quietly into Mr. Emerson's study to get a volume of Pliny's letters. Expecting to see no one, and accustomed to attend without distraction to the business at hand, he was as quietly going out, when the host spoke to him, and without surprise, and with unsmiling courtesy, Thoreau greeted his friends. He seated himself, maintaining the same habitual erect posture, which made it seem impossible that he could ever lounge or slouch, and that made Hawthorne speak of him as "cast-iron," and immediately began to talk in the strain so familiar to his friends. It was a staccato style of speech, every word coming separately and distinctly, as if preserving the same cool isolation in [p. 62] the sentence that the speaker did in society; but the words were singularly apt and choice, and Thoreau had always something to say. His knowledge was original. He was a Fine-ear and a Sharp-eye in the woods and fields; and he added to his knowledge of nature the wisdom of the most ancient times and of the best literature. His manner and matter both reproved trifling, but in the most impersonal manner. It was like the reproof of Pan's statue. There seemed never to be any loosening of the intellectual tension, and a call from Thoreau in the highest sense "meant business."

On the morning of which we are speaking the talk fell upon the Indians, with whom he had a profound sympathy, and of whose life and ways and nature he apparently had an instinctive knowledge. In the slightly contemptuous inference against civilization which his remarks left, rather than in any positively scornful tone, there was something which rather humorously suggested the man who spoke lightly of the equator, but with the difference that there would have [p. 63] been if the light speaking had left a horrible suspicion of that excellent circle. For Thoreau so ingeniously traced our obligations to the aborigines that the claims of civilization for what is really essential palpably dwindled. He dropped all manner of curious and delightful information as he went on, and it was sad to see in the hollow cheek and the large, unnaturally lustrous eye the signs of the disease that very soon removed him from among us. Those who remember him, and were familiar with his truly heroic and virtuous life, or those who perceive in his works that spirit of sweetness and content which made him at the last say that he was as happy to be sick as to be well, will apply to him the words of his own poem in the first number of the *Dial:*

> "Say not that Caesar was victorious,
>   With toil and strife who stormed the House of fame;
> In other sense this youth was glorious,
>   Himself a kingdom wheresoe'er he came."

His talk of the Indians left an impres[p. 64]sion entirely unlike that of the Cooper novel and the red man of the theatre. It was untouched by romance or sentimentality. It made them a grave, manly race, intimately familiar with nature, with a lofty scorn of feebleness. The sylvan shade and the leafy realm and Arden and pastoral poetry were wholly wanting in the picture he drew, quite as much as the theory that they are vermin to be exterminated as fast as possible. He said that the pioneers of civilization, as it is called, among the Indians are purveyors of every kind of mischief. We graft the sound native stock with a sour fruit, then denounce it bitterly and cut it down. What was most admirable in Daniel Boone, he said, was his Indian nature and sympathy; and the least admirable part was his hold, such as it was, upon civilization. He seemed to imply that if Boone could only have succeeded in becoming an Indian altogether, it would have been a truly memorable triumph. Thoreau acknowledged that the Indian was not only doomed, but, as he gravely said, damned, because his enemies were [p. 65] his historians; and he could only say, "Ah, if we lions had painted the picture!"

—George William Curtis, *From the Easy Chair* (New York: Harper, 1892), pp. 62-66.

ᗍᗌ ᗌᗍ

Last evening we had the "Conversation," though, owing to the bad weather, but few attended. The subjects were: What is Prophecy? Who is a Prophet? and The Love of Nature. Mr. Lane decided, as for all time and the race, that this same love of nature—of which Henry [Thoreau] was the champion, and Elizabeth Hoar and Lidian (though L. disclaimed possessing it herself) his faithful squiresses— that this love was the most subtle and dangerous of sins; a refined idolatry, much more to be dreaded than gross wickednesses, because the gross sinner would be alarmed by the depth of his degradation, and come up from it in terror, but the unhappy idolaters of Nature were deceived by the refined quality of their sin, and would be the last to enter the kingdom. Henry frankly affirmed to both the wise men that they were wholly deficient in the faculty in question, and therefore could not judge of it. And Mr. Alcott as frankly answered that it was because they went beyond the mere material objects, and were filled with spiritual love and perception (as Mr. T. was not), that they seemed to Mr. Thoreau not to appreciate outward nature. I am very heavy, and have spoiled a most excellent story. I have given you no idea of the scene, which was ineffably comic, though it made no laugh at the time; I scarcely laughed at it myself,—too deeply amused to give the usual sign. Henry was brave and noble; well as I have always liked him, he still grows upon me.

—Mrs. Ralph Waldo Emerson, Letter to Ralph Waldo Emerson, Concord, February 20, 1843, in "The Emerson-Thoreau Correspondence," *Atlantic Monthly*, LXIX (May, 1892), 585.

∽ ⌒

More than forty years ago half a dozen boys were on the east bank of the Assabet river taking a sun bath after their swimming in the stream. They were talking about the conical heaps of stone in the river, and wishing that that [*sic*] they knew what built them. There were about as many theories as there were boys, and no conclusion had been arrived at, when one of the boys said, "Here comes Henry Thoreau, let us ask him." So when he came near, one of the boys asked him 'What made those heaps of stones in the river?' "I asked a Penobscot Indian that question," said Thoreau, "and he said, 'The musquash did,' but I told him that I was a better Indian than he, for I knew and he did not," and with that reply he walked off. John —— said, "That is just like him, he never will tell a fellow anything unless it is in his lectures, darn his old lectures about chipmunks and Injuns, I won't go to hear him," and the unanimous conclusion of the boys was, that when they got left again, another man would do it. The boys could not understand Thoreau, and he did not understand boys, and both were losers by it.

While looking over Thoreau's "Autumn" lately, the writer was reminded of the time when Thoreau and the writer's father spent some two or three weeks running anew the boundary lines in Sudbury woods. I think it was in 1851, and there were grave disputes and law suits seemed probable but after a while these two men were selected to fix the bounds. The real trouble was owing to the variations of the compass, the old lines having been run some 200 years before; but Thoreau understood his business thoroughly and settled the boundary question so that peace was declared. Thoreau's companion was an old lumberman and woodchopper and a close observer of natural objects, but he said that Thoreau was the best man he had ever known in the woods. He would climb a tree like a squirrel, knew every plant and shrub and really seemed to have been born in the forest. Thoreau asked many questions; one of them was, "Do you know where there is a white grape, which grows on high land, which bears every year and is of superior quality?" "Yes," was the reply. "It is a little north of Deacon Dakins' rye field and when the grapes are ripe if you are not on the windward side your nose will tell you where they are." Thoreau laughed and appeared satisfied.

About this time Thoreau went to a party in Concord, and he says in his journal or diary, that he would rather eat crackers and cheese with his old companion in the woods.

It is a great mistake to suppose that Thoreau was a solitary student of natural history in Concord and vicinity at that time. He was better equipped for his work, and could record his observations and discoveries better than his fellow students and this was enough to make him famous in later years. . . .

There was a great intermediate class between Emerson and the Canadian wood chopper who would have gladly aided Thoreau if he had been a little more human in his dealings with them.

—[Horace R. Hosmer], "Reminiscences of Thoreau," *Concord Enterprise,* April 15, 1893.

Thoreau often visited the west part of Concord, passing along the east bank of the Assabet river from Derby's bridge up the stream, along the high banks which overlook the river to the land formerly owned by Timothy Shehan, and from there to the Ministerial swamp and vicinity where he first found the climbing fern. The writer saw him the day he found the rare plant while returning home with his prize. I never saw such a pleased, happy look on his face as he had that day. He took off his hat, in the crown of which the fern was coiled up, and showed me the dainty, graceful glory of the swamp. He said it had never been seen before in the New England states, outside of the botanical gardens in Cambridge, and he volunteered the information that it grew in a swamp between the place we were on and Sudbury.

Soon after, perhaps two weeks, two men, who said they came from Cambridge came to me and asked where the climbing fern grew. I did not tell them for many reasons, perhaps the best one was that which Thoreau gave while speaking of the pink lilies which grew on the Cape. In reply to my question whether he had seen the pink lilies which grew in Hayward's pond in Westvale, he said he had never seen them there or on the Concord river, but there was a place on the Cape, a sort of creek, where they had grown unnoticed by the inhabitants until Theodore Parker saw them one summer and gathered them, and "after that," said Thoreau, "the bumpkins grubbed them up root and branch, and almost exterminated them."

—*Ibid.*, II, April 22, 1893.

∽ ⚮

He used to flit in and out of the house with long, ungainly, Indian-like stride, and his piercing large orbs, staring, as it were in vacancy.

—Rose Hawthorne, in George Parsons Lathrop, "Lecture," *Brooklyn Citizen*, December 12, 1894.

∽ ⚮

I told Thoreau that he would have to come along with me, and he went without any trouble and was locked up. When his tax had been paid by some one (since ascertained to have been Thoreau's aunts,) I told him he was free to go but he would not, until finally I said, "Henry, if you will not go of your own accord I shall put you out, for you cannot stay here any longer." He was the only prisoner that I ever had that did not want to leave when he could.

—Samuel Staples, in Anonymous, "An Evening with Thoreau," *High School Voice* (Concord, Mass.), November 15, 1895.

∽ ⚮

Thoreau used to walk through Concord with the long step of an Indian, looking straight before him, but at the same time observing everything. Occasionally he would stop, make an incision in the bark of a tree with his knife, or pick up a [p. 24] stone and examine it. It was not often that he was met with in anybody's house, or seen in company with other men.

His profession was that of a surveyor; and it is easy to imagine how, with his poetic temperament, while laying out roads and measuring woodlots, he came to be what he was. Many people thought his peculiar ways were an affectation, but I believe that he was one of the plainest and simplest of men; as plain and single-minded as President Lincoln himself. It was his theory of the way men should live. He was a Diogenes without being a cynic.

—Frank Preston Stearns, *Sketches from Concord and Appledore* (New York: Putnam, 1895), pp. 24-25.

He had a strong dislike of matrimony. Once while walking across a field with David A. Wasson he kicked a skunk-cabbage with his boot and said, "There, marriage is like that."

—*Ibid.*, p. 26.

He delivered a lecture one winter before the Concord lyceum on wild apple-trees. The subject made his audience laugh, but their laughter was [p. 27] of short duration. The man who had lived there so long unknown was at last revealed before them. It was the best lecture of the season, and at its close there was long continued applause.

—*Ibid.*, pp. 27-28.

Mr. [George] Bartlett told me one story of Thoreau which I have not seen in print. . . . A number of loafers jeered at him as he passed one day, and said:

"Halloo, Thoreau, and don't you really ever shoot a bird then when you want to study it?"

"Do you think," replied Thoreau, "that I should shoot you if I wanted to study you?"

—Hector Waylen, "A Visit to Walden Pond," *Natural Food* (Rowerdenan, Merton Park, Surrey, England), July, 1895.

His humorous, sarcastic, but ever entertaining talks, rather than lectures, were received with more favor [than those of Emerson], but with perhaps even less comprehension. It was under the roof of old city hall, and to an audience of less than 100 persons, that his famous lecture on "Beans" was delivered. This was afterwards incorporated in his famous work "Walden." . . .

Thoreau's few visits to Worcester were made generally at the invitation of his friends, the Browns, Chamberlains, Blakes, John Wyman and Augustus Tucker, who formed the nucleus of what might have been called the literary salon of the infant city of Worcester. His lectures were delivered principally in city hall, Brinley hall (where the new State Mutual building now stands), and in the drawing room of his friend Harrison Gray Otis Blake. These were never well attended. If at the earnest solicitations of his friends an audience of 100 people could be gotten together to hear him, it was considered a compliment to him, and he was well satisfied. For these lectures he asked nothing, only stipulating that his expenses should be paid. He, like Alcott, cared nothing for money, and it was one of his proudest boasts that he had once lived a year on an actual cash expenditure of $65.99. People could not understand him, and in his secret consciousness he was inclined to be proud of the fact.

He made no effort whatever to pay regard to the conventionalities. On his visits to Worcester he never troubled to bring a trunk or even a traveling bag. His hostess would often be mortified, after his arrival, to find his personal belongings reposing on the table in the hall tied up in a red bandanna, or in a greasy sheet of brown paper.

—Anonymous, "Early Worcester Literary Days," *Worcester Telegram,* October 26, 1896.

There are evidently two Thoreaus—one that of his admirers, and the other that of his detractors. His admirers include such persons as Mr. Frank B. Sanborn and Mr. H. S. Salt, who have both written biographies of Thoreau, and who cannot easily accept any criticism of one they love almost to excess. Whatever of genius there was in him they are quick to recognize; but his faults they ignore or prefer to overlook. The other class, whose chief representative is Lowell, are inclined to see what was odd in Thoreau; they emphasize his excesses, and do not fully credit the genius which he undoubtedly possessed.

A willingness to recognize both phases of Thoreau's nature led me, the other day, to seek out two persons who knew him well—the one a most ardent admirer, and the other, not so much a detractor as one who is inclined to emphasize his faults. I will permit the detractor to speak first, in order that the admirer may give the last and most important word.

The detractor said that he went to school with Thoreau in the Concord Academy, that he was an odd stick, not very studious or devoted in his lessons, but a thoughtful youth and very fond of reading. He was not given to play or to fellowship with the boys; but he was shy and silent. When he was in college at Harvard he was not inclined to hard study, but spent much of his time in the library, had no special rank in his class, and took no part in commencement [Error: He read an honors paper.] As a teacher in Concord Academy he was a failure, and only remained for a short time.

Then Thoreau spent a year or two in Emerson's family, as the tutor of his children and as his literary assistant. This resulted in his becoming a thorough-going imitator of Emerson, whose manner, speech, and ideas he copied with great fidelity and success. This was carried to such an extent as to make a decided change in Thoreau's life; and the change was for the better. When he sometimes gave lectures, as he did before the Concord Lyceum, and on other occasions, his manner of speaking was a coarse imitation of Emerson's, and so badly done as to make it painful to listen to him. He caught Emerson's hesitating manner, with all that was ungraceful and awkward in it. On these occasions Thoreau had but a small audience, no one but his personal friends turning out to hear him; and he had only a small personal following in the village.

Thoreau was an odd, shy recluse man, an intense egotist, who thoroughly believed in himself and his own ideas. He was an Indian in his nature, with the advantages of Harvard library and Plato's philosophy. He was a good deal of a Stoic; and he always judged of everything, even that Nature which he loved so well, with reference to himself. He could not see anything except with his own personality as its test, and with reference to what bearings it had upon his own life and thought. In his books he loved to play upon words, and cultivated a punning, alliterative style. The mere jingle of words seemed to attract him; and what was odd or bizarre gave him much pleasure.

The detractor went to visit Thoreau half-a-dozen times while he was living in his hut on Walden Pond. His life there was helped out by many tea-drinkings and dinners to which he was invited by his relatives and friends in the village, as well as by food which was frequently sent to him. He enjoyed his stay there, and had the feeling that he was performing a great feat to live without the trappings of civilization. He did not much care for the conventionalities of life, and readily broke away from its customs and ceremonies. In the last years of his life he became a thorough convert to not blacking his shoes, but never did anything to them until they were worn out. He thought it a waste of time to blacken and polish them, and a useless concession to mere custom.

His attitude toward society was shown in his refusal to pay taxes. Being an extreme individualist, he felt that he had no use for Government; that it hampered him, and did not permit him to do as he liked. He refused to yield obedience to it, or to add anything to its means of support. When called upon by the tax gatherer he excused himself on the ground of not caring to pay. After repeated requests for the dollar and a half which the tax roll had put down against his name, the tax collector, who was also the constable, grew impatient of the delay, and took Thoreau away to jail. In a few hours the tax was paid by one of his friends, and he was liberated. He protested against any one paying for him, but walked away as if nothing had happened.

Thoreau greatly enjoyed talking with the quaint people of the town, those who were racy in speech and personal in character. The more of oddity he found in them the greater liking he had for their society, and the greater enjoyment he found in their expressions and ideas. He talked with the old farmers of nature and outdoor life, of what they had learned on their farms, and of what they had gained of practical wisdom. He seldom came into close contact with the educated people of the village, with the exception of Emerson, Hawthorne, Channing, and the few others who were his special admirers and friends.

The detractor said that he knew quite well that his way of regarding Thoreau was that of the Philistine; but it was that of the people generally in Concord who knew Thoreau intimately. He said that he had all of Thoreau's books, had read them carefully, and enjoyed much of what was in them. He procured "Walden" and "The Week" when they first appeared, and he had recently read the books on the four seasons. Thoreau's descriptions he regards as accurate and delightful; but his philosophy he always skips, as he does not care for it or agree with it. Those who knew Thoreau personally have found nothing so surprising as the cult which has grown up about him or so difficult of a rational explanation.

The admirer gave me a very different account of Thoreau, for he grew up with him, being only a few years younger. He had a boy's admiration for his friend, took lessons of him in woodcraft, came to love the woods and its creatures under his guidance, and had that enthusiasm about him which the boy conceives for his hero. Even now he does not like to hear a word said against Thoreau; and he has never yet forgiven Lowell for his cruel word of detraction and misrepresentation. By the admirer Thoreau is regarded with that fondness which would have been natural if he had been an older brother; and this is, in reality, the relation in which they stand to each other, not by blood, but in the feeling which is cherished for the intimate friend of now so many years past. Thoreau's memory is not only cherished, but most warmly defended by this admirer of whatever [p. 1671] was good and noble in him. He is talked of with the keenest zest, and all his bright qualities, his genius, his gifts which appealed to a boy's admiration, are described with strong appreciation.

Thoreau's room in his later years was in a back attic of the house in Concord where he died, and which was afterward owned by the Alcott family. It was sparsely furnished, with Spartan-like simplicity. There was in it a bureau, in which he kept a collection of birds' eggs and one of arrowheads. A rude cot on which he slept, a chair or two, and a washstand, bowl and pitcher, made up all the room contained.

He was a true companion of the boys of the village, entered into their sports, and was delighted in their outdoor life. He was pleased to show them birds'-nests; but he was shy of those who had not a genuine love of the life of the wood, and who hunted merely because they followed the other boys. Those who loved outdoor life found in him a true companion, one who was always willing and glad to serve them, and who entered into all their interests with a delight equal to their own. He was ready to initiate them into a knowledge of the country around, and into all the mysteries of woodcraft and the hidden secrets of Nature.

According to his admirer Thoreau was an impressive speaker, and had a large hearing whenever he spoke in Concord. There was a tang, something queer, in his manner of speech and in his ideas, which attracted people. On the day when John Brown was hanged he sent a boy about to notify people that he would speak in the vestry of the church. The boy returned, and said that Mr. Sanborn thought it a bad thing to do, that the time was dangerous, and it would be better to wait until there was a better feeling among the people. Thoreau sent the boy back with this message: "Tell Mr. Sanborn that he has misunderstood the announcement, that there is to be a meeting in the vestry, and that Mr. Thoreau will speak."

The vestry was full, but people came in shyly, as if afraid to be seen there; but they listened to the end, and then went out without discussion or comment. Thoreau was full of his subject on this occasion, was deeply agitated, and was so moved by his feelings as scarcely to be able to speak or to control his voice. It was a bold, strong argument he made, but in a time of fear and doubt. He had no hesitation himself, knew clearly his own attitude, and what he wished to say. Few other persons had a definite opinion or dared utter their thoughts openly. He was himself a non-resistant, decidedly preferred the interests of the individual to those of the State, would not pay taxes because he did not believe in the attitude of the nation on the great moral questions of the hour; but he saw at once to the core of Brown's character, was his earnest champion, and had for him the greatest admiration.

Thoreau's lectures were listened to with delight, and admired for their fresh and unique qualities. His descriptions of scenery and outdoor life were much appreciated and admired, and were fully understood by the farmers and other such people. He had a poetic fervor and charm which made his speaking attractive and pleasant for the listener.

The gossip about his being furnished with doughnuts, pies, and other delicacies, while he was living at Walden, is not worth listening to; for he was quite capable of living in the woods on his own fare. He did in no sense depend upon the supplies from the village; but these were accepted out of good will to the donors, not from any desire on his part to receive them. The fact is, he loved society in a way of his own, desired the companionship of people, cared for all simple, sincere and genuine persons, and went to see them at their houses from time to time. He could depend upon himself, but he was no misanthrope, no mere recluse, certainly not one to distrust or to hate his kind. He sought the company of the people of the village when he found it convenient to do so or the impulse called. He did not shun good food, but accepted it willingly; yet he was not in any degree dependent upon it. He did not seek it or beg for it; when it was offered he used it, but not to his own detriment.

He was a genuine man, sound, wholesome, thoroughly natural, and of noble impulses and purposes. His life was without any mortal taint, and it was clean throughout. He was not narrow or warped, but sound in his principles and upright in his conduct. There was no deceit about him, no pretense, no stunted elements of character; but he was genuinely loyal and faithful in all the relations of life. In his relations to his friends he was fidelity itself; and to those who were in any way dependent upon him or who appealed to his sympathies he gave the most unfailing loyalty. To an elderly woman, a dependent and complaining person, he gave much of his time, made great efforts to cheer her and to give her courage, constituted himself her protector, and was persistent in his acts of kindness. He was patient, sympathetic and self-forgetful in her behalf, would run on errands for her, and did not fail in even the most lowly service.

Thoreau loved the society of boys, he knew boy character intimately, and he thoroughly sympathized with them; but he would not tolerate bad language or meanness in any boy who was in his company. Evil habits he scorned, and he used his best effort to destroy them in all the boys who associated with him. He sought to develop whatever was good in the characters of his boy friends, and to give them moral backbone and manliness.

By nature Thoreau was independent in character and opinion, institutions were indifferent to him, while social forms and requirements repulsed him. He was an individualist of the most pronounced type, maintaining that institutions oppressed the individual, and were not to be trusted or their arbitrary laws obeyed. This faith of his he carried into daily life, not in an aggressive or offensive manner, but in his disregard of mere conventionalities. He was one of the most sturdy and uncompromising democrats who ever lived. He dressed plainly, like a farmer, not slovenly, but with no extra care or nicety. He fitted his dress to his outdoor life and its requirements. He was scrupulously clean, but did not love show or parade.

When Thoreau lived at Walden he read and wrote much, carried there the best books and read them diligently. It was a time of quiet thought with him, and of putting his thoughts upon paper. He had many visitors; and all of those who had raciness of speech or any native force of character he was glad to welcome. He loved native fruit, at least among men, that with the flavor of the soil. One such man in Concord, the constable and tavern-keeper, had the warmest appreciation of Thoreau, and said of him that he was a good fellow and a delightful man to meet. Such was the testimony of all who knew him intimately on any side of his life, and who got close to that which was best within him.

Thoreau must be understood from the point of view of the detractor as well as from that of the admirer, in order fully to appreciate him. He was a genuine product of the soil of New England, a crab apple from the woods, transplanted to a cultivated garden, but retaining the old flavor along with the new. He was a hunter and backwoodsman, who knew Plato and could talk the language of the latest form of intellectual speculation. Through it all, however, there is something so racy, genuine and incisive about him that he commands our admiration, in spite of all his limitations. The very defects give us a great love for him; and we read him with the more delight that he is always himself, wild, rebellious and scornful. There is a raciness about his books, a manly robust quality, and a freshness as of a spring morning, which commands them, and will keep them alive.

—George W. Cooke, "The Two Thoreaus," *Independent*, XLVIII (December 10, 1896), 1671-1672. [It is only fair to point out that F. B. Sanborn, in reply to this article, denied he had sent a message to Thoreau on the occasion of the John Brown address but that it had been sent by another Abolitionist. The constable, mentioned later, was undoubtedly Sam Staples.]

∾ ᔆ

He played with much expression on the flute, and in his early years sang in a pleasing voice, although he had no special training in music. After his brother's death he could not be induced to sing. The musical quality of his voice made him a charming reader. He often came to my father's house to read a new poem or description that pleased him; and those that had ever listened could never forget the pleasure of such occasions. Doubtless his musical ability gave him the power to imitate bird notes so closely that the feathered songsters would answer to his call, and perhaps helped him to a keener perception of the sweetness of a life lived in harmonious accord with nature's laws.

—S. E. Rena, "Thoreau's Voice," *Boston Transcript*, February 15, 1896.

∾ ᔆ

Just before the Civil War there was a famous muster at Con[p. 3] cord, and the peaceful acres, usually vexed with the diligent plow, and possibly even more vexed by the gentle philosophers of those days, became for one week a glittering plain. It was a goodly show, and filled the mere citizen with a just pride in national glory. On the last day of the encampment a certain militiaman from Boston, clad in all the splendid regalia of war, and not dissatisfied with his personal appearance, climbed a neighboring height with Thoreau, who during the week had been conspicuously absent from the inspiring scene. The top gained, they looked long and earnestly at the great human panorama before them, each filled with his own reflection. At length Thoreau said, "Mr. D——, did it ever occur to you what a small place in Nature a camp fills!"

—The Taverner, "Here in Boston," *Time and the Hour*, I (April 18, 1896), 3-4.

∾ ᔆ

Another peculiar spirit now and then haunted us, usually sad as a pine-tree—Thoreau. His enormous eyes, tame with religious intellect and wild with the loose rein, making a steady flash in this strange unison of forces, frightened me dreadfully at first. The unanswerable argument which he unwittingly made to soften my heart towards him was to fall desperately ill. During his long illness my mother lent him our sweet old music-box, to which she had danced as it warbled at the Old Manse, in the first year of her marriage, and which now softly dreamed forth its tunes in a time-mellowed tone. When he died, it seemed as if an anemone, more lovely than any other, had been carried from the borders of a wood into its silent depths, and dropped, in solitude and shadow, among the recluse ferns and mosses which are so seldom disturbed by passing feet. Son of freedom and opportunity that he was, he touched the heart by going to nature's peacefulness like the saints, and girding upon his American sovereignty the hair-shirt of service to self-denial. He was happy in his intense discipline of the flesh, as all men are when they have once tasted power—if it is the power which awakens perception of the highest concerns. His countenance had an April pensiveness about it; you would never have guessed that he could write of owls so jocosely. His manner was such as to [p. 420] suggest that he could mope and weep *with* them. I never crossed an airy hill or broad field in Concord, without thinking of him who had been the companion of space as well as of delicacy; the lover of the wood-thrush, as well as of the Indian. Walden woods rustled the name of Thoreau whenever we walked in them.

—Rose Hawthorne Lathrop, *Memories of Hawthorne* (Boston: Houghton Mifflin, 1897), pp. 420-421.

∽ ∾

December 30 [1842].

One afternoon, Mr. Emerson and Mr. Thoreau went with him [Hawthorne] down the river. Henry Thoreau is an experienced skater, and was figuring dithyrambic dances and Bacchic leaps on the ice—very remarkable, but very ugly, methought. Next him followed Mr. Hawthorne who, wrapped in his cloak, moved like a self-impelled Greek statue, stately and grave. Mr. Emerson closed the line, evidently too weary to hold himself erect, pitching headforemost, half lying on the air.

—Sophia Peabody Hawthorne, Letter to Mrs. Caleb Foote, in *ibid.*, p. 53.

᠃   ᠃

This evening Mr. Thoreau is going to lecture, and will stay with us. His lecture before was so enchanting; such a revelation of nature in all its exquisite details of wood-thrushes, squirrels, sunshine, mists and shadows, fresh, vernal odors, pine-tree ocean melodies, that my ear rang with music, and I seemed to have been wandering through copse and dingle! Mr. Thoreau has risen above all his arrogance of manner, and is as gentle, simple, ruddy, and meek as all geniuses should be; and now his [p. 92] great blue eyes fairly outshine and put into shade a nose which I once thought must make him uncomely forever.

—Sophia Peabody Hawthorne, Letter of February 28, 1849, in *Ibid.*, pp. 92-93.

᠃   ᠃

"While I was at the Thoreaus in Concord, Mass., in the fall of '63," says C. H. Greene, of Rochester, Mich., who is one of the poet-naturalist's strongest admirers, "Miss Sophia Thoreau related, among others, the following anecdotes of her brother during his last illness."

Some boys of the vicinity were in the habit of bringing game for him to eat, presenting it at the kitchen door, and then gently withdrawing so as not to disturb the sick man. On one occasion he was told of it soon after their leaving, when he earnestly inquired: "Why did you not invite them in? I want to thank them for so much that they are bringing me." And then adding, thoughtfully: "Well, I declare; I don't believe they are going to let me go after all."

At another time he requested some lads who had been robbing birds' nests to be called into his sick room that he might lecture them about it. In the interview he was heard asking them if they knew what a wail of sorrow and anguish their cruelty had sent all over the fields and through the woods.

Speaking of one's hair turning gray, and to what cause it is sometimes attributed, Thoreau remarked: "I never had any trouble in all my life, or only when I was about fourteen; then I felt pretty bad a little while on account of my sins, but no trouble since that I know of. That must be the reason why my hair doesn't turn gray faster. But there is Blake; he is as gray as a rat."

Near the close of his life one of his dearest friends, who had been in the habit of visiting him occasionally, ceased coming to see him, as the family understood, only through fear of his own ability to endure the strain on his nerves at seeing Thoreau's then emaciated appearance, and the leave-taking that would follow. His sister alluding to this friend's absence, Thoreau said, in an emphatic whisper, his voice having already failed him, "Now, Ricketson ought to come and see me; it would do him good." . . .

He had no belief whatever in Christianity; on the contrary, his attitude toward it was almost contemptuous, as though it were too childish for serious men to talk about. He included it among the tricks and trades which he denounced by telling the story of the boy who was building the model of a church in dirt as the minister was passing. "Why, my little lad," said the minister, "why, making a meeting-house of that stuff? Why, why!" "Yes," answered the youth; "yes, I am; and I expect to have enough left over to make a Methodist minister besides."

—*The Truth Seeker,* November 20, 1897, p. 144.

∽ ∾

I remember well that when I endeavored to enlist Judge Hoar, the leading citizen of Concord, in an effort to persuade Miss Thoreau to allow her brother's journals to be printed, he heard me partly through, and then quickly said, "But you have left unsettled the preliminary question, Why should any one care to have Thoreau's journals put in print?"

—Thomas Wentworth Higginson, *Cheerful Yesterdays* (Boston: Houghton Mifflin, 1898), p. 170.

∽ ∾

It seems that a question had arisen regarding the boundary line between land owned by Emerson and Mr. S[taples] himself, which the latter told me had recently become his through a "dicker" with someone whose name I did not catch. Thoreau was employed to make the necessary survey ("and he did it right slick, I tell you"); and having finished his work, he had appointed a meeting at Emer[p. 97] son's house to make his report. I can never forget how Mr. S. in his statement of that meeting made me feel the bland mildness of Emerson's nature. "He was a man, sir, that wouldn't hurt a fly," said Mr. S. most emphatically. Then he went on to explain that there had been no "quarrel" between Emerson and himself; they only "just wanted to know, you know, which was which."

Thoreau was already at Emerson's house when Mr. S. arrived, and they plunged into business without delay. Much to Emerson's surprise, Thoreau said and proved by a map of the survey that his, Mr. Emerson's, partition fence intruded several feet upon the adjoining property; and without waiting for a word from the utterly unconscious intruder, he went on to declare that the appropriation of the land was intentional, only Mr. S. had proven too sharp to be imposed upon; and all these years you've been holding up your nose as an upright citizen and an example to everybody, yet every time you reset your fence you knowingly shoved it in a little farther and a little farther, until you've stolen land enough to almost feed a yearling heifer; but Mr. S. has been too smart for any of you sly fellows, and I'm glad to have a hand in exposing you; though its an awful disappointment to me."

"Why," said Mr. S., "if Emerson hed been ketched pickin' pockets at town meetin' he could n't a looked more streaked. Thoreau was talkin' in downright earnest, and you could have heard him way out on the Lexin'ton road. I felt so all-fired mean, I could n't do nothin' but look at the floor; but whilst Thoreau was a rakin' of him and had just said somthin' darned haa'sh, I just had to look at him, and when I saw his eye I laughed 'til you could a heard it up to the top of the Hill buryin' ground. You see, he was just guyin' Mr. Emerson, and when he see it, he did n't take it amiss at all. He was the nicest man that ever lived."

—Samuel Arthur Jones, "Thoreau's Incarceration," *Inlander*, IX (December, 1898), 97-98.

"Henry knew that I had a warrant for him, but I did n't go to hunt for him, 'cause I knew I could git him when I wanted to."

Thoreau was arrested early in the evening, while on his way to get a shoe that was being repaired preparatory to his piloting a huckleberry party on the morrow. The serving of the warrant had no novelty in it for the reminiscential jailer, so he mentioned no details of the arrest, but simply stated that he locked up Thoreau "and the rest of the boys" for the night. A little later he himself went up town on some business. During his brief absence someone rapped at the door of the jailer's private apartments. His daughter opened it, when a veiled young woman said: "Here is the money to pay Mr. Thoreau's tax," and immediately departed. The demand of the law being satisfied, Thoreau was no longer a culprit, and should have been instantly set free on the jailer's return; but when telling me of it, that worthy, in the coolest manner imaginable, said, "I had got my boots off and was sittin' by the fire when my daughter told me, and I was n't goin' to take the trouble to unlock after I'd got the boys all fixed for the night, so I kep' him in 'till after breakfast next mornin' and then I let him go." [p. 99] . . .

He said Thoreau was "as mad as the devil when I turned him loose."

—*Ibid.*, IX, 99-100.

∽ ∾

He [Emerson] showed from the car window where Thoreau's hut had stood. "More like an Indian," said he, speaking of the hermit, "than a white man. He was free and strange. If he found the sky clear when he got up in the morning he might say, 'This is a good day to go to the White Mountains,' and shut his door and trudge off to the White Mountains just as he would go to the spring for a drink. He used to come up through the woods and call on us without ceremony, and help himself to any axe or spade or bucket that he found on my premises, and would keep it until he was through with it." A reminiscent twinkle here. Thoreau was neither romantic nor misanthropic, nor was he unhappy. His nature had nothing [p. 58] of the morbid or unhealthful, his sympathies were fresh and keen, he was content to be alone, yet he delighted in tramps and boating trips with his college chums, and would walk to Worcester to ask his friend, Mr. Blake, to take a jaunt up-country to the mountains. For prying strangers and supercilious people he lacked courtesy. He disliked pretense of all kinds, but restrained himself to reproof of wrong and folly rather than enlarged his energies as an active reformer. A creature of impulses, he was still a hard worker, after his fashion, wrote much in his cabin, and left a chest of manuscript, but made next to nothing by his writing. He did get a job of surveying, now and then, and gave an occasional lecture, and the few dollars that he made in that way seemed to satisfy him. Thus Mr. Emerson.

—Charles M. Skinner, *With Feet to the Earth* (Philadelphia: Lippincott, 1898), pp. 58-59.

∽ ∾

A comical illustration of his [Thoreau's] readiness to cope with sudden emergencies occurred late one warm afternoon in summer, just as a short, sharp thunder-storm had passed and the sun was breaking through the dispersing clouds. We had finished supper, but were lingering at the table, when the servant threw open the door, exclaiming, with wild excitement, "Faith! the' pig's out o'th' pin, an' th'way he's tearin' roun' Jege Hoore's fluer-bids es enuf ter scare er budy." Henry and his father at once rushed out in pursuit of the marauder, and the ladies flew to the windows to see the fray. Never was practical strategy more in evidence; plotting and counterplotting on both sides, repeated circumvention of well-laid plans, and a final cornering and capture of the perverse beast, who, after his delicious taste of freedom, protested loudly and vigorously against being forced to return to his prison pen. It was truly a triumph of the intellectual over the animal nature, whose brief enjoyment of wild destructive liberty was suddenly ended by the power of a superior will. It was remarked at the time how much mental and physical strength had to be expended to subdue so inferior an animal.

—Anonymous, "Reminiscences of Thoreau," *Outlook*, LXIII (December 2, 1899), 816.

∽ ∾

If Henry happened to be with us, although we were unobservant of what was beneath our feet, his acute eyes, ever active, would detect Indian arrow-heads, or some implement for domestic purposes made of flint or other hard stone. I have seen him with a stick bring to light great [p. 818] numbers of clam-shells, remnants of Indian feasts of long ago. It was noticeable that these shell deposits were always found in places evidently selected for their pleasant situation and outlook.

Occasionally Henry would invite us to go with him in his boat. One of these excursions was in late November, and the weather was of almost unearthly beauty; bees in great multitudes hummed loudly as they lazily floated in the golden slumberous haze only seen in the true Indian summer. At a particular spot Henry turned the boat toward the bank, saying: "We will make a call upon a wild flower that is not ordinarily at home at this date, but the unusually warm days and nights of the past fortnight may have prevented its departure; so we will knock at its door," tapping at the upper leaves of a low-growing plant; and, verily, there was the shy, dainty little blossom underneath—welcomed by at least one pair of alert, sympathetic eyes.

—*Ibid.*, LXIII, 818-819.

It was often amusing to observe Henry's want of gallantry; in getting in or out of a boat, or if a fence or wall were to be surmounted. no hand did he stretch forth; he assumed that a woman should be able to help herself in all such matters; but if she were defenseless, his inborn chivalry could be relied on; as in the case of a terrified girl pursued through the woods by a couple of young ruffians, sons of influential parents, Henry's valiant rescue was most timely; and by his persistent efforts due punishment was inflicted upon the shameless offenders. Again, when a weary mother with a heavy child in her arms was struggling to reach the station, where the train had already arrived, her feet sinking in the hot sand at every step, with one glance Henry took in the situation. He bounded over the fence, transferred the child to his own arms, and, with strides that seemed to disdain the shifting sand, he moved over the ground with a conquering air that appeared to impress [p. 819] the inanimate engine and compel it to tarry till the belated mother and child were safely aboard the train.

No one could more heartily enjoy his family life than Henry. He invariably came down from his study for a while in the evening for conversation; the sound of the piano was sure to draw him.

Tears dim my eyes as those scenes arise before me; Sophia play-ing the old-time music, notably Scotch melodies, which so well suited her flexible voice, and those quaint ballads of a past generation, whose airs were often so plaintive and with so much of heartbreak in the words. All the family had rich, sweet voices. If the song was a fa-vorite, the father would join in, and thrilling was their singing of that gem, "Tom Bowline." I hear now the refrain:

His soul has gone aloft.

Often Henry would suddenly cease singing and catch up his flute, and, musical as was his voice, yet it was a delight never to be for-gotten to listen to the silvery tones that breathed from the instrument.

—*Ibid.*, LXIII, pp. 819-820.

Once, after a day so stormy that he had not taken his customary outdoor exercise, Henry came flying down from his study when the evening was half spent. His face was unusually animated; he sang with zest, but evidently needed an unrestricted outlet for his pent-up vitality, and soon began to dance, all by himself, spinning airily round, displaying remarkable litheness and agility; growing more and more inspired, he finally sprang over the center-table, alighting like a feather on the other side—then, not in the least out of breath, con-tinued his waltz until his enthusiasm abated.

I know not why I was surprised at hearing his mother refer to his "dancing days," for I had never associated Henry with any fashionable follies, even in his boyhood; but it seems he had been taught the usual accomplishments of well-bred children.

In sad contrast to the memory of Henry in his strength arises another, some years later—of him in his decline; he had returned from the West, whither he had been in search of health, and by eve-ning a flush had come to his cheeks and an ominous brightness and beauty to his eyes, painful to behold. His conversation was unusually brilliant, and we listened with a charmed attention which perhaps stimulated him to continue talking until the weak voice could no longer articulate.

This was the autumn before his death; in a few months his life on earth was ended. I was told that he retained his splendid courage and fortitude to the last.

—*Ibid.*, LXIII, 820.

>o c<

The last two evenings we had in Worcester, we were at two parlour lectures given by Mr. Henry D. Thoreau, the author of that odd book, *Walden, or Life in the Woods.* The first lecture was upon "Autumnal Tints," and was a beautiful and, I doubt not, a faithful report of the colours of leaves in October. Some of you may have read his "Chesuncook," in the *Atlantic Monthly;* if so you can fancy how quaint and observing, and humorous withal, he is as traveller— or excursionist-companion in wild solitudes. Several gentlemen, friends of his, tell us much of their tour with him to the White Mountains last summer, of his grand talk with their guide in "Tuckerman's Ravine," where they had their camp. He paid us the compliment of a nice long morning call after we heard him read his "Autumnal Tints," and remembered our being once at his mother's to tea, and Miss Putnam's looking over his herbarium with his sister.

—Sallie Holley, Letter to Mrs. Porter, February 28, 1959, in John White Chadwick, ed., *A Life for Liberty* (New York: Putnam, 1899), p. 167.

>o c<

Why, this room [Thoreau's sickroom] did not seem like a sickroom. My son wanted flowers and pictures and books all around here; and he was always so cheerful and wished others to be so while about him. And during the nights he wanted the lamp set on the floor and some chairs put around it so that in his sleepless hours he could amuse himself with watching the shadows.

—Mrs. Cynthia Thoreau, in S. A. Jones, *Some Unpublished Letters of Henry D. and Sophia E. Thoreau* (Jamaica: Marion Press, 1899), p. 75.

>o c<

Mr. Thoreau was a land-surveyor in Concord. I knew him well. He had a way of his own, and he didn't care much about money; but if there ever was a gentleman alive, he was one.

—Barney Mullins, in David Starr Jordan, *Imperial Democracy* (New York: Appleton, 1899), p. 280.

I hope you will find Mr. Thoreau a pleasant companion. I have met him at Mr. Hoar's, and was pleased with the accuracy of his botanical observations. He seemed to know what he knew—by no means, I think, the most common of characteristics.

—John Witt Randall, Letter to Francis Ellingwood Abbott, January 9, 1857, in *Poems of Nature and Life* (Boston: Ellis, 1899), p. 109.

He [Thoreau] seemed rather less than the medium height, well-proportioned, and noticeably straight and erect. His shoulders were not square but sloping, like those of Mr. Emerson. His head was not large, nor did it strike me as handsome: it was covered with a full growth of rather dark hair somewhat carelessly brushed after no particular style. His face was very striking whether seen in the front or profile view. Large perceptive eyes—blue, I think, large and prominent nose; his mouth concealed by a full dark beard, worn natural but not untrimmed; these features pervaded by a wise, serious and dignified look. The expression of his countenance was not severe or commanding, but it certainly gave no hint of shallowness or trifling.

In speech he was deliberate and positive. The emphatic words seemed to "hang fire" or to be held back for an instant as if to gather force and weight. Although he r[e]sembled Emerson in this, there was no appearance of affectation about it; he appeared to be looking at his thought all the time he was selecting and uttering his words.

Perhaps Thoreau talked rather like one who was accustomed to be listened to than to listen, though this was by no means prominent, and there was not the slightest lack of courtesy in his manner. His conversation was easy and interesting, but it was of the kind that proceeds by a succession of short paragraphs deliberately constructed, lecturewise, rather than by suggestive sentences and phrases neatly and sympathetically adjusted to what is said by others. He gave you a chance to talk, attended to what you said, and then made his reply, but did not come to very close quarters with you or help you out with your thought after the manner of skilled and practiced conversers. Emerson says of him that "he coldly and fully stated his opinion without affecting to believe that it was the opinion of the company." Thoreau was always interesting, often entertaining, but never what you would call charming.

—E. Harlow Russell, "Unitarian Club," *Leominster* [Mass.] *Daily Enterprise*, December 28, 1899. ["An account of an evening passed with Thoreau more than 30 years ago, at the house of a common friend."]

‥⃗ ⃖‥

"Henry often reminded me of an animal in human form. He had the eye of a bird, the scent of a dog, the most acute, delicate intelligence. But no soul. No," [p. 565] he repeated, shaking his head with decision, "Henry could not have had a human soul."

—Ralph Waldo Emerson, in a conversation with Rebecca Harding Davis in 1862, in Rebecca Harding Davis', "A Little Gossip," *Scribner's Magazine*, XXVIII (November, 1900), 565-566.

‥⃗ ⃖‥

When I first saw Thoreau, in the College yard at Cambridge, striding along the path, away from my room in Holworthy, [p. 5] where he had left a copy of *Walden* for me, I knew him not, but was struck with his short and rustic appearance, and that peculiar stride which all who have walked with him remember.

—F. B. Sanborn, *The Personality of Thoreau* (Boston: Goodspeed, 1901), pp. 5-6.

‥⃗ ⃖‥

One day as I entered the front hall of the Thoreau house for my noonday dinner, I saw under the stairs a pile of books; and when we met at the table, Henry said, "I have added several hundred volumes to my library lately, all of my own composition." In fact, he had received from his first publisher the last parcel of his unsold *Week*, [p. 30] and for a year or two afterwards he sold them himself upon orders through the mail.

—*Ibid.*, pp. 30-31. [Since Sanborn testifies himself that he did not meet Thoreau until 1855, and since Thoreau records the receipt of the unsold copies of *A Week* in his *Journal* for October 27, 1853 (V, 459), it is obvious that this incident is a fabrication of Sanborn's unreliable memory.]

When I first heard Thoreau lecture, as he did every year at the Concord Lyceum, and frequently at Worcester and elsewhere, I did not find his spoken essays so interesting as his conversations. He had few of the arts of the orator, in which Emerson and Phillips excelled; his presence on the platform was not inspiring, nor was his voice specially musical, though he had a musical ear and a real love of melody. But for the thought and humor in his lectures they would have been reckoned dull,—and that was the impression often made. He appeared to best advantage reading them in a small room; or when, as with the John Brown Address, he was [p. 37] mightily stirred by the emotions that a life so heroic excited in his fearless heart. At the age of forty, or thereabout, I heard him sing his favorite song, *Tom Bowline*, by Dibdin, which to Thoreau was a reminiscence of his brother John, so early lost and so dearly loved. The voice was unpractised and rather harsh, but the sentiment made the song interesting.

—*Ibid.*, pp. 37-38.

My children think Henry rather snubs them. He said the *Linnoea borealis* did not flower in Concord, till E. carried it to him, gathered near one of our paths in the park. Why is he never frank? That was an excellent saying of Elizabeth Hoar's, "I love Henry, but I can never like him." What is so cheap as politeness? Never had I the least social pleasure with him, though [p. 61] often the best conversation, in which he goes along accumulating one thing upon another so lavishly—when he is not pugnacious. And in matters practical he makes it worth my while to pay him surveyor's wages for doing other things . . . ; he is so thoughtful, has such a conscience about it, and does so much more than he bargained to do. When he undertakes anything, you may be sure the thing will be done; he has the common sense of Shakespeare.

—Ralph Waldo Emerson, in *ibid.*, pp. 61-62.

ഗ ഇ

His illness might be passed over by some persons, but not by me; it was most impressive. To see one in middle life, with nerves and muscles and will of iron, torn apart piecemeal by that which was stronger than all, were enough to be described, if pen had the power to do it. It was a saying of his, not unfrequent, that he had lived and written as if to live forty years longer; his work was laid out for a long life. Therefore his resignation was great, true, and consistent; great, too, was his suffering. "I have no wish to live, except for my mother and sister," was one of his conclusions. But still, as always, work, work, work! During his illness he enlarged his calendar, made a list of birds, drew [p. 66] greatly on his Journals; at the same time he was writing or correcting several articles for printing, till his strength was no longer sufficient even to move a pencil. Nevertheless, he did not relax, but had the papers still laid before him. I am not aware that anywhere in literature is a greater heroism; the motive, too, was sacred, for he was doing this that his family might reap the advantage. One of his noblest and ablest associates was a philosopher (Alcott) whose heart was like a land flowing with milk and honey; and it was affecting to see this venerable man kissing his brow, when the damps and sweat of death lay upon it, even if Henry knew it not. It seemed to me an extreme unction, in which a friend was the best priest.

—Ellery Channing, in *ibid.*, pp. 66-67.

ഗ ഇ

Yes, truly, "One world at a time" was the very word, almost the last word to me, of our lamented Thoreau. And in tone too sweet and tender for me to suspect that he deemed my question impertinent, or even in questionable taste; as it would have been if dictated by idle curiosity, or, still worse, by religious spleen or sectarian bigotry. He was very weak and low; he saw but very few more setting suns. He sat pillowed in an easy chair. Behind him stood his patient, dear, devoted mother, with her fan in one hand, and phial of ammonia or cologne in the other, to sustain him in the warm morning. At a table near him, piled with his papers and other articles related to them and him, sat his sister, arranging them, as I understood, for Ticknor and Fields, who had been to Concord and bought the copyright.

When I entered Thoreau was looking deathly [p. 68] weak and pale. I saw my way but for the fewest words. I said, as I took his hand, "I suppose this is the best you can do now." He smiled and only nodded, and gasped a faint assent. "The outworks," I said, "seem almost ready to give way." Then a smile shone on his pale face, and with an effort he said, "Yes,—but as long as she cracks she holds" (a common saying of boys skating).

Then I spoke only once more to him, and cannot remember my exact words. But I think my question was substantially this: "You seem so near the brink of the dark river, that I almost wonder how the opposite shore may appear to you." Then he answered: "One world at a time." All this did not occupy more than two minutes, or three at farthest; he needed all his little remaining strength for more important work.

Mrs. Thoreau told me subsequently that in revising for the press he was throwing out almost everything that tended to mirthfulness, as not becoming to the deep seriousness with which he then viewed human existence.

—Parker Pillsbury, Letter to F. B. Sanborn, in *ibid.*, pp. 68-69.

Shortly before he [Thoreau] passed away, in the season of returning birds, and awakening blossoms, he said to a dear friend [Edmund Hosmer] who came to visit him, and who was describing his walk through the country, and across a field in which he had just seen a robin,—

"Yes! This is a beautiful world; *but I shall see a fairer.*"

—Emily R. Lyman, *Thoreau* (Concord: Privately printed, 1902), p. 5.

His mother had expressed a wish for a pine-tree of certain size for the yard and Henry, always eager to give pleasure to his family, found the desired tree one morning, pulled it up by the roots, and, balancing it upon his shoulder, started for his Concord home. Arrived at the town-centre, he noticed a number of people coming out of the church and then, for the first time, he remembered it was Sunday. Fifty years ago, in a village community, such disregard of the Sabbath seemed most culpable, both to Trinitarians and Unitarians. When he first realized his position, he might have stopped at any house on the road, where he was always welcome, . . . [p. 134] but any such concealment or device would be contrary to his open, sincere nature. With good motive he had started to bring home the pine-tree and, justifying his conscience, he sturdily bore his burden past the church amid the gaping, horrified people to his mother's yard.

—"A friend of the Thoreaus," in Annie R. Marble, *Thoreau: His Home, Friends and Books* (New York: Crowell, 1902), pp. 134-135.

ᔓ ᔕ

He always reminded me of an eagle, ready to soar to great heights or to swoop down on anything he considered evil.

—"A lady who was his hostess on occasions in Worcester," in *ibid.*, p. 152.

ᔓ ᔕ

My first interview with him was so peculiar that I will venture to state it. The season was winter, a snow had lately fallen, and I was engaged in shovelling the accumulated mass from the entrance to my house, when I perceived a man walking towards me bearing an umbrella in one hand and a leather travelling-bag in the other. So unlike my ideal Thoreau, whom I had fancied, from the robust nature of his mind and habits of life, to be a man of unusual vigor and size, that I did not suspect, although I had expected him in the morning, that the slight, quaint-looking person before me was the Walden philosopher. There are few persons who had previously read his works that were not disappointed by his personal appearance. As he came near to me I gave him the usual salutation, and supposing him to be either a pedler or some way-traveller, he at once remarked,

"You don't know me." The truth flashed on my mind, and conceal[p. 11]ing my own surprise I at once took him by the hand and led him to the room already prepared for him, feeling a kind of disappointment—a disappointment, however, which soon passed off, and never again obtruded itself to the philosopher's disadvantage. In fact, I soon began to see that Nature had dealt kindly by him, and that this apparently slender personage was physically capable of enduring far more than the ordinary class of men, although he had then begun to show signs of failure of strength in his knees. [p. 12] . . .

Many a long ramble have I taken with him, and although I am a pretty good walker, he usually quite fatigued me before he had accomplished his object, perhaps the pursuit of some rare plant. In a boat of his own construction I have sailed with him up and down the slow gliding Concord River, and found him a good boatman, both in sailing and sculling. Once, during a winter visit to him, we took a tramp through the snow to White Pond, some two or three miles beyond Walden, then surrounded by heavy wood, and frequented by huntsmen. He was fond of hardy enterprises, and few of his companions could compete with him. In fact I have heard that he quite tired out an Indian guide, on one of his excursions in Maine. I do not remember of ever seeing him laugh outright, but he was ever ready to smile at anything that pleased him; and I never knew him to betray any tender emotion except on one occasion, when he was narrating to me the death of his only brother, John Thoreau, from lockjaw, strong symptoms of which, from his sympathy with the sufferer, he himself experienced. At this time his voice was choked, and he shed tears, and went to the door for air. The subject was of course dropped, and never recurred to again.

—Daniel Ricketson, *Daniel Ricketson and His Friends* (Boston: Houghton Mifflin, 1902), pp. 11-12, 14.

October 7, 1855

Last Sunday my friend Thoreau and I spent most of the day visiting Sassaquin and Long Pond, "Joe's Rocks." I enjoyed the visit of Thoreau very much; he improves, unlike most people, upon an intimate acquaintance—modest and gentle in his manner, the best read and most intelligent man I ever knew. He is also a very good naturalist, and very much interested while here in wild plants, shells, etc. He took away with him quite a little collection of curiosities he had collected during our rambles. In Indian history I found him well informed, and as a classical scholar but few, I should judge, could compete with him. My respect for his character and talents is greater than for any man I know.

—Ibid., p. 283.

❧ ❧

August 20, 1861

At home this A.M. talking a good deal with Thoreau in the Shanty. Rode with Thoreau this P.M., visited the old house at Thomas Wood's farm. In relation to my friend Thoreau's health my impression is that his case is a very critical one as to recovery; he has a bad cough and expectorates a good deal, is emaciated considerably, his spirits, however, appear as good as usual, his appetite good. Unless some favorable symptom shows itself soon I fear that he will gradually decline. He is thinking of going to a warm climate for the winter, but I think a judicious hydropathic treatment at home would be much better for him.

—Ibid., p. 318.

❧ ❧

You ask for some particulars relating to Henry's illness. I feel like saying that Henry was never affected, never reached by it. I never before saw such a manifestation of the power of spirit over matter. Very often I have heard him tell his visitors that he enjoyed existence as well as ever. He remarked to me that there was as much comfort in perfect disease as in perfect health, the mind always conforming to the condition of the body. The thought of death, he said, could not begin to trouble him. His thoughts had entertained him all his life, and did still.

When he had wakeful nights, he would ask me to arrange the furniture so as to make fantastic shadows on the wall, and he wished his bed was in the form of a shell, that he might curl up in it. He considered occupation as necessary for the sick as [p. 141] for those in health, and has accomplished a vast amount of labor during the past few months in preparing some papers for the press. He did not cease to call for his manuscripts till the last day of his life.

During his long illness I never heard a murmur escape him, or the slightest wish expressed to remain with us; his perfect content- ment was truly wonderful. None of his friends seemed to realize how very ill he was, so full of life and good cheer did he seem. One friend, as if by way of consolation, said to him, "Well, Mr. Thoreau, we must all go." Henry replied, "When I was a very little boy I learned that I must die, and I sat that down, so of course I am not disappointed now. Death is as near to you as it is to me."

There is very much that I should like to write you about my precious brother, had I time and strength. I wish you to know how very gentle, lovely, and submissive he was in all his ways. His little study bed was brought down into our front parlor, when he could no longer walk with our assistance, and every arrangement pleased him. The devotion of his friends was most rare and touching; his room was made fragrant by the gift of flowers from young and old; fruit of every kind which the season afforded, and game of all sorts was sent him. It was really pathetic, the way in which the town was moved to minister to his comfort. Total strangers sent grateful mes- sages, remembering the good he had done them. All this attention was fully [p. 142] appreciated and very gratifying to Henry; he would sometimes say, "I should be ashamed to stay in this world after so much had been done for me, I could never repay my friends." And they so remembered him to the last. Only about two hours before he left us, Judge Hoar called with a bouquet of hyacinths fresh from his garden, which Henry smelled and said he liked, and a few minutes after he was gone, another friend came with a dish of his favorite jelly.

I can never be grateful enough for the gentle, easy exit which was granted him. At seven o'clock Tuesday morning he became rest- less and desired to be moved; dear mother, Aunt Louisa, and myself were with him; his self-possession did not forsake him. A little after eight he asked to be raised quite up, his breathing grew fainter and fainter, and without the slightest struggle, he left us at nine o'clock.

—Sophia Thoreau, Letter to Daniel Ricketson, May 20, 1862, in *ibid.*, pp. 141-143.

∽ ∾

It may interest you to hear of the last visit which I with Blake made at his (Thoreau's) house a short time before he died. We took our skates, and then the cars as far as Framingham. From some two miles north of Framingham we took to the river and [p. 213] skated nearly to Thoreau's house. We found him pretty low, but well enough to be up in his chair. He seemed glad to see us. Said we had not come much too soon. We spent some hours with him in his mother's parlor, which overlooks the river that runs all through his life. There was a beautiful snowstorm going on the while which I fancy inspired him, and his talk was up to the best I ever heard from him,—the same depth of earnestness and the same infinite depth of fun going on at the same time.

I wish I could recall some of the things he said. I do remember some few answers he made to questions from Blake. Blake asked him how the future seemed to him. "Just as uninteresting as ever," was his characteristic answer. A little while after he said, "You have been skating on this river; perhaps I am going to skate on some other." And again, "Perhaps I am going up country." He stuck to nature to the last.

He seemed to be in an exalted state of mind for a long time before his death. He said it was just as good to be sick as to be well,—just as good to have a poor time as a good time.

—Theo Brown, Letter to Daniel Ricketson, January 19, 1868, in *ibid.*, pp. 213-214.

❧ ❧

He was a man of rare courage, physically and intellectually. In the way of the former, he arrested two young fellows with horse and wagon on the lonely road leading to his hermitage at Walden pond, who were endeavoring to entrap a young woman on her way home, and took them to the village; whether they were brought to court I do not remember, and [p. 252] may not have given an exact account of the affair, but it is circumstantially correct.

—Daniel Ricketson, Letter to Henry Salt, December 9, 1889, in *ibid.*, pp. 252-253.

❧ ❧

A little over fifty years ago, I was well acquainted with Thoreau and used to get him to survey wood land, which I bought by the acre, and paid him three dollars per day. He was always very pleasant[,] talkative, and very ingenious [*sic*]. I recollect one day late in the autumn, of employing him to survey a lot I had bought. We had been bothered about finding the bounds, and before we were ready to run the last line, it was quite dark. I was wondering how he would be able to see the last bound to take bearings. When he was ready to do so, and had his compass set, he took from his pocket a tallow candle and a match, lighted the candle, gave it to me and told me to hold it on top of the stick on the last bound. In that way he finished the work, and saved our going another day.

Thoreau once asked me if I knew that a white pine tree had a beautiful blossom on its very top. I told him I had never seen one. He said that once in June, he had climbed to the top of a pine tree and found the blossom, but he had never found any person who had ever seen one. I think in one of his books he mentions this blossom.

About forty-nine years ago, I bought a large tract (several thousand acres) of wood and timber land in Vermont on the top of the Green Mountains, and went there to live. I frequently came to Concord to visit my friends and always made it a point to see Thoreau.

When I told him I was cutting off the Primeval Forest, he was quite interested in my work and said he would come up to see me sometime. I began to tell him how he could get to Vermont, and he said, "Oh, I sha'n't go by rail, I shall take a bee line and walk."

—James B. Wood, "Thoreau and the Pines," *Middlesex Patriot* (Concord, Mass.), February 21, 1902.

∾ ⌒

Thoreau was already there [at Ralph Waldo Emerson's house]. I think he had ended his experiment at Walden Pond some years before. Thoreau was dressed, I remember, in a plain, neat suit of dark clothes, not quite black. He had a healthy, out-of-door appearance, and looked like a respectable husbandman. He was rather silent; when he spoke, it was in either a critical or a witty vein. I did not know who or what he was; and I find in my old diary of the day that

I spelled his rare name phonetically, and heard afterward that he was a man who had been a hermit. I observed that he was much at home with Emerson; and as he remained through the afternoon and evening, and I left him still at the fireside, he appeared to me to belong in some way to the household. I observed also that Emerson continually deferred to him and seemed to anticipate his view, preparing himself obviously for a quiet laugh at Thoreau's negative and biting [p. 27] criticisms, especially in regard to education and educational institutions. He was clearly fond of Thoreau; but whether in a human way, or as an amusement, I could not then make out. Dear, indeed, as I have since learned, was Thoreau to that household, where his memory is kept green, where Emerson's children still speak of him as their elder brother. In the evening Thoreau devoted himself wholly to the children and the parching of corn by the open fire. I think he made himself very entertaining to them. Emerson was talking to me, and I was only conscious of Thoreau's presence as we are of those about us but not engaged with us. A very pretty picture remains in my memory of Thoreau leaning over the fire with a fair girl on either side, which somehow did not comport with the sub[p. 28]sequent story I heard of his being a hermit. [p. 29] . . .

As soon as I could I introduced the problem I came to propound —what [p. 30] course a young man must take to get the best kind of education. Emerson pleaded always for the college; said he himself entered at fourteen. This aroused the wrath of Thoreau, who would not allow any good to the college course. And here it seemed to me Emerson said things on purpose to draw Thoreau's fire and to amuse himself. When the curriculum at Cambridge was alluded to, and Emerson casually remarked that most of the branches were taught there, Thoreau seized one of his opportunities and replied: "Yes, indeed, all the branches and none of the roots." At this Emerson laughed heartily. So without conclusions, or more light than the assertions of two representative men can give, I heard agitated for an hour my momentous question. [p. 31] . . .

He [Emerson] said [p. 44] we needed some great poets, orators. He was always looking out for them, and was sure the new generation of young men would contain some. Thoreau here remarked he had found one, in the woods, but it had feathers and had not been to Harvard College. Still it had a voice and an aerial inclination, which was pretty much all that was needed. "Let us cage it," said Emerson.

"That is just the way the world always spoils its poets," responded Thoreau. Then Thoreau, as usual, had the last word; there was a laugh, in which for the first time he joined heartily, as the perquisite of the victor.

—John Albee, *Remembrances of Emerson* (New York: Cooke, 1903), pp. 27-45.

ᔥ ᔐ

I knew Henry Thoreau very intimately. I went to school with him when I was a little boy and he was a big one. Afterward I was a scholar in his school.

He was very fond of small boys, and used to take them out with him in his boat, and make bows and arrows for them, and take part in their games. He liked also to get a number of the little chaps of a Saturday afternoon and take them out in his boat, or for a long walk in the woods.

He knew the best places to find huckleberries and blackberries and chestnuts and lilies and cardinal and other rare flowers. We used to call him Trainer Thoreau, because the boys called the soldiers the "trainers," and he had a long, measured stride and an erect carriage which made him seem something like a soldier, although he was short and rather ungainly in figure. He had a curved nose which reminded one a little of the beak of a parrot.

His real name was David Henry Thoreau, although he changed the order of his first two names afterward. He was a great finder of Indian arrow-heads, spear-heads, pestles, and other stone implements which the Indians had left behind them, of which there was great abundance in the Concord fields and meadows.

He knew the rare forest birds and all the ways of birds and wild animals. Naturalists commonly know birds and beasts and flowers as a surgeon who has dissected the human body, or perhaps sometimes a painter who has made pictures of them knows men and women. But he knew birds and beasts as one boy knows another—all their delightful little habits and fashions. He had the most wonderful good [p. 70] fortune. We used to say that if anything happened in the deep woods which only came about once in a hundred years, Henry Thoreau would be sure to be on the spot at the time and know the whole story. [p. 71] . . .

It is a singular fact that Emerson did not know Henry Thoreau until after Thoreau had been some years out of college. Henry walked to Boston, eighteen miles, to hear one of Emerson's lectures, and walked home again in the night after the lecture was over. Emerson heard of it, and invited him to come to his house and hear the lectures read there, which he did. People used to say that Thoreau imitated Emerson, and Lowell has made this charge in his satire, "A Fable for Critics":

> There comes—, for instance; to see him's rare sport,
> Tread in Emerson's tracks with legs painfully short.

I think there is nothing in it. Thoreau's style is certainly fresh and original. His tastes and thoughts are his own. His peculiarities of bearing and behavior came to him naturally from his ancestors of the isle of Guernsey.

I retained his friendship to his death. I have taken many a long walk with him. I used to go down to see him in the winter days in my vacations in his hut near Walden. He was capital company. He was a capital guide in the wood. He liked to take out the boys in his boat. He was fond of discoursing. I do not think he was vain. But he liked to do his thinking out loud, and expected that you should be an auditor rather than a companion.

I have heard Thoreau say in private a good many things which afterward appeared in his writings. One day when we were walking, he leaned his back against a rail fence and discoursed of the shortness of the time since the date fixed for the creation, measured by human lives. "Why," he said, "sixty old women like Nabby Kettle" (a very old woman in Concord), "taking hold of hands, would span the whole of it." He repeats this in one of his books, adding, "They would be but a small tea-party, but their gossip would make universal history."

—George F. Hoar, *Autobiography of Seventy Years* (New York: Scribner's, 1903), pp. 70-72.

∽ ∾

Thoreau ate no meat; he told me his only reason was a feeling of the filthiness of flesh-eating. A bear huntsman he thought was entitled to his steak. He had never attempted to make any general principle on the subject, and later in life ate meat in order not to cause inconvenience to the family .

On our first walk I told him the delight with which I read his book, "A Week on the Concord and Merrimack Rivers." He said that the whole edition remained on the shelf of his publisher, who wished to get rid of them. If he could not succeed in giving them away they would probably be sold as old paper. I got from him valuable hints about reading. He had studied carefully the old English Chronicles, and Chaucer, Froissart, Spenser, and Beaumont and Fletcher. He recognized kindred spirits in George Herbert, Cowley, and Quarles, considering the latter a poet but not an artist. He explored the old books of voyages—Drake, Purchas, and others, who assisted him in his circumnavigation of Concord. The Oriental books were his daily bread; the Greeks (especially Æschylus, whose "Prometheus" and "The Seven against Thebes" he translated finely) were his luxuries. He was an exact Greek scholar. Of moderns he praised Wordsworth, Coleridge, and to a less extent, Carlyle and Goethe. He admired Ruskin's "Modern Painters," though he thought the author bigoted, but in the "Seven Lamps of Architecture" [p. 142] he found with the good stuff "too much about art for me and the Hottentots. Our house is yet a hut." He enjoyed William Gilpin's "Hints on Landscape Gardening: Tour of the River Wye." He had read with care the works of Franklin. He had as a touchstone for authors their degree of ability to deal with supersensual facts and feelings with scientific precision. What he admired in Emerson was that he discerned the phenomena of thought and functions of every idea as if they were *antennae or stamina.*

It was a quiet joke in Concord that Thoreau resembled Emerson in expression, and in tones of voice. He had grown up from boyhood under Emerson's influence, had listened to his lectures and his conversations, and little by little had grown this resemblance. It was the more interesting because so superficial and unconscious. Thoreau was an imitator of no mortal; but Emerson had long been a part of the very atmosphere of Concord, and it was as if this element had deposited on Thoreau a mystical moss.

—Moncure Daniel Conway, *Autobiography* (Boston: Houghton Mifflin, 1904), pp. 142-143. [By permission of Columbia University.]

The children of Emerson, of Judge Rockwood Hoar, of the Loring and Barrett families, mostly girls between ten and twelve years, were all pretty and intelligent, and as it was vacation time they were prepared for walks, picnics, boating, etc. Other of their elders beside myself found delight in the society of these young people, especially Thoreau. He used to take us out on the river in his boat, and by his scientific talk guide us into the water-lilies' fairyland. He showed us his miracle of putting his hand into the water and bringing up a fish. I remember Ellen Emerson asking her father, "Whom shall we invite to the picnic?"—his answer being, "All children from six years to sixty." Then there were huckleberrying parties. These were under the guidance of Thoreau, because he alone knew the precise locality of every variety of the berry. I recall an occasion when little Edward Emerson, carrying a basket of fine huckleberries, had a fall and spilt them all. Great was his distress, and our offers of berries could not console him for the loss of those gathered by himself. But Thoreau came, put his arm around the troubled child, and explained to him that if the crop of huckleberries was to continue it was necessary that some should be scattered. Nature had provided that little boys should now and then stumble and sow the berries. We shall have a grand lot of bushes and berries in this spot, and we shall owe them to you. Edward began to smile.

—*Ibid.*, p. 148.

❧ ❧

On July 4, 1854, the annual gathering of the abolitionists in Framingham Grove occurred. . . . Thoreau had come all the way from Concord for this meeting. It was a rare thing for him to attend any meeting outside of Concord, and though he sometimes lectured in the Lyceum there, he had probably never spoken on a platform. He was now clamoured for and made a brief and quaint speech. He began with the simple words, "You have my sympathy; it is all I have to give you, but you may find it important to you." It was impossible to associate egotism with Thoreau; we all felt that the time and trouble he had taken at that crisis to proclaim his sympathy with the "Disunionists" was indeed important. He was there a representative of Concord, [p. 184] of science and letters, which could not quietly pursue their tasks while slavery was trampling down the rights of mankind. Alluding to the Boston commissioner who had surrendered Anthony Burns, Edward G. Loring, Thoreau said, "The fugitive's case was already decided by God,—not Edward G. God, but simple God." This was said with such serene unconsciousness of anything shocking in it that we were but mildly startled.

—*Ibid.*, pp. 184-185.

I am not sure whether you had personal knowledge of Thoreau, whom I had seen a little of from time to time, and a good deal more about thirty years ago, when I spent several Sundays at his mother's house (having the same expectation of becoming a resident of Concord), and had a good many talks with him. He was a surveyor by profession, and kept a local map, which served him for a guide in his long tramps. He avoided the highways, and was reluctant even to have his feet off the turf or out of the woods. One may believe that he knew every rabbit-burrow and squirrel-hole in Concord, if not the individual physiognomy of each wild creature. He watched them as individuals; would bring turtles' eggs in his pocket to hatch in the garden, and had an undue contempt for book-and-study naturalists, unjustly disparaging Agassiz. As Mr. Emerson said to me, he was "so good—and so bad!" [p. 12]

His hermit-like and ascetic theories were eked out by frequent sharing of Emerson's conversation and hospitality. Before "Walden" was published I heard him give a lecture before a small audience, which began: "I have been a good deal of a traveler—about my native village," and went on with a very entertaining account of his experiments in living. Noncomformist as he was, he once spent a week [*sic*] in Concord jail for refusing to pay his taxes. His mother lived very quietly near the railroad station, and took occasional boarders—like myself. His sister was (I believe) a nurse by profession, and a grave woman of bright intelligence. She used to beat me easily at chess. His out-door life probably kept at bay the consumption he died of; though his hermitage could hardly have been good for him.

—Anonymous, in Joel Benton, *Persons and Places* (New York: Broadway, 1905), pp. 12-13.

I was made very happy to-day by seeing Miss Thoreau, whose brother died such a happy, peaceful death,—leaving them all so fully possessed of his faith in the Immortal Life that they seem almost to have entered it with him. They said they never could be sad in his presence for a moment; he had been the happiest person they had ever known, [p. 103] all through his life, and was just as happy in the presence of death. This is the more remarkable as he was still in the prime of life, with a vivid sense of its enjoyments. But he was nearer to the heart of Nature than most men. Sophia said to-day that he once told her when looking at a pressed flower that he had walked 10,000 miles to verify the day on which that flower bloomed. It grew four miles from his home, and he walked there every day in the season of it for many years. . . . He seemed to walk straight into Heaven. It is animating and inspiring to see a great or a good man take that last step with his thoughts about him, and intent upon the two worlds whose connection he sees with the clairvoyance that death gives. I know it well, and I could fully sympathize in her sense of her brother's continued presence. Death is not the word to use for such a transit,—but more life,—for which we as yet have no word.

—Mary Mann, Letter to Mrs. Nathaniel Hawthorne, May, 1862, in H. D. Thoreau, *Sir Walter Raleigh* (Boston: Bibliophile Society, 1905), pp. 103-104.

It was a hot sweltering day in late June, when E[d] W[atson] at Hillside said he must go home to the island and shear the poor suffering sheep. With a slightly sarcastic tone Thoreau said: 'Ah! you gentlemen of property must look after it.' 'Why,' said E. W., 'everybody has something to go home to,—you have your desk, or something, have n't you?' This arrow, shot at a venture, hit the mark, for Thoreau could scarcely write a line away from his green desk. One evening at the island he described the early Norse voyagers and the coming over of some of his own family who were shipwrecked. He said he asked a shopkeeper on Cape Cod by what route he came to Provincetown. 'I was cast ashore here,' was the pat answer. Thoreau gave a fine account of the early voyagers, strong and breezy; it carried you along with it. We had always thought our Pilgrim Fathers were worthy of some notice; they too had a right to fame; they colonized a country. But the daring enterprise of the Vikings took for the time the wind out of their sails. What were liberty, religion, a good constitution, wise laws? Why, nothing to that bold, adventurous spirit of the Norsemen. Not one word that he said can be now remembered, but it took hold of us and carried us along as with an 'o'ertaking blast' from the north. Thoreau sat in a chair by the open window, and his long arms went out in gestures as he described the voyage. One after another the island boys looked in at the window, and sat down outside, their earnest weather-beaten faces turned towards the speaker. Their circle of bright, adventurous spirits listened eagerly; they too would one day spread the sail to the breeze and visit far-off lands. I think Thoreau was a true sailor.

—F. B. Sanborn, "A Concord Note-Book," *Critic*, XLVII (November, 1905), 446.

∾ ⌒

March 28, 1853.

My Aunt Maria asked me to read the life of Dr. Chalmers, which however I did not promise to do. Yesterday, Sunday, she was heard through the partition shouting to my Aunt Jane, who is deaf, "Think of it! He stood half an hour to-day to hear the frogs croak, and he would n't read the life of Chalmers."

—Henry David Thoreau, *Journal* (Boston: Houghton Mifflin, 1906), V, 58.

∾ ⌒

November 6, 1858.

I guessed at Goodwin's age on the 1st. He is hale and stout and looks younger than he is, and I took care to set him high enough. I guessed he was fifty-five, and he said that if he lived two or three months longer he would be fifty-six. He then guessed at my age, thought I was forty. He thought that Emerson was a very young-looking man for his age. "But," said he, "he has not been out o' nights as much as you have."

—*Ibid.*, XI, 289.

∾ ⌒

Thoreau had his own odd ways. Once he got to the house while I was out—went straight to the kitchen where my dear mother was baking some cakes—took the cakes hot from the oven. He was always doing things of the plain sort—without fuss. I liked all that about him. But Thoreau's great fault was disdain—disdain for men (for Tom, Dick and Harry): inability to appreciate the average life—even the exceptional life: it seemed to me a want of imagination. He couldn't put his life into any other life—realize why one man was so and another man was not so: was impatient with other people on the street and so forth. We had a hot discussion about it—it was a bitter difference: it was rather a surprise to me to meet in Thoreau such a very aggravated case of superciliousness. It was egotistic—not taking that word in its worst sense. . . . We could not agree at all in our estimate of men—of the men we meet here, there, everywhere—the concrete man. Thoreau had an abstraction about man—a right [p. 212] abstraction: there we agreed. We had our quarrel only on this ground. Yet he was a man you would have to like—an interesting man, simple, conclusive. . . . When I lived in Brooklyn—in the suburbs—probably two miles distant from the ferries—though there were cheap cabs, I always walked to the ferry to get over to New York. Several times when Thoreau was there with me we walked together.

—Walt Whitman, in Horace Traubel, *With Walt Whitman in Camden* (Boston: Small, Maynard, 1906), I, 212-213. [By permission of Gertrude Traubel.]

∽ ∾

He struck me as being very odd, very wise and exceedingly observing. He roamed about the country at his own sweet will, and I was fortunate enough to be his companion on a walk up Wantastiquet Mt. I was well acquainted with the flora and could meet him understandingly there, but was somewhat abashed by the numerous questions he asked about all sorts of things, to which I could only reply "I do not know." It appealed to my sense of humor that a person with such a fund of knowledge should seek information from a young girl like myself, but I could not see that he had any fun in him. The only question I can now recall is this. As we stood on the summit of Wantastiquet, he fixed his earnest gaze on a distant point in the landscape, which he designated, asking "How far is it in a bee line to that spot?"

—Mary Brown Dunton, in Elizabeth B. Davenport, "Thoreau in Vermont in 1856," *Vermont Botanical Club Bulletin*, III (April, 1908), 37.

❧ ☙

I will gladly come on Thursday. Thoreau is to be at my house, and I shall take the liberty to bring him with me, unless he has scruples about intruding [p. 28] on you. You would find him well worth knowing; he is a man of thought and originality, with a certain iron-pokerishness,—an uncompromising stiffness,—in his mental character, which is interesting, though it grows rather wearisome on close and frequent acquaintance.

—Nathaniel Hawthorne, Letter to Henry Wadsworth Longfellow, November 21, 1848, in F. B. Sanborn, *Hawthorne and His Friends* (Cedar Rapids: Torch Press, 1908), pp. 28-29.

❧ ☙

Gov. Banks's grand muster in 1859 . . . was the opportunity for a jest by Thoreau at the expense of the State authorities. A friend met him on his way from his mother's house to the Village, and said, "I hear the Governor comes to Concord today." "Yes," said the philosopher, "I am going down to buy a lock for our front-door." "But the Legislature are coming too." "Indeed?" said Thoreau, "then I must put a lock on our back-door."

—F. B. Sanborn, *Recollections of Seventy Years* (Boston: Badger, 1909), I, 44.

❧ ☙

It once happened that Alcott and Thoreau spent some days together at Hillside, and in their walks through the surrounding wood encountered the remains of a dead hog—his white, firm jawbone, and his bristles quite untouched by decay. "You see," said Thoreau to his vegetarian friend, "here is something that succeeded, beside spirituality, and thought,—here is the tough child of nature,"—and they fell into high converse respecting the bristly darling of the Great Mother.

—*Ibid.*, II, 320.

∾∾

The Ricketsons said, when asked about the visit of Thoreau, Alcott, and Channing at their New Bedford house (Brooklawn) in April, 1857, that Thoreau sang and danced there to the accompaniment of Mrs. Ricketson's piano. Mr. Alcott, then giving Conversations in New Bedford, visited the Ricketsons for two or three weeks. Thoreau went there April 2d, and returned April 15th; but was at Plymouth and elsewhere part of the time. Channing, then living in New Bedford, came out to dine or take tea at Brooklawn several times a week. On this particular evening, Daniel Ricketson and Channing, after tea, had gone out to the "shanty," where the friends smoked and talked, while Alcott and Thoreau remained with Mrs. R. and Walton. Anna was taking her usual walk on the verandas, before going to bed. As Mrs. R. struck up a lively Scotch air ("The Campbells are Comin' "), Thoreau felt moved to try a dance, and did so,— keeping time to the music perfectly, but executing some steps more like Indian dances than the usual ball-room figures. Anna was so amused at the sight, which she saw through the window, that she ran and called her father and Channing, who came and looked on,— Alcott sitting on the sofa, meanwhile, and watching the dance. Thoreau continued the performance for five or ten minutes; it was earnest and spontaneous, but not particularly graceful.

—*Ibid.*, II, 397.

∾∾

It was in the spring of 1858 or 1859, when I was working at the grist-and-saw-mill of Samuel Barrett, that one day, as I was grinding corn, Mr. Thoreau came into the grist mill to inquire for Mr. Barrett, Now, thinks I, is the time to find out whether or no the water snakes will harm us boys when we go in swimming; for we always felt a little shy of them. So I said, "Mr. Thoreau, can the snakes in the mill pond hurt me if I go in where they are?" "No," said he, "they cannot; if you can find me one I will show you why not." Now up at the reservoir dam was a plank bridge, and in such warm days in April the water snakes would come out of the pond and lie on the bridge in the sun, and go to sleep; so I said to Mr. Thoreau that we could find one up there. He said he would go along and show me they were harmless, if I could go then. I shut down the water gate at once and walked with him to the bridge; and behold, there was a [p. 389] big snake fast asleep. Mr. T. quietly stept up and clasped him around the body, a little below the head; whereat Mr. Snake began to wake up and squirm, and coil himself about the arm of his captor. He then called my attention to the open mouth of the reptile, and said, "You see he has no jawbone; he cannot bite; he sucks in his food; and as for a sting in his tail that you may have heard the boys talking of,— you can see for yourself there is none,"—pinching the tail. "So you may be assured you will get no harm if you come in contact with the very king of the water snakes." And I never had any fear of them after that day.

—Mr. [?] Carr, in *ibid.*, II, 389-390.

He was very reticent of biographical recollections; yet I recall that he well remembered a certain field, through which we walked in Concord, a good distance from the village, to which he used to drive his cow, with bare feet, like the other village boys. He did not dwell on the past. I am confident he rarely read a book over twice, and he loved not to repeat a story after its first freshness. His talent was onward, vigorous, in the moment, which was perfectly filled, and then he went to the next with great speed.

But I doubt not he loved to linger in mind over the old familiar things of boyhood; and he occasionally let fall some memory of the "Mill Dam" when he was a boy, and of the pond behind it, now a meadow. Of the many houses in which he lived (for his was a very moving family), I heard him rarely speak: that one, now torn away, at the corner of the slaughter-house street (Walden Road); another, where the Library now stands (the Parkman house), farther towards the railroad; and still another which had been "fixed over" for more aspiring villagers than the Irish, who succeeded the Thoreaus in the

Parkman house. Three of these mansions he passed in his daily walks
to the Post Office, a duty he fulfilled after the death of his father, for
the benefit of his family,—for he was a martinet in the family service,—but I never heard him say more than, "I used to live in that
house," or, "There it was that so-and-so took place"; thus refreshing
his memory by the existing locality. In the year before he built for
himself at Walden his only true house, he assisted in making a house
in that western part of the village called "Texas," not far from the
River. To this [p. 400] spot he was always much attached; it commanded an excellent view toward the southwest, was retired, and he
had planted a small orchard there.

—Ellery Channing, in *ibid.*, II, 400-401.

∽ ∾

Sunday, January 15, 1848.

We had a nice pleasant time at Mr. Alcott's Conversation last
night, although I could hardly say it was very fine. . . . Thorault
[*sic*] amused me the most. He is all overlaid by an imitation of
Emerson; talks like him, puts out his arm like him, brushes his hair
in the same way, and is even getting up a caricature nose like Emerson's. Yet he has something in himself,—else he would be altogether
disgusting and ridiculous; as it is, 'tis funny. I really enjoyed it all
the evening, and wanted to say to him, as the child did to Judge
Smith, of Exeter,—"Man, talk more!" He was not a living man,—he
was a phenomenal creature. This is, of course, surface criticism, but
true as far as it goes.

—Ednah Littlehale Cheney, in *ibid.*, II, 469.

∽ ∾

Thoreau has just come back from reading to Parker's company
a revolutionary Lecture on Osawatomie [John] Brown, a hero and
martyr after his own heart and style of manliness. It was received
here by our Concord folks with great favor, and by the Worcester
friends of his. I wish the towns might be [p. 130] his auditors
throughout the length and breadth of states and country. He thinks

of printing it in pamphlet and spreading it far and wide, North and South.

—A. Bronson Alcott, Letter to Daniel Ricketson, November 7, 1859, in Anna and Walton Ricketson, eds., *Daniel Ricketson: Autobiographic and Miscellaneous* (New Bedford: Anthony, 1910), pp. 130-131.

◡ ◠

Henry D. Thoreau is a great man in Concord, a man of original genius & character, who knows Greek, & knows Indian also,—not the language quite as well as John Eliot—but the history monuments & genius of the Sachems, being a pretty good Sachem himself, master of all woodcraft, & an intimate associate of the birds, beasts, & fishes, of this region. I could tell you many a good story of his forest life.— He has written what he calls "A Week on the Concord & Merrimack Rivers," which is an account of an excursion made by himself & his brother (in a boat which he built) some time ago, from Concord, Mass., down the Con[p. 60]cord river & up the Merrimack, to Concord, N.H.—I think it a book of wonderful merit, which is to go far & last long. It will remind you of Izaak Walton, and, if it have not all his sweetness, it is rich, as he is not, in profound thought.

—Ralph Waldo Emerson, Letter to William Henry Furness, August 6, 1847, in H. H. F., ed., *Records of a Lifelong Friendship* (Boston: Houghton Mifflin, 1910), pp. 60-61.

◡ ◠

I was glad to see Mr. Thoreau. He was full of interesting talk for the little while that we saw him, & it was amusing to hear your intonations. And then he looked so differently from my idea of him. . . . He had a glimpse of the Academy [of Natural Sciences] as he will tell you—I could not hear him lecture for which I was sorry. Miss Caroline Haven heard him, & from her report I judge the audience was stupid & did not appreciate him.

—W. H. Furness, Letter to Ralph Waldo Emerson, November 26, 1854, in *ibid.*, p. 101.

◡ ◠

February 11, 1838.

I delight much in my young friend [Thoreau], who seems to have as free and erect a mind as any I have ever met.

—Ralph Waldo Emerson, *Journals* (Boston: Houghton Mifflin, 1910), IV, 395.

~ ~

February 17, 1838.

My good Henry Thoreau made this else solitary afternoon sunny with his simplicity and clear perception. How comic is simplicity in this double-dealing, quacking world. Everything that boy says makes merry with society, though nothing can be graver than his meaning. I told him he should write out the history of his college life, as Carlyle has his tutoring. We agreed that the seeing the stars through a telescope would be worth all the astronomical lectures. Then he described Mr. Quimby's electrical lecture here, and the experiment of the shock, and added that "college corporations are very blind to the fact that that twinge in the elbow is worth all the lecturing."

—*Ibid.,* IV, 397.

~ ~

November, 1838.

My brave Henry Thoreau walked with me to Walden this afternoon and complained of the proprietors who compelled him, to whom, as much as any, the whole world belonged, to walk in a strip of road and crowded him out of all the rest of God's earth. He must not get over the fence: but to the building of that fence he was no party. Suppose, he said, some great proprietor, before he was born, had bought up the whole globe. So had he been hustled out of nature. Not having been privy to any of these arrangements, he does not feel called on to consent to them, and so cuts fishpoles in the woods without asking who had a better title to the wood than he. I defended, of course, the good institution as a scheme, not good, but the best that could be hit on for making the woods and waters and fields available to wit and worth, and for restraining the bold, bad man. At all events,

I begged him, having this maggot of Freedom and Humanity in his brain, to write it out into good poetry and so clear himself of [p. 128] it. He replied, that he feared that that was not the best way, that in doing justice to the thought, the man did not always do justice to himself, the poem ought to sing itself: if the man took too much pains with the expression, he was not any longer the Idea himself.

—*Ibid.*, V (1911), 128-129.

∾ ∾

March, 1843.

Elizabeth Hoar says, "I love Henry, but do not like him." Young men, like Henry Thoreau, owe us a new world, and they have not acquitted the debt. For the most part, such die young, and so dodge the fulfillment. One of our girls said, that Henry never went through the kitchen without coloring.

—*Ibid.*, VI, 371.

∾ ∾

May, 1844.

Henry Thoreau's conversation consisted of a continual coining of the present moment into a sentence and offering it to me. I compared it to a boy, who, from the universal snow lying on the earth, gathers up a little in his hand, rolls it into a ball, and flings it at me.

—*Ibid.*, VI, 515.

∾ ∾

May, 1844.

Henry said that the other world was all his art; that his pencils would draw no other; that his jackknife would cut nothing else. He does not use it as a means. Henry is a good substantial Childe, not encumbered with himself. He has no troublesome memory, no wake, but lives *ex tempore*, and brings to-day a new proposition as radical and revolutionary as that of yesterday, but different. He is a good Abbot Samson: and carries counsel in his breast. If I cannot show his performance much more manifest than that of the other grand promisers, at least I can see that, with his practical faculty, he has declined all the kingdoms of this world. Satan has no bribe for him.

—*Ibid.*

※ ※

July, 1846.

My friend Mr. Thoreau has gone to jail rather than pay his tax. On him they could not calculate. The Abolitionists denounce the war and give much time to it, but they pay the tax.

—*Ibid.*, VII (1912), 219.

※ ※

July, 10, 1847.

Thoreau sometimes appears only as a *gendarme*, good to knock down a cockney with, but without that power to cheer and establish which makes the value of a friend.

—*Ibid.*, VII, 303.

※ ※

August, 1847.

Henry Thoreau says that twelve pounds of Indian meal, which one can easily carry on his back, will be food for a fortnight. Of course, one need not be in want of a living wherever corn grows, and where it does not, rice is as good.

Henry, when you talked of art, blotted a paper with ink, then doubled it over, and safely defied the artist to surpass his effect.

—*Ibid.*, VII, 321.

※ ※

September 1, 1850.

Nature, Ellery thought, is less interesting. Yesterday Thoreau told me it was more so, and persons less. I think it must always combine with man.

—*Ibid.*, VIII, 122.

∻ ∻

July, 1852.

Henry Thoreau rightly said, the other evening, talking of lightning-rods, that the only rod of safety was in the vertebrae of his own spine.

—*Ibid.*, VIII, 300.

∻ ∻

July, 1852.

Thoreau gives me, in flesh and blood and pertinacious Saxon belief, my own ethics. He is far more real, and daily practically obeying them, than I; and fortifies my memory at all times with an affirmative experience which refuses to be set aside.

—*Ibid.*, VIII, 303.

∻ ∻

July, 1852.

Lovejoy, the preacher, came to Concord, and hoped Henry Thoreau would go to hear him. "I have got a sermon on purpose for him." [p. 305] "No," the aunts said, "we are afraid not." Then he wished to be introduced to him at the house. So he was confronted. Then he put his hand from behind on Henry, tapping his back, and said, "Here's the chap who camped in the woods." Henry looked round, and said, "And here's the chap who camps in a pulpit." Lovejoy looked disconcerted, and said no more.

—*Ibid.*, VIII, 305-306.

December, 1852.

At home, I found Henry himself, who complained of Clough or somebody that he or they recited to every one at table the paragraph just [p. 352] read by him and by them in the last newspaper and studiously avoided everything private. I should think he was complaining of one H.D.T.

—*Ibid.*, VIII, 352-353.

‰ ʒ

September, 1853.

Henry Thoreau says he values only the man who goes directly to his needs; who, wanting wood, goes to the woods and brings it home; or to the river, and collects the drift, and brings it in his boat to his door, and burns it: not him who keeps shop, that he may buy wood. One is pleasing to reason and imagination; the other not.

—*Ibid*, VIII, 415.

‰ ʒ

March, 1854.

Henry Thoreau charged Blake, if he could not do hard tasks, to take the soft ones, and when he liked anything, if it was only a picture or a tune, to stay by it, find out what he liked, and draw that sense or meaning out of it, and do *that:* harden it, somehow, and make it his own. Blake thought and thought on this, and wrote afterwards to Henry, that he had got his first glimpse of heaven. Henry was a good physician.

—*Ibid.*, VIII, 450.

‰ ʒ

May, 1854.

Thoreau thinks 't is immoral to dig gold in California; immoral to leave creating value, and go to augmenting the representative of value, and so altering and diminishing real value, and, that, of course, the fraud will appear.

—*Ibid.*, VIII, 467.

⤲ ⤳

February, 1856.

If I knew only Thoreau, I should think cooperation of good men impossible. Must we always talk for victory, and never once for truth, for comfort, and joy? Centrality he has, and penetration, strong understanding, and the higher gifts,—the insight of the real, or from the real, and the moral rectitude that belongs to it; but all this and all his resources of wit and invention are lost to me, in every experiment, year after [p. 15] year, that I make, to hold intercourse with his mind. Always some weary captious paradox to fight you with, and the time and temper wasted.

—*Ibid.*, IX (1913), 15-16.

⤲ ⤳

April, 1856.

It is curious that Thoreau goes to a house to say with little preface what he has just read or observed, delivers it in lump, is quite inattentive to any comment or thought which any of the company offer on the matter, nay, is merely interrupted by it, and when he has finished his report departs with precipitation.

—*Ibid.*, IX, 34.

⤲ ⤳

May 2, 1857.

Walk yesterday, first day of May, with Henry Thoreau to Goose Pond, and to the "Red Chokeberry Lane." . . . From a white birch, Henry cut a strip of bark to show how a naturalist would make the best box to carry a plant or other [p. 91] specimen requiring care,

and thought the woodman would make a better hat of birch-bark
than of felt,—hat, with cockade of lichens thrown in.

—*Ibid.*, IX, 91-92.

∾ ∾

March 24, 1862.

Sam Staples yesterday had been to see Henry Thoreau. "Never
spent an hour with more satisfaction. Never saw a man dying with
so much pleasure and peace." Thinks that very few men in Concord
know Mr. Thoreau; finds him serene and happy.

—*Ibid.*, IX, 413.

∾ ∾

September, 1864.

Thoreau was with difficulty sweet.

—*Ibid.*, X (1914), 65.

∾ ∾

Thoreau himself, who had so clear a vision of the falsity and
folly of society as we still have it, threw himself into the tide that was
already, in Kansas and Virginia, reddened with war; he aided and
abetted the John Brown raid, I do not recall how much or in what
sort; and he had suffered in prison for his opinions and actions. It
was this inevitable heroism of his that, more than his literature even,
made me wish to see him and revere him; and I do not believe that
I should have [p. 58] found the veneration difficult, when at last I
met him in his insufficient person, if he had otherwise been present
to my glowing expectation. He came into the room a quaint, stump
figure of a man, whose effect of long trunk and short limbs was
heightened by his fashionless trousers being let down too low. He had
a noble face, with tossed hair, a distraught eye, and a fine aquilinity
of profile, which made me think at once of Don Quixote and of Cer-
vantes; but his nose failed to add that foot to his stature which Lamb
says a nose of that shape will always give a man. He tried to place

me geographically after he had given me a chair not quite so far off as Ohio, though still across the whole room, for he sat against one wall, and I against the other; but apparently he failed to pull himself out of his revery by the effort, for he remained in a dreamy muse, which all my attempts to say something fit about John Brown and Walden Pond seemed only to deepen upon him. I have not the least doubt that I was needless and valueless about both, and that what I said could not well have prompted an important response; but I did my poor best, and I was terribly disappointed in the result. The truth is that in those days I was a helplessly concrete young person, and all forms of the abstract, the air-drawn, afflicted me like physical discomforts. I do not remember that Thoreau spoke of his books or of himself at all, and when he began to speak of John Brown, it was not the warm, palpable, loving, fearful old man of my conception, but a sort of John Brown type, a John Brown ideal, a John Brown principle, which we were somehow (with long pauses between the vague, orphic phrases) to cherish, and to nourish ourselves upon.

It was not merely a defeat of my hopes, it was a rout, and I felt myself so scattered over the field of thought [p. 59] that I could hardly bring my forces together for retreat. I must have made some effort, vain and foolish enough, to rematerialize my old demigod, but when I came away it was with the feeling that there was very little more left of John Brown than there was of me. His body was not mouldering in the grave, neither was his soul marching on; his ideal, his type, his principle alone existed, and I did not know what to do with it. I am not blaming Thoreau; his words were addressed to a far other understanding than mine, and it was my misfortune if I could not profit by them. I think, or I venture to hope, that I could profit better by them now; but in this record I am trying honestly to report their effect with the sort of youth I was then.

—William Dean Howells, *Literary Friends and Acquaintance* (New York: Harper, 1911), pp. 58-60.

಼ ಼

Thoreau in those days was known in the town as an irregular, eccentric spirit, rather hopeless for any practical purpose. He could make a good lead-pencil but having mastered the art he dropped it, preferring to lead a vagabond life, loitering on the river and in the woods, rather to the disquietude of the community, though he had a comfortable home cared for by his good mother and sister. He housed himself in a wigwam at Walden Pond and was suspected of having started from the brands of his camp a forest fire which had spread far. This strange man, rumour said, had written a book no copy of which had ever been sold. It described a week on the Concord and Merrimac rivers. The edition fell dead from the press, and all the books, one thousand or more, he had collected in his mother's house, a queer library of these unsold books which he used to exhibit to visitors laughing grimly over his unfortunate venture in the field of letters. My aunt sent me one day to carry a message to Mrs. Thoreau and my rap on her door was answered by no other man than this odd son who, on the threshold received my message. He stood in the doorway with hair which looked as if it had been dressed with a pine-cone, inattentive grey eyes, hazy with far-away musings, an emphatic nose and disheveled attire that bore signs of tramps in woods and [p. 235] swamps. Thinking of the forest fire I fancied he smelled of smoke and peered curiously up the staircase behind him hoping I might get a glimpse of that queer library all of one book duplicated one thousand times.

—James Kendall Hosmer, *The Last Leaf* (New York: Putnam, 1912), pp. 235-236.

❧ ❧

Thirty-one years ago last June a man came to see me in Chicago whom I was very glad and proud to meet. It was Henry Thoreau of Concord, the Diogenes of this new world, the Hermit of Walden Woods. The gentle and loving misanthropist and apostle of individualism so singular and separate that I do not know where to look for his father or his son—the most perfect instance to be found I think of American independence run to seed, or shall we say to a mild variety which is very fair to look on but can never sow itself for another harvest. The man of a natural mind which was *not* enmity against God, but in a great and wide sense was subject to the law of God and to no other law. The saint of the *bright* ages and the own brother in this to the Saint of the dark ages, who called the wild creatures that run and fly his sisters and brothers, and was more intimate with them than he was with our human kind. The man of whom, so far as pure seeing goes, Jesus would have said "blessed are your eyes, for *they see*," and whose life I want to touch this evening for some lessons that as it seems to me he alone could teach those who would learn. [p. 294]

As I remember Henry Thoreau then, he was something over forty years of age but would have easily passed for thirty-five, and he was rather slender, but of a fine, delicate mold, and with a presence which touched you with the sense of perfect purity as newly opened roses do. It is a clear rose-tinted face he turns to me through the mist of all these years, and delicate to look on as the face of a girl; also he has great gray eyes, the seer's eyes full of quiet sunshine. But it is a strong face, too, and the nose is especially notable, being as [Moncure] Conway said to me once of Emerson's nose, a sort of interrogation mark to the universe. His voice was low, but still sweet in the tones and inflections, though the organs were all in revolt just then and wasting away and he was making for the great tablelands beyond us Westwards, to see if he could not find there a new lease of life. His words also were as distinct and true to the ear as those of a great singer, and he had Tennyson's splendid gift in this, that he never went back on his tracks to pick up the fallen loops of a sentence as commonplace talkers do. He would hesitate for an instant now and then, waiting for the right word, or would pause with a pathetic patience to master the trouble in his chest, but when he was through the sentence was perfect and entire, lacking nothing, and the word was so purely one with the man that when I read his books now and then I do not hear my own voice within my reading but the voice I heard that day. [p. 295] . . .

We are not sure it would be best to meet some men who have touched us by their genius, but it seems to me now that to see Thoreau as I did that day in Chicago and hear him talk was the one thing needful to me, because he was so simply and entirely the man I had thought of when I read what he had written. There was no lapse, no missing link; the [p. 296] books and the man were one, and I found it was true of him also that "the word was made flesh and dwelt among us."

—Robert Collyer, "Thoreau," in *Clear Grit* (Boston: Beacon Press, 1913), pp. 294-297.

∽ ∾

Thoreau had a number of matrimonial proposals. On one occasion he read one of these missives in a joking manner to Emerson—to which the sage rebukingly said, "Henry, we will have no more regarding the matter." . . .

[Speaking of Thoreau's mental condition during his last illness:] He was of singular good cheer, and a philosopher to the end. When his corpulent full-faced aunt came to his chamber door to inquire about his welfare, he remarked: "Whenever Aunt ———— comes to the door I think it is the rising full moon."

—F. B. Sanborn, in C. T. Ramsey, "A Pilgrimage to the Haunts of Thoreau," *New England Magazine*, L (December, 1913), 435.

≈   ≈

In Concord I went to see Thoreau; he is more human and polite than I supposed, and said he had heard Mr. Emerson speak of me; he is a little bronzed spare man; he makes lead pencils with his father on Monday and Tuesday and was in the midst of work. On other days he surveys land, both mathematically and meditatively; lays out houselots in Haverhill and in the moon. He talks sententiously and originally; his manner is the most unvarying facsimile of Mr. Emerson's, but his thoughts are quite his own. . . . He does not seem particularly affected by applause, but rather by his own natural egotism. I find nobody who enjoys his book as I do (this I did not tell him). . . . I saw his mother, a gaunt and elderly Abolitionist who had read my Thanksgiving sermon with comfort, and told me anecdotes of 'Henry's' ways which are more domestic and filial than one would suppose.

—Thomas Wentworth Higginson, *Journal*, in Mary Higginson, *Thomas Wentworth Higginson* (Boston: Houghton Mifflin, 1914), p. 98.

≈   ≈

"You know my father worked for Henry's father when he was in the pencil business. Father helped to furnish the graphite. I tell ye, that fellow Henry was a lazy lad, and it was well he could write an essay on economy as they say he did—many a piece of pie he ate from my pail."

—Pat Flannery, in C. T. Ramsey, "A Pilgrimage to the Haunts of Thoreau," *New England Magazine*, LI (April, 1914), 68.

∽ ∾

Thoreau, in Brooklyn, that first time he came to see me, referred to my critics as 'reprobates.' I asked him: 'Would you apply so severe a word [p. 318] to them?' He was surprised: 'Do you regard that as a severe word? reprobates? what they really deserve is something infinitely stronger, more caustic: I thought I was letting them off easy.'

—Walt Whitman, in Horace Traubel, *With Walt Whitman in Camden* (New York: Mitchell Kennerley, 1914), III, 318-319. [By permission of Gertrude Traubel.]

∽ ∾

Henry was not all for me—he had his reservations: he held back some: he accepted me—my book—as on the whole something to be reckoned with: he allowed that I was formidable: said so to me much in that way: over in Brooklyn: why, that very first visit: 'Whitman, do you have any idea that you are rather bigger and outside the average—may perhaps have immense significance?' That's what he said: I did not answer. He also said: 'There is much in you to which I cannot accommodate myself: the defect may be mine: but the objections are there.'

—*Ibid.*, III, 403.

∽ ∾

I have a keen recollection of the first time I met Henry David Thoreau. It was upon a beautiful day in July, 1847, that Mrs. Alcott told us we were to visit Walden. We started merrily a party of seven, Mr. and Mrs. Alcott, the four girls and myself, for the woods of oak and pine that encircled the picturesque little lake called Walden Pond. We found Thoreau in his cabin, a plain little house of one room containing a wood stove.

He gave us gracious welcome, asking us within. For a time he talked with Mr. Alcott in a voice and with a manner in which, boy as I was, I detected a something akin with Emerson. He was a tall and rugged-looking man, straight as a pine tree. His nose was strong, dominating his face, and his eyes as keen as an eagle's. He seemed to speak with them, to take in all about him in one vigorous glance. His brows were shaggy as in people who observe rather than see.

He was talking to Mr. Alcott of the wild flowers in Walden woods when, suddenly stopping, he [p. 91] said: "Keep very still and I will show you my family." Stepping quickly outside the cabin door, he gave a low and curious whistle; immediately a woodchuck came running towards him from a nearby burrow. With varying note, yet still low and strange, a pair of gray squirrels were summoned and approached him fearlessly. With still another note several birds, including two crows, flew towards him, one of the crows nestling upon his shoulder. I remember it was the crow resting close to his head that made the most vivid impression upon me, knowing how fearful of man this bird is. He fed them all from his hand, taking food from his pocket, and petted them gently before our delighted gaze; and then dismissed them by different whistling, always strange and low and short, each little wild thing departing instantly at hearing its special signal.

Then he took us five children upon the Pond in his boat, ceasing his oars after a little distance from the shore and playing the flute he had brought with him, its music echoing over the still and beautifully clear water. He suddenly laid the flute down and told us stories of the Indians that "long ago" had lived about Walden and Concord; delighting us with simple, clear explanations of the wonders of Walden woods. Again he interrupted himself suddenly, speaking of the various kinds of lilies grow[p. 92]ing about Walden and calling the wood lilies, stately wild things. It was pond lily time and from the boat we gathered quantities of their pure white flowers and buds; upon our return to the shore he helped us gather other flowers and laden with many sweet blossoms, we wended our way homewards rejoicingly. As we were going he said to me: "Boy, you look tired and sleepy; remember, sleep is half a dinner."

I saw him afterwards very many times in the company of his most intimate friends, Mr. Emerson and Mr. Alcott. He often came to our home; indeed, aside from visits to his father, mother, sisters, and Mr. Emerson, he visited no one else. Upon some of these occasions I remember him saying "that he had a great deal of company in the morning when nobody called;" and "I have never found the companion who is so companionable as solitude." I also remember, "in Walden Woods I hunt with a glass; for a gun gives you but the body while a glass gives you the bird." He possessed to an uncanny degree a knowledge of flowers, plants, and trees. He kept a careful calendar of the shrubs and flora about Walden and showed it me in explanation many times.

The land upon which his cabin was built had been given him by Emerson; the cabin he built himself at a cost of less than thirty dollars and for [p. 93] the first nine months of his life in it his expenses amounted to sixty-two dollars. He thus proved that most of us waste our time and substance upon superficialities, that one hundred dollars per year will suffice for one's living expenses, and that, best of all, one could really live and still have two-thirds of one's time to one's self. . . .

This is but a record of youthful memory; its aim is to compass nothing else. During the nearly sixty years since Thoreau's death I have read, I think, all that has been said about him. But among it nothing has, nor do I believe ever will, be better said than a paragraph from Emerson's funeral tribute to his dead friend: "He has in a short life exhausted the capabilities of this world; wherever there is knowledge, wherever there is virtue, wherever there is beauty, he will find a home."

—Frederick L. H. Willis, *Alcott Memoirs* (Boston: Badger, 1915), pp. 91-94. [By permission of Bruce Humphries, Inc.]

In childhood I had a friend [Thoreau],—not a house friend, domestic, stuffy in association; nor yet herdsman, or horseman, or farmer, or slave of bench, or shop, or office; nor of letters, nor art, nor society; but a free, friendly, youthful-seeming man, who wandered in from unknown woods or fields without knocking,—

"Between the night and day
When the fairy king has power,"—

as the ballad says, passed by the elders' doors, but straightway sought out the children, brightened up the wood-fire forthwith; and it seemed as if it were the effect of a wholesale brave north wind, more than of the armful of "cat-sticks" which he would bring in from the yard. His type was Northern,—strong fea[p. 1]tures, light brown hair, an open-air complexion with suggestion of a seafaring race; the mouth pleasant and flexible when he spoke, aquiline nose, deep-set but very wide-open eyes of clear blue grey, sincere, but capable of a twinkle and again of austerity, but not of softness. Those eyes could not be made to rest on what was unworthy, saw much and keenly (but yet in certain worthy directions hardly at all), and did not fear the face of clay. A figure short and narrow, but thick; a carriage assuring of sturdy strength and endurance. When he walked to get over the ground one thought of a tireless machine, seeing his long, direct, uniform pace; but his body was active and well balanced, and his step could be light, as of one who could leap or dance or skate well at will.

His dress was strong and plain. He was not one of those little men who try [p. 2] to become great by exuvial methods of length of hair or beard, or broad collars, or conspicuous coat.

This youthful, cheery figure was a familiar one in our house, and when he, like the "Pied Piper of Hamelin," sounded his note in the hall, the children must needs come and hug his knees, and he struggled with them, nothing loath, to the fireplace, sat down and told stories, sometimes of the strange adventures of his childhood, or more often of squirrels, muskrats, hawks, he had seen that day, the Monitor-and-Merrimac duel of mud-turtles in the river, or the great Homeric battle of the red and black ants. Then he would make our pencils and knives disappear, and redeem them presently from our ears and noses; and last, would bring down the heavy copper warming-pan from the oblivion of the garret and unweariedly shake it over [p. 3] the blaze till reverberations arose within, and then opening it, let a white-blossoming explosion of popcorn fall over the little people on the rug.

—Edward Emerson, *Henry Thoreau as Remembered by a Young Friend* (Boston: Houghton Mifflin, 1917), pp. 1-4.

∞ ∞

And yet another [Friend] tells how, though this [p. 4] being sometimes looked uncouth to her, like a " 'long-shore-man,"—she could never quite forgive the sin that his garments sat strangely on him,—when he told his tale to the ring of children it was, as it were, a defence, for he seemed abashed by them. Perhaps as the years came on him he began to feel with the sad Vaughan concerning childhood—

> "I cannot reach it, and my striving eye
> Dazzles at it, as at Eternity";

and his hope was with him to keep

> that innocence alive,
> The white designs that children drive."

And it was this respect for unspoiled nature in the creatures of the wood that was his passport to go into their dwelling-places and report to the children that were like enough to them to care to hear.

This youth, who could pipe and sing himself, made for children pipes of all sorts, of grass, of leaf-stalk of squash [p. 5] and pumpkin, handsome but fragrant flageolets of onion tops, but chiefly of the golden willow-shoot, when the rising sap in spring loosens the bark. As the children grew older, he led them to choice huckleberry hills, swamps where the great high-bush blueberries grew, guided to the land of the chestnut and barberry, and more than all, opened that land of enchantment into which, among dark hemlocks, blood-red maples, and yellowing birches, we floated in his boat, and freighted it with leaves and blue gentians and fragrant grapes from the festooning vines.

A little later, he opened another romantic door to boys full of Robin Hood; made us know for ourselves that nothing was truer than

> " 'T is merry! 't is merry in the good green wood
> When mavis and merle are singing!"—[p. 6]

told us how to camp and cook, and especially how, at still midnight, in the middle of Walden, to strike the boat with an oar,—and, in another minute, the hills around awoke, cried out, one after another with incredible and startling *crash*, so that the Lincoln Hill and Fairhaven, and even Conantum, took up the tale of the outrage done to their quiet sleep. He taught us also the decorum and manners of the wood, which gives no treasures or knowledge to the boisterous and careless; the humanity not to kill a harmless snake because it was ugly, or in revenge for a start; and that the most zealous collector of eggs must always leave the mother-bird most of her eggs, and not go too often to watch the nest.

He showed boys with short purses, but legs stout, if short, how to reach the nearer mountains,—Wachusett, then Monadnoc,— and live there in a bough-[p. 7]house, on berries and meal and beans, happy as the gods on Olympus, and like them, in the clouds and among the thunders.

He always came, after an expedition afar, to tell his adventures and wonders, and all his speech was simple and clean and high. Yet he was associated with humble offices also, for, like the friendly Troll in the tale, he deftly came to the rescue when any lock or hinge or stove needed the hand of a master.

I saw this man ever gravely and simply courteous, quietly and effectively helpful, sincere, always spoken of with affection and respect by my parents and other near friends;—knew him strongly but not noisily interested on the side of Freedom in the great struggle that then stirred the country.

When the red morning began to dawn in Kansas and at Harper's Ferry, I saw [p. 8] him deeply moved, and though otherwise avoiding public meetings and organized civic action, come to the front and, moved to the core, speak among the foremost against oppression.

Fatal disease laid hold on him at this time and I saw him face his slow death with cheerful courage.

—*Ibid.*, pp. 4-9.

∽ ∾

This little picture of Henry Thoreau's childhood survives, told by his mother to an old friend: John and Henry slept together in the trundlebed, that obsolete and delightful children's bed, telescoping on large castors under the parental four[p. 14]poster. John would go to sleep at once, but Henry often lay long awake. His mother found the little boy lying so one night, long after he had gone upstairs, and said, "Why, Henry dear, why don't you go to sleep?" "Mother," said he, "I have been looking through the stars to see if I couldn't see God behind them."

—*Ibid.*, pp. 14-15.

∽ ∾

The story which one of Thoreau's friends told me was, that with a queer humour,—he was very young,—he, to avoid taking the town's money, without giving the expected equivalent, in the afternoon punished six children, [p. 20] and that evening resigned the place where such methods were required. One of the pupils, then a little boy, who is still living, all through life has cherished his grievance, not understanding the cause. But we may be sure his punishment would not have been cruel, for Henry Thoreau always liked and respected children. Later this pupil came to know and like him. He said "he seemed the sort of a man that wouldn't willingly hurt a fly," and, except on this occasion, had shown himself mild and kindly.

—*Ibid.*, pp. 20-21.

∽ ∾

After his father's death his mother said, "But for this I should never have seen the tender side of Henry," who had nursed him with loving care.

—*Ibid.*, p. 60.

∽ ∾

I must not fail to record the pleasant circumstances that the tax collector, good Sam Staples, also constable and jailor, before arresting him said, "I'll pay your tax, Henry, if you're hard up," not understanding, as he found by Henry's refusal, and, later, by Mr. Alcott's, that " 'Twas nothin' but principle." He always liked and respected Thoreau, but when he told me the story, he added, "I would n't have done it for old man Alcott."

—*Ibid.* p. 64.

∽ ∾

An incident, not there [in "Civil Disobedience"] told, I learned from a friend. He was kept awake by a man in the cell below ejaculating, "What is life?" and, "So this is life!" with a painful monotony. At last, willing to get whatever treasure of truth this sonorous earthen vessel might hold, Thoreau put his head to the iron window-bars and asked suddenly, "Well, What *is* life, then?" but got no other reward than the sleep of the just, which his fellow-martyr did not further molest.

—*Ibid.*, p. 65.

Another [assistant to Thoreau as a surveyor], born on a farm, who knew and had worked in the black-lead mill many years, said, when I asked what he thought of Thoreau: "Why, he was the best friend I ever had. He was always straight in his ways: and was very particular to make himself agreeable. Yes, he was always straight and true: you could depend upon him: all was satisfactory." Was he a kindly and helpful man? "Yes, he was all of that: what we call solid and true, but he couldn't bear any gouge-game and dishonesty. When I saw him crossing my field I always wanted to go and have a talk with him. He was more company for me than the general run of neighbours. I liked to hear his ideas and get information from him. He liked to talk as long as you did, and what he said was new; mostly about Nature. I think he went down to Walden to pry into the arts of Nature and get something that wasn't open to the public. He liked the creatures. He seemed to think their nature could be improved. Some people called him, lazy: I didn't deem it so. I called him industrious, and he was a first-rate mechanic. He was a good neighbour and very entertaining. I found him a particular friend."

—*Ibid.*, p. 77.

To his Calvinistic Aunt who felt obliged to ask, "Henry, have you made your peace with God?" "I did not know we had ever quarrelled, Aunt," was the pleasant answer.

—*Ibid.*, p. 117.

For the last months he was confined to the house, he was affectionate, and utterly brave, and worked on his manuscript until the last days. When his neighbour, Reverend Mr. Reynolds, came in he found him so employed, and he looked up cheerfully and, with a twinkle in his eye, whispered—his voice was gone—"you know it's respectable to leave an estate to one's friends."

—*Ibid.*

His friend and companion, Edward Hoar, said to me, "With Thoreau's life something went out of Concord woods and fields and river that never will return. He so loved Nature, delighted in her every aspect and seemed to infuse himself into her." Yes, something went. But our woods and waters will always be different because of this man. Something of him abides and truly "for good" in his town. Here he was born, and within its borders he found a wealth of beauty and interest—all that he asked—and shared it with us all.

—*Ibid.*, p. 118.

[Reporting on a conversation on profanity between Thoreau and some of the pupils in his school:] "Boys, if you went to talk business with a man, and he persisted in thrusting words having no connection with the subject into all parts of every sentence—Boot-jack, for instance,—wouldn't you think he was tak[p. 128]ing a liberty with you, and trifling with your time, and wasting his own?" He then introduced the "Boot-jack" violently and frequently into a sentence, to illustrate the absurdity of street bad language in a striking way.

—*Ibid.*, pp. 128-129.

On my birthday, in the early summer, just before I went to take my examination for Harvard, my father and mother invited Thoreau and Channing, both, but especially Thoreau, friends from my babyhood, to dine with us. When we left the table and were passing into the parlour, Thoreau asked me to come with him to our East door—our more homelike door, facing the orchard. It was an act of affectionate courtesy, for he had divined my suppressed state of mind and remembered that first crisis in his own life, and the wrench that it seemed in advance, as a gate leading out into an untried world. With serious face, but with a very quiet, friendly tone of voice, he reassured me, told me that I should be really close to home; very likely should pass my life in Concord. It was a great relief.

—*Ibid.*, p. 147.

Mr. Reynolds also told how, [p. 147] speaking of Indian arrowheads, he asked Thoreau if they were not rather hard to find. He said, "Yes, rather hard, but at six cents apiece I could make a comfortable living out of them."

Mr. Reynolds added: "Thoreau was one of the pleasantest gentlemen, most social and agreeable, I ever met. When I officiated at his father's funeral he came over the next evening as a courteous acknowledgment, and spent two hours, and told his Canada story far better than in his book."

—*Ibid.*, pp. 147-148.

It [Thoreau's school] was a peculiar school, there was never a boy flogged or threatened, yet I never saw so absolutely military discipline. How it was done I scarcely know. Even the incorrigible were brought into line.

—Horace R. Hosmer, in *ibid.*, p. 22.

Henry was not loved. He was a conscientious teacher, but rigid. He would not take a man's money for nothing: if a boy were sent to him, he could make him do all he [p. 22] could. No, he was not disagreeable. I learned to understand him later. I think that he was then in the green-apple stage.

—*Ibid.*, pp. 22-23.

What impressed me, then and later, was Henry's knowledge of Natural History; a keen observer and great student of things, and a very pleasant talker. He reminded me more of Gilbert White of Selborne than any other character.

—George Keyes, in *ibid.*, p. 24.

We boys used to visit him on Saturday afternoons at his house by Walden, and he would show us interesting things in the woods near by. I did not see the philosophical side. He was never stern or pedantic, but natural and very agreeable, friendly,—but a person you would never feel inclined to fool with. A face that you would long remember. Though short in stature, and inconspicuous in dress, you would not fail to notice him in the street, as more than ordinary.

—*Ibid.*, p. 129.

Henry lived in a lofty way. I loved to hear him talk, but I did not like his books so well, though I often read them and took what I liked. They do not do him justice. I liked to see Thoreau rather in his life. Yes, he was religious; he was more like the ministers than others; that is, like what they would wish and try to be. I loved him, but . . . always felt a little in awe of him.

He loved to talk, like all his family, but not to gossip: he kept the talk on a high plane. He was cheerful and pleasant.

—Mrs. Minot Pratt, in *ibid.*, p. 80.

I have seen children catch him by the hand, as he was going home from school, to walk with him and hear more.

—Dr. Thomas Hosmer, in *ibid.*, p. 128.

⁝ ⁞

When I asked Marston Watson, of Plymouth, who was Sophomore while Thoreau was Senior, what he knew of the Concord youth in college, he replied that he remembered him at the Chapel in a green coat, "green, I suppose, because the rules required black."

—F. B. Sanborn, *The Life of Henry David Thoreau* (Boston: Houghton Mifflin, 1917), p. 154.

⁝ ⁞

Mr. [Henry] Warren remembered an instance of Henry's close observation in the matter of Indian antiquities, of which both brothers early became connoisseurs. As they were sailing through the Great Meadows, past Ball's Hill . . . Henry Thoreau called attention to a spot on the river-shore, where he fancied the Indians had made their fires, and perhaps had a fishing village. There, he said, if he had a spade, he could perchance uncover one of their rude fireplaces. "We cannot find one to-day, for we have no spade; but the next time we come I will see if that was the place of habitation." Coming to land there the next week, they drew the boat to shore, and moved up the bank a little way. "Do you see," said Henry, "anything here that would be likely to attract Indians to this spot?" One boy said, "Why, here is the river for their fishing"; another pointed to the woodland near by, which could give them game. "Well, is there anything else?" pointing out a small rivulet that must come, he said, from a spring not far off, which could furnish water cooler than the river in summer; and a hillside above it that would keep off the north and northwest wind in winter. [p. 205]

Then, moving inland a little farther, and looking carefully about, he struck his spade several times, without result. Presently, when the boys began to think their young teacher and guide was mistaken, his spade struck a stone. Moving forward a foot or two, he set his spade in again, struck another stone, and began to dig in a circle. He soon uncovered the red, fire-marked stones of the long-disused Indian fire-place; thus proving that he had been right in his conjecture. Having settled the point, he carefully covered up his find and replaced the turf,—not wishing to have the domestic altar of the aborigines profaned by mere curiosity.

On another walk he suddenly stopped, knelt down, and examined the ground with some care; then, plucking a minute something, he asked Henry Warren if he could see that? "Yes,—but what about it?" Drawing his microscope, Thoreau showed the boy that, thus magnified, this little thing was a perfect flower, just then in the season of its blossoming; and he went on to say that he had become so well acquainted with the flowers, large and small, of Concord and Acton and Lincoln, that without looking in the almanac, he could tell by the blooming of the flowers in what month he was. All this with no [p. 206] evident wish to display his own superior knowledge, but only to impress on the youthful mind how immense is the sum of Nature's activities, and to impart to others his own skill in such matters.

—*Ibid.*, pp. 205-207.

My first intimacy with Henry began after his graduation in 1837. Mrs. Brown, Mrs. Emerson's sister from Plymouth, then boarded with Mrs. Thoreau and her children in the Parkman house, where the [p. 128] Library now stands, and saw the young people every day. She would bring me verses of Henry's,—the "Sic Vita," for instance, which he had thrown into Mrs. Brown's window, tied round a bunch of violets gathered in his walk,—and once a passage out of his Journal, which he had read to Sophia, who spoke of it to Mrs. Brown as resembling a passage in one of my Concord lectures. He always looked forward to authorship as his work in life, and fitted himself for that. Finding he could write prose so well,—and he talked equally well,—he soon gave up much verse-writing, in which he was not patient enough to make his lines smooth and flowing.

—Ralph Waldo Emerson, in *ibid.*, pp. 128-129.

He is a man of incorruptible integrity, and of great ability and industry; and we shall yet hear much more of him. But he affects manners rather brusque, does not think it worth while to use the cheap service of courtesy; is pugnacious about trifles; likes to contradict, likes to say No, and to be on the other side. You cannot always tell what will please him. He was ill, and I sent him a bottle of wine, which I doubt if he ever tasted. I regret these oddities. He needs to fall in love, to sweeten him and straighten him.

—*Ibid.*, p. 239.

He said to me once, standing at the window,—"I cannot see on the outside at all. We thought ourselves great philosophers in those wet days when we used to go out and sit down by the wall-sides." This was absolutely all he was ever heard to say of that outward world during his illness; neither could a stranger in the least infer that he had ever a friend in wood or field.

—Ellery Channing, in *ibid.*, p. 344.

Henry was fond of making an ado, a wonder, a surprise, of all facts that took place out of doors; but a picture, a piece of music, a novel, did not affect him in that fashion. This trait of exaggeration was as pleasing as possible to his companions. Nothing was more delightful than the enormous curiosity, the effervescing wonder, of this child of Nature—glad of everything its mother said or did. This joy in Nature is something we can get over, like love. And yet love,— that is a hard toy to smash and fling under the grate, for good. But Henry made no account at all of love, apparently; he had notions about friendship.

—*Ibid.*, p. 353.

Friday, May 18 [*1855*].

To-night Mr. Thoreau came in as I was reading Demosthenes, and we fell to talking about Greek, Latin, Milton, Wordsworth, Emerson, Ellery Channing, and other things. But first of all let me describe Thoreau. . . . He is a sort of pocket edition of Mr. Emerson, as far as outward appearance goes, in coarser binding and with woodcuts instead of the fine steel-engravings of Mr. Emerson. He is a little under size, with a huge Emersonian nose, bluish gray eyes, brown hair, and a ruddy, weather-beaten face [p. 834] which reminds one of that of some shrewd and honest animal, some retired philosophic woodchuck or magnanimous fox. He dresses very plainly, wears his collar turned over like Mr. Emerson, and often an old dress-coat, broad in the skirts, and by no means a fit. He walks about with a brisk rustic air, and never seems tired. He talks like Mr. Emerson and so spoils the good things which he says; for what in Mr. Emerson is charming, becomes ludicrous in Thoreau, because an imitation.

—Frank Sanborn, "An Unpublished Concord Journal," *Century,* CII (April, 1922), 834-835.

∽ ∾

Like all boys, I was intensely interested in birds and animals. One day I was playing in the grass in front of the Old Manse, when I suddenly looked up to see a short man with a blond beard leaning over me.

"What have you there, Eddie?"

"A great crested flycatcher's egg," I replied.

This was a very rare find.

He wanted me to give it to him, but I would not. Then he proposed a swap.

"If you will give it to me, I will show you a live fox," he said. This was too much to resist. We made a rendezvous for the next Sunday.

Although descended from a line of parsons, I had already learned that Sunday was, for me, merely a holiday, and it was evidently the same for him. This man was Henry W. [*sic*] Thoreau.

Accordingly, the following Sabbath I trudged down to his place at Walden Pond, and he, who had "no [p. 5] walks to throw away on company," proceeded to devote his entire afternoon to a boy of ten. After going a long way through the woods, we both got down on our bellies and crawled for miles, it seemed to me, through sand and shrubbery. But Mr. Fox refused to show himself—and worse luck than all, I never got my egg back! I have always had a grudge against Thoreau for this.

—Edward Simmons, *From Seven to Seventy: Memories of a Painter and a Yankee* (New York: Harpers, 1922), pp. 5-6.

❧ ❧

On the occasion of my lecture . . . Mr. Thoreau, . . . that gentle Arcadian of the nineteenth century, gave me his hand gravely, and said with solemn emphasis, "You have spoken!" which good Mr. Alcott interpreted to mean, "You have brought an oracle."

—Elizabeth Oakes Smith, *Autobiography* (New York: Columbia University Press, 1924), p. 140.

❧ ❧

Henry Thoreau . . . furnished me a good deal of companionship. He was a college graduate of high culture, but still more intimately versed in nature. He was thoroughly unselfish, truly refined, sincere, and of a pure spirit. His minute and critical knowledge of the everyday affairs of nature, as well as his poetical [p. 221] appreciation of her fleeting graces, not only attracted me, but helped my education. Thoreau abounded in paradox. This led me to review the grounds of opinions rather than change them.

I saw it was his humor, and his vane would whip round and set in the opposite quarter if the world should conform to his statements.

Of Indian relics and history he was a careful student, and of the savage character an inveterate admirer; he had a good deal to say too of the Indian over the sea, which I thought better unsaid, as his natural bent rather apprehended the North American than the Asiatic.

His books, like his conversation, have veins of pure gold. Time

will probably dip out his paradoxes and present his nice appreciation
and beautiful sense of nature.

—Richard Frederick Fuller, "The Younger Generation in 1840: From the
Diary of a New England Boy," *Atlantic Monthly*, CXXXVI (August, 1925),
221-222.

∾ ᧞

Those who thought of Thoreau as cold or indifferent little understood the depth of feeling that lay beneath his undemonstrative exterior. During his father's illness his devotion was such that Mrs.
Thoreau in recalling it said, "If it hadn't been for my husband's illness, I should never have known what a tender heart Henry had." He
mourned deeply for this beloved brother. He laid aside his flute and
for years refused to speak his name. A friend told me that twelve
years later Thoreau started, turned pale, and could hardly overcome
his emotion when some reference to John was made.

—Mary Hosmer Brown, *Memories of Concord* (Boston: Four Seas, 1926),
p. 92. [By permission of Bruce Humphries, Inc.]

∾ ᧞

On stormy days his familiar step was wont to be heard on our
doorstep. He knew that if the weather was bad farm duties must be
suspended and that Grandfather would probably be at leisure.

The children hailed his coming with delight. It was better than
any fairy tale to listen to his stories of the woods or the river. To
hear him talk they would gather around as still as mice. What marvelous ways the birds and squirrels had which no one else had discovered. Who but Mr. Thoreau could tame the fishes in the pond,
feed the little mice from his fingers, keep up a whistling fire of conversation with the birds till they alighted on his head and shoulders,
wondering what friend could be so very familiar with bird language.
Who else received calls from the moles,—and how the children's eyes
would brighten as he told them of the tamed partridge so proud of
her family that she brought them all to show him and how in return
for her kindness he shared his breakfast with the brood. He knew

every spot were the wild flowers grew, every sheltered nook where the maiden-hair or climbing fern hid their treasures of gracefulness. One day he came in with a rare nettle which he could not place. Aunt Abby was immediately sent for the botany [p. 96]. Nothing could be said till the nettle problem was settled.

He liked to read to the children from the *Canterbury Tales.* Often he would stop and think about a line, saying, "You can sometimes catch the sense better by listening than by reading."

In later life when my Aunt Jane became a teacher and read these same tales to her pupils, she said she could distinctly recall that melodious voice and the wonderful sense of rhythm he could impart as he read.

Unlike Emerson, Thoreau was a natural musician. He played the flute well and had a musical voice for singing. His ears were so keenly attuned to the various melodies of nature that sounds unheard by others were easily distinguished by him. It was this musical sense that enabled him to discern so accurately the notes of birds and the calls of other animals.

He had fitted a lyre in one of his windows and he noticed that in a deep cut in the woods certain trees formed a natural aeolian lyre when the wind blew through them. Aunt Eliza, when a small girl, tried to make an aeolian lyre and was quite disconsolate because it wouldn't work as the one at the Thoreau home did.

—*Ibid.*, pp. 96-97.

❧ ❧

On a Sunday afternoon the children loved to go to the Walden shack. Thoreau sat at his desk, Grandfather was given a chair, while they arranged themselves along the edge of the cot bed, the youngest child still remembering that her feet couldn't quite reach the floor. If the conversation grew too abstruse or they were tired of sitting still, one by one they slipped out to amuse themselves in the woods. They might be rewarded later by a glimpse of friendly animals, or Mr. Thoreau would give them a row on the pond.

To take a walk with Thoreau, one must rigidly adhere to the manners of the woods. He could lead one to the ripest berries, the hidden nest, the rarest flowers, but no plant life could be carelessly destroyed, no mother bird lose her eggs.

First he would give a curious whistle and a woodchuck would appear—a different whistle and two squirrels would run to him. A different note yet and birds would fly and even so shy a bird as a crow would alight on his shoulder. The children must be mute and very motionless till each pet was [p. 98] fed from his pocket and had departed. Thus the children were introduced to his family, as he called them.

When boating, he could name all the lilies of the pond or the wood lilies, and he could delight them with stories of the Indians who once lived around Walden.

—*Ibid.*, pp. 98-99.

∞ ∞

Sometimes the owner of that familiar grey homespun suit, made by his aunt to suit the needs of a perennial tramper, would appear at the farm late [p. 99] in the afternoon. That meant a simple supper with the ten children and a long evening for talk.

Aunt Jane said that Thoreau and her father discussed Scandinavian mythology so much that she became an adept in those legends. Such a deep impression was made on her mind that in later life she was compelled to translate Greek and Roman myths back into her early models of Thor, Woden, and Igdrasil. Grandmother told me that sometimes the two men would get into a lively discussion over some vital question. Neither would give in, each could well sustain his own side of the argument, time would pass unheeded and the hour of midnight strike before they realized it. If however Thoreau departed unconvinced or unconvincing and could think during the following day of a fresh argument wherewith to overwhelm Grandfather's point of view, he would come back and they would go at it again the next night.

After the trips to Maine or Canada there were fascinating evenings when no child wanted to go to bed, so interesting were the new experiences in forest lore and the stories about the Indians.

—*Ibid.*, pp. 99-100.

∞ ∞

The children all loved Mr. Thoreau and had no fear of him. Doubtless no liberties were taken, for "seen and not heard" was Grandfather's motto for them. Thoreau himself resented too great familiarity.

—*Ibid.*, p. 101.

∽ ∝

One forenoon Thoreau and a companion [Edward Hoar] went by boat to explore the sources of the Sudbury river. In cooking their lunch on the bank in some way the dry grass got on fire and in spite of their efforts spread so fast that a hundred cords of wood belonging to a Mr. Wheeler were burned. A few years ago the latter's daughter was calling at our house and in the course of the conversation Thoreau's name was mentioned. "Don't talk to me about Henry Thoreau," she said. "Didn't I all that winter have to go to school with a smootched apron or dress because I had to pitch in and help fill the wood box with partly charred wood."

—*Ibid.*, p. 103.

∽ ∝

The afternoon before he died, as one of my aunts was passing the house, Sophia called her in. "Mr. B____," she said, "has offered to sit up with my brother tonight, but Henry wants your father." So after supper Grandfather walked over to spend the night with him.

The next day he passed on, trustfully expectant of renewed vision. When Grandfather said, "I heard the robins sing as I came along," Thoreau answered, "This is a beautiful world, but soon I shall [p. 105] see one that is fairer," and again he said to him, "I have so loved nature."

When Grandfather started to go home in the morning Thoreau called Sophia and asked her to give him a copy of one of his first editions.

—*Ibid.*, pp. 105-106.

∽ ∝

I loved to hear the farmers talk about him. One of them used to say:

'Henry D. Thoreau—Henry D. Thoreau,' jerking out the words with withering contempt. 'His name ain't no more Henry D. Thoreau than my name is Henry D. Thoreau. And everybody knows it, and he knows it. His name's *Da*-a-vid Henry and it ain't never been nothing [p. 94] but *Da*-a-vid Henry. And he knows that! Why, one morning I went out in my field across there to the river, and there, beside that little old mud pond, was standing *Da*-a-vid Henry, and he wasn't doin' nothin' but just standin' there—lookin' at that pond, and when I came back at noon, there he was standin' with his hands behind him just lookin' down into that pond, and after dinner when I come back again if there wan't *Da*-a-vid standin' there just like as if he had been there all day, gazin' down into that *pond*, and I stopped and looked at him and I says, "Da-a-vid Henry, what air you a-doin'?" And he didn't turn his head and he didn't look at me. He kept on lookin' down at that pond, and he said, as if he was thinkin' about the stars in the heavens, "Mr. Murray, I'm a-studyin' —the habits—of the bullfrog!" And there that darned fool had been standin'—the livelong day—*a-studyin'*—the habits—of the *bull*-frog!'

—Mrs. Daniel Chester French, *Memories of a Sculptor's Wife* (Boston: Houghton Mifflin, 1928), pp. 94-95.

∾ ∾

He is three and twenty, has been through college and kept a school, is very fond of the classics and an earnest thinker, yet intends being a farmer. He has a great deal of practical sense, and as he has bodily sense to boot, he may look to be a successful and happy man. He has a boat which he made himself, and rows me out on the pond.

—Margaret Fuller, Letter to her brother Richard, in Margaret Bell, *Margaret Fuller* (New York: Boni, 1930), p. 123.

∾ ∾

Mrs. Gilchrist told me she visited Emerson last fall in Concord, twice. He is very serene and cheerful, remembers earlier things and events, but is fast losing his hold upon later. . . .

"What was the name of my best friend?" he will inquire of his wife. [p. 181]

"Henry Thoreau," she will answer.

"Oh, yes, Henry Thoreau."

—John Burroughs, Letter to Benton, February 9, 1879, in Clara Barrus, *Whitman and Burroughs: Comrades* (Boston: Houghton Mifflin, 1931), pp. 181-182.

Thoreau taught me one thing: not to fill my bucket too full. Told me to fetch a bucket of water. When I found it was too heavy to lift out of the well, he wouldn't help me. No, sir, he wouldn't help me. I learned then not to fill my bucket too full. I was only a lad of six or seven then. He always said there were only two naturalists. He was *the* naturalist, and I was the other one. We used to talk about birds and eggs and things we found in the woods.

—Howard Melvin, in Helen E. Glutsch, "Interesting Reminiscences," *Saturday Review of Literature*, VIII (August 29, 1931), 92.

"Thoreau? . . . Yes, I remember him. We boys liked to run up to him and ask questions about animals and fishes. He was a queer kind of a duck. Always used to wear a gray shirt and tramp through the woods every day."

—[Frank] Pierce, in Robert Whitcomb, "The Thoreau 'Country,'" *Bookman*, LXXIII (July, 1931), 461.

Sept. 1st. [1842] Thursday.

Mr. Thorow [*sic*] dined with us yesterday. He is a singular character—a young man with much of wild original nature still remaining in him; and so far as he is sophisticated, it is in a way and method of his own. He is as ugly as sin, long-nosed, queer-mouthed, and with uncouth and somewhat rustic, although courteous manners, corresponding very well with such an exterior. But his ugliness is of an honest and agreeable fashion, and becomes him much better than beauty. He was educated, I believe, at Cambridge, and formerly kept school in this town; but for two or three years back, he has repudiated all regular modes of getting a living, and seems inclined to lead a sort of Indian life among civilized men—an Indian life, I mean, as respects the absence of any systematic effort for a livelihood. He has been for sometime an inmate of Mr. Emerson's family; and, in requital, he labors in the garden, and performs such other offices as may suit him—being entertained by Mr. Emerson for the sake of what true manhood there is in him. Mr. Thorow is a keen and delicate observer of nature—a genuine observer, which, I suspect, is almost as rare a character as even an original poet; and Nature, in return for his love, seems to adopt him as her especial child, and shows him secrets which few others are allowed to witness. He is familiar with beast, fish, fowl, and reptile, and has strange stories to tell of adventures, and friendly passages with these lower brethren of mortality. Herb and flower, likewise, wherever they grow, whether in garden, or wild wood, are his familiar friends. He is also on intimate terms with the clouds, and can tell the portents of storms. It is a characteristic trait, that he has a great regard for the memory of the Indian tribes, whose wild life would have suited him so well; and strange to say, he seldom walks over a ploughed field without picking up an arrow-point, a spear-head, or other relic of the red men—as if their spirits willed him to be the inheritor of their simple wealth.

With all this he has more than a tincture [p. 166] of literature—a deep and true taste for poetry, especially the elder poets, although more exclusive than is desirable, like all other Transcendentalists, so far as I am acquainted with them. He is a good writer—at least, he has written one good article, a rambling disquisition on Natural History in the last Dial,—which, he says, was chiefly made up from journals of his own observations. Methinks this article gives a very fair image of his mind and character—so true, minute, and literal in observation, yet giving the spirit as well as letter of what he sees, even as a lake reflects its wooded banks, showing every leaf, yet giving the wild beauty of the whole scene;—then there are passages in the article of cloudy and dreamy metaphysics, partly affected, and partly the natural exhalations of his intellect;—and also passages where his thoughts seem to measure and attune themselves into spontaneous verse, as they rightfully may, since there is real poetry in him. There is a basis of good sense and moral truth, too, throughout the article, which also is a reflection of his character; for he is not unwise to think and feel, however imperfect in his own mode of action. On the whole, I find him a healthy and wholesome man to know.

After dinner (at which we cut the first water-melon and musk melon that our garden has ripened) Mr. Thorow and I walked up the bank of the river; and, at a certain point, he shouted for his boat. Forthwith, a young man paddled it across the river, and Mr. Thorow and I voyaged further up the stream, which soon became more beautiful than any picture, with its dark and quiet sheet of water, half shaded, half sunny, between high and wooded banks. The late rains have swollen the stream so much, that many trees are standing up to their knees, as it were, in the water; and boughs, which lately swung high in air, now dip and drink deep of the passing wave. As to the poor cardinals, which glowed upon the bank, a few days since, I could see only a few of their scarlet caps, peeping above the water. Mr. Thorow managed the boat so perfectly, either with two paddles or with one, that it seemed instinct with his own will, and to require no physical effort to guide it. He said that, when some Indians visited Concord a few years since, he found that he had acquired, without a teacher, their precise method of propelling and steering a canoe. Nevertheless, being in want of money the poor fellow was desirous of selling the boat, of which he is so fit a pilot, and which was built by his own hands; so I agreed to give him his price (only seven dollars) and accordingly became possessor of the Musketaquid. I wish I could acquire the aquatic skill of its original owner at as a reasonable a rate.

Sept. 2d. Friday.

Yesterday afternoon, while my wife, and Louisa, and I, were gathering the windfallen apples in our orchard, Mr. Thorow arrived with the boat. The adjacent meadow being overflowed by the rise of the stream, he had rowed directly to the foot of the orchard, and landed at the boards, after floating over forty or fifty yards of water, where people were making hay, a week or two since. I entered the boat with him, in order to have the benefit of a lesson in rowing and paddling. My little wife, who was looking on, cannot feel very proud of her husband's proficiency. I managed, indeed, to propel the boat by rowing with two oars; but the use of the single paddle is quite beyond my present skill. Mr. Thorow had assured me that it was only necessary to will the boat to go in any particular direction, and she would immediately take that course, as if imbued with the spirit of the steersman. It may be so with him, but certainly not with me; the boat seemed to be bewitched, and turned its head to every point of the compass except the right one. He then took the paddle himself, and though I could observe nothing peculiar in his management of it, the Musketaquid immediately became as docile as a trained steed. I suspect that she has not yet transferred her affections from her old master to her new one. [p. 167] By and by, when we are better acquainted, she will grow more tractable; especially after she shall have had the honor of bearing my little wife, who is loved by all things, living or inanimate. We propose to change her name from Musketaquid (the Indian name of Concord river, meaning the river of meadows) to the Pond Lily—which will be very beautiful and appropriate, as, during the summer season, she will bring home many a cargo of pond lilies from along the river's weedy shore. It is not very likely that I shall make such long voyages in her as Mr. Thorow has. He once followed our river down to the Merrimack, and thence, I believe, to Newburyport—a voyage of about eighty miles, in this little vessel.

—Nathaniel Hawthorne, *The American Notebooks*, Randall Stewart, ed., pp. 166-168. (Copyright 1932, 1960, by the President and Fellows of Harvard College)

April 7th. [*1843*] *Friday.*

. . . I arose, and began this record in the journal, almost at the commencement of which I was interrupted by a visit from Mr. Thoreau, who came to return a book, and to announce his purpose of going to reside at Staten Island, as private tutor in the family of Mr. Emerson's brother. We had some conversation upon this subject, and upon the spiritual advantages of change of place, and upon the Dial, and upon Mr. Alcott, and other kindred or concatenated subjects. I am glad, on Mr. Thoreau's own account, that he is going away; as he is physically out of health, and, morally and intellectuallly, seems not to have found exactly the guiding clue; and in all these respects, he may be benefitted by his removal;—also, it is one step towards a circumstantial position in the world. On my account, I should like to have him remain here; he being one of the few persons, I think, with whom to hold intercourse is like hearing the wind among the boughs of a forest-tree; and with all this wild freedom, there is high and classic cultivation in him too.

—*Ibid.*, p. 175.

∾ ∾

April 11th, 1843.

Just when I was on the point of choking with a huge German word, Molly announced Mr. Thoreau. He wanted to take a row in the boat, for the last time, perhaps, before he leaves Concord. So we emptied the water out of her, and set forth on our voyage. She leaks; but not more than she did in the autumn. We rowed to the foot of the hill which borders the north-branch, and there landed, and climbed the moist and snowy hillside, for the sake of the prospect. Looking down the river, it might well have been mistaken for an arm of the sea, so broad is now its swollen tide; and I could have fancied that, beyond one other headland, the mighty ocean would outspread itself before the eye. On our return, we boarded a large cake of ice, which was floating down the river, and were borne by it directly to our own landing-place, with the boat towing behind.

—*Ibid.*, p. 180.

∾ ∾

I have just returned, (most 10 o'clock,) from hearing a sort of lecture from Henry Thoreau, on the subject of the affair at Harper's Ferry, or rather on the character of Capt. Brown. Henry spoke of him in terms of the most unqualified eulogy. I never heard him before speak so much in praise of any man, and did not know that his sympathies were so strong in favor of the poor slave. He thinks Capt.

Brown has displayed heroic qualities that will cause him to be remembered wherever and whenever true heroism is admired. The lecture was full of Henry's quaint and strong expressions: hitting the politicians in the hardest manner, and showing but little of that veneration which is due to our beloved President and all the government officials, who are laboring so hard and so disinterestedly for the welfare of the dear people. The church also, as a body, came in for a share of whipping, and it was laid on right earnestly. In the course of his remarks on Capt. Brown's heroic character, and actions in the service of freedom and the probability of his being killed therefor, he said he had been very strongly impressed with the *possibility* of a man's *dying*—very few men *can* die—they never *lived*, how then can they die! The life they lived was not life—that constant endeavor after selfgratification, with no high aspiration and effort for the race, was too mean an existence to be called life. Brown was a man of *ideas* and *action;* whatever he saw to be right, that he endeavored to do with energy, without counting the cost to himself. Such a real, live man could *die.*

The lecture was full of noble, manly ideas, though, perhaps, a little extravagant in its eulogy of Capt. Brown.

—Minot Pratt, Letter to Mrs. Minot Pratt, October 30, 1859, in "When Thoreau Lectured on John Brown," *Concord Journal,* December 8, 1932.

☙ ❧

[Thoreau] was literally the most childlike, unconscious and unblushing egotist it has ever been my fortune to encounter in the ranks of manhood; so that, if he happened to visit you on a Sunday morning, when possibly you were in a devout frame of mind, as like as not you would soon find yourself intoning subaudible praises to the meticulous skill which had at last succeeded in visibly marrying such sheer and mountainous inward self-esteem with such harmless and beautiful force of outward demeanour. [p. 182] I have not had the advantage, to be sure, of knowing Thoreau well, through the medium of his books, which so many competent persons praise as singularly witty and sagacious. I have, however, honestly try to read them, but owing, I suppose, to prejudice derived from personal contact with him, their wit always seemed more or less spoiled, to my taste, by intention, and even their sagacity seemed painfully aggressive and alarming; so I relinquished my task without any edifying result.

—Henry James, Sr., Letter to the *Boston Herald* of April 24, 1881, in Austin Warren, *The Elder Henry James* (New York: Macmillan, 1934), pp. 182-183.

಼ ಼

January 26, 1848.

Heard Thoreau's lecture before the Lyceum on the relation of the individual to the State—an admirable statement of the rights of the individual to self-government, and an attentive audience.

His allusions to the Mexican War, to Mr. Hoar's expulsion from Carolina, his own imprisonment in Concord Jail for refusal to pay his tax, Mr. Hoar's payment of mine when taken to prison for a similar refusal, were all pertinent, well considered, and reasoned. I took great pleasure in this deed of Thoreau's.

—Bronson Alcott, *Journals* (Boston: Little, Brown, 1938), p. 201.

಼ ಼

September 11, 1856.

Thoreau is persistently manly and independent as of old. His criticisms on men and the times as characteristic, individual, and urged with all the honest pertinacity befitting a descent of the Scandinavian Thor. A man of a genealogy like his—Franko-Norman-Scottish-American—may well be forgiven for a little foolhardiness, if not pugnacity, amidst his great common sense and faithfulness to the core of natural things. [p. 284] ...

In the evening Thoreau reads Dr. Bellow's Historical Sketch of the Founder's Family, and takes all there is known of Walpole [New Hampshire] to bed with him, to be used for such ornaments of his jaunt this day as our traveller's humour shall dictate.

—*Ibid.*, pp. 284-285. [Written at Walpole, New Hampshire, where Thoreau was visiting Alcott.]

಼ ಼

November 2, 1856.

Thoreau reads his lecture on "Walking," and interests his company deeply in his treatment of nature. Never had such a walk as this been taken by any one before, and the conversation so flowing and lively and curious—the young people enjoying it particularly.

—*Ibid.*, p. 287. [Written at the Fourier community, Eagleswood, Perth Amboy, New Jersey, where both Alcott and Thoreau were visiting.]

∽ ∾

November 10, 1856.

I hoped to put him [Walt Whitman] in communication direct with Thoreau, and tried my hand a little after we came down stairs and sat in the parlour below; but each seemed planted fast in reserves, surveying the other curiously,—like two beasts, each wondering what the other would do, whether to snap or run; and it came to no more than cold compliments between them. Whether Thoreau was [p. 290] meditating the possibility of Walt's stealing away his "out-of-doors" for some sinister ends, poetic or pecuniary, I could not well divine, nor was very curious to know; or whether Walt suspected or not that he had here, for once, and the first time, found his match and more at smelling out "all Nature," a sagacity potent, penetrating and peerless as his own, if indeed not more piercing and profound, finer and more formidable. I cannot say. At all events, our stay was not long.

—*Ibid.*, pp. 290-291. [Written at Eagleswood after Alcott had taken Thoreau to Brooklyn to visit Walt Whitman.]

∽ ∾

April 11, 1859.

Comes Thoreau and sups with us. We discuss thought and style. I think his more primitive than that of any of our American writers —in solidity, in organic robust quality unsurpassed, as if Nature had built them out for herself and and breathed into them free and full, seasoning every member, articulating every sense with her salubrities and soul of soundness. He is rightly named *Thorough, Through,* the pervading *Thor,* the sturdy sensibility and force in things.

—*Ibid.,* p. 315.

∾ ◠

June 9, 1859

Sanborn, Henry Thoreau, and Allen take tea and pass the evening with us. We discuss questions of philosophy and the Ideal Theory as applied to education. Thoreau is large always and masterly in his own wild ways. With a firmer grasp of the shows of Nature, he has a subtler sense of the essence and personality of the flowing life of things than most men, and he defended the Ideal Theory and Personal Identity to my great delight.

—*Ibid.,* p. 317.

∾ ◠

July 3, 1859.

Thoreau comes and stays an hour or two. Students of Nature alike, our methods differ. He is an observer of Nature pure, and I discern her as exalted and mingled in Man. Her brute aspects and qualities interest him, and these he discriminates with a sagacity unsurpassed. He is less thinker than observer; a naturalist in tendency but of a mystic habit, and a genius for detecting the essence in the form and giving forth the soul of things seen. He knows more of Nature's secrets than any man I have known, and of Man as related to Nature. He thinks and sees for himself in way eminently original, and is formidably individual and persistent.

—*Ibid.,* p. 318.

∾ ◠

August 21, 1859.

Henry Thoreau is here and spends the evening conversing in his remarkable way on Nature and naturalists. I think him the naturalist by birth and genius, seeing and judging by instinct and first sight, as none other I have known. I remark this in Thoreau, that he discerns objects individually and apart, never in groups and collectively, as a whole, as the artist does. Nature exists separately to him and individually. He never theorizes; he sees only and describes; yet, by a seventh sense as it were, dealing with facts shooting forth from his mind and mythologically, so that his page is a creation. His fancy is ever the complement of his understanding, and finishes Nature to the senses even. If he had less of fancy, he would be the prose naturalist and no more; and had he less of understanding he would be a poet— if, indeed, with all this mastery of things concrete and sensible, he be not a poet, as Homer was.

—*Ibid.,* p. 319.

∾ ʠ

October 30, 1859.

Thoreau reads a paper of his on John Brown, his virtues, spirit, and deeds, at the Vestry this evening, and to the delight of his company I am told—the best that could be gathered on short notice, and among them Emerson.

—*Ibid.,* p. 320.

∾ ʠ

February 8, 1860.

Thoreau and his lecture on "Wild Apples" before the Lyceum. It is a piece of exquisite sense, a celebrating of the infinity of Nature, exemplified with much learning and original observation, beginning with the apple in Eden and down to the wildings in our woods. I listened with uninterrupted interest and delight, and it told on the good company present.

—*Ibid.,* p. 326.

∾ ʠ

January 28, 1861.

Channing writes tenderly of Thoreau's confinement, and I see him this morning and find his hoarseness forbids his going out as usual.

'Tis a serious thing to one who has been less a house-keeper than any man in town, has lived out of doors for the best part of his life, has harvested more wind and storm, sun and sky, and has more weather in him, than any—night and day abroad with his leash of keen senses, hounding any game stirring, and running it down for certain, to be spread on the dresser of his page before he sleeps and served as a feast of wild meats to all sound intelligences like his. If any can make game for his confinement it must be himself, and for solace, if sauce of the sort is desired by one so healthy as he has seemed hitherto. We have been accustomed to consider him the salt of things so long that we are loath to believe it has lost savor; since if it has, then "Pan is dead" and Nature ails throughout.

I find him in spirits—busied, he tells me, with his Journals, and, bating his out-of-doors, in his usual working trim. Fair weather and spring time, I trust, are to prove his best physicians, and the woods and fields know their old friend again presently.

—*Ibid.,* p. 333.

∽ ᓚ

January 1, 1862.

To Thoreau, and spend the evening, sat to find him failing and feeble. He is talkative, however; is interested in books and men, in our civil troubles especially, and speaks impatiently of what he calls the temporizing policy of our rulers; blames the people too for their indifferency to the true issues of national honor and justice. Even Seward's letter to Earl Grey respecting Mason's and Liddell's case, comforting as it is to the country and serving as a foil to any hostile designs of England for the time at least, excites his displeasure as seeming to be humiliating to us, and dishonorable.

We talk of Pliny, whose books he is reading with delight. Also of Evelyn and the rural authors. If not a writer of verse, Thoreau is a poet in spirit, and has come as near to the writing of pastorals as any poet of his time. Were his days not numbered, and his adventures in the wild world once off his hands, then he might come to orchards and gardens, perhaps treat these in manner as masterly, uniting the spirit of naturalist and poet in his page. But the most he may hope for is to prepare his manuscripts for others' editing, and take his leave of them and us. I fear he has not many months to abide here, and the spring's summons must come for him soon to partake of "Syrian peace, immortal leisure."

—*Ibid.*, p. 343.

∾ ᴄ

May 7, 1862.

I am at Mrs. Thoreau's. She tells me about Henry's last moments and his sister Sophia showed me his face, looking as when I last saw him, only a tinge of paler hue. 44 years last July.

—*Ibid.*, p. 347.

∾ ᴄ

Thoreau had told me one day when we were standing on the rock at North Branch, where a smaller stream joins Concord River— a picturesque spot, where a tall, precipitous bank overhung the still, black surface of the water, crowned with dark pines, and with scarlet cardinal flowers on the opposite bank, sheaves of which my father used to gather for his bride, in their Old Manse honeymoon in the 1840's: and where white water-lilies with golden hearts lay on their broad green pads on the smooth sable mirror—Thoreau, I say, had told me that the lilies closed their petals at sunset, but in the morning, as the first rays of the sun touched them, they stirred and awoke, and, from green buds, became glorious blooms. "Worth seeing!" said Thoreau, turning upon me his "terrible blue eyes," as Emerson called them. All the strange man said was gospel to me, and I silently resolved to get up early some morning, and witness that exquisite drama.

—Julian Hawthorne, *Memoirs* (New York: Macmillan, 1938), p. 64.

∾ ᴄ

Human fellowship is necessary to human beings; that was something which Thoreau never fully achieved—he thought perhaps that he didn't care for it. If he had lived longer, he might have modified his heresy—if it was heresy, and not inspiration.

—*Ibid.*, p. 114.

❧ ❧

Once, when I was nearly seven years old, Thoreau came to the Wayside to make a survey of our land, bringing his surveying apparatus on his shoulder. I watched the short, dark, unbeautiful man with interest and followed him about, all over the place, never losing sight of a movement and never asking a question or uttering a word. The thing must have lasted a couple of hours; when we got back, Thoreau remarked to my father: "Good boy! Sharp eyes, and no tongue!" On that basis I was admitted to his friendship; a friendship or comradeship which began in 1852 and was to last until his death in 1862.

In our walks about the country, Thoreau saw everything, and would indicate the invisible to me with a [*p. 114*] silent nod of the head. The brook that skirted the foot of our meadow was another treasure-house which he discovered to me, though he was too shy to companion me there; when he had given me a glimpse of Nature in her privacy, he left me alone with her; he was not very successful in writing poetry, but he felt it. "Books in the running brooks," said Shakespeare, and I found plenty. Beside that brook on a hot August day, I would often sit, hidden from the world, thinking boy thoughts.

I learned how to snare chub, and even pickerel, with a loop made of a long-stemmed grass; dragon-flies poised like humming-birds, and insects skated zigzag on the surface, casting odd shadows on the bottom. In spring, delightful little fairy turtles would come up out of the water, with red and yellow spots on their shells—creatures no larger than a five-cent piece. Yes, Thoreau showed me things, and though it didn't aid me in the Harvard curriculum, it helped me through life.

Truly, Nature absorbed his attention, but I don't think he cared much for what is called the beauties of nature; it was her way of working, her mystery, her economy in extravagance; he delighted to trace her footsteps toward their source, and to watch her growths and developments. He liked to feel that the pursuit was endless, with mystery at both ends of it. But of color or form as valued by artists I doubt whether he took heed. He was able to say of a girl's smile, "What is it but showing me bare bones?" That may indicate a radical defect.

—*Ibid.*, pp. 114-115.

∽ ∾

Nothing bothered him so much as the friendships. Those and his moral sensitiveness. I have never been able to understand what he meant by his life. . . . Why was he so disappointed with everybody else &c. Why was he so much interested in the river and the woods and the sky &c. Something peculiar I judge.

—Ellery Channing, in Henry Seidel Canby, *Thoreau* (Boston: Houghton Mifflin, 1939), p. xii.

∽ ∾

I wish he could find something better to do than walking off every now and then.

—Aunt Maria Thoreau, Letter to the Ward family, September 7, 1948, in *ibid.*, p. 22.

∽ ∾

Henry will have to take care that he don't hurt himself seasoning—a very common occurence. When he gets settled on his farm—I should like to look in upon him . . . & sing with him & John—'In good old [?] times'. . . . We will 'do up' the glee & other matters with as hearty a will at least, as ever.

—George Ward, Letter to his mother, February 22, 1841, in *ibid.*, p. 176. [Question mark indicates illegible word.]

∽ ∾

Henry T[.] has built him a house of one room a little distance from Walden pond & in view of the public road. There he lives—cooks, eats, studies & sleeps & is quite happy. He has many visitors, whom he receives with pleasure & does his best to entertain. We talk of passing the day with him soon.

—Prudence Ward, Letter of January 20, 1846, in *ibid.*, p. 216.

～ ～

When his mother heard of his arrest, she hastened to the Jail, then to the Thoreau house in the Square, at which Misses Jane and Maria Thoreau then lived, and one of the latter, putting a shawl over her head, went to the jailer's door, and paid the tax and fees to Ellen Staples, her father the jailer being absent.

—Jane Hosmer, in *ibid.*, p. 234.

～ ～

Mr. Emerson is going to Europe soon to *lecture* there, and in consequence Henry has sold his house [the Walden cabin] to him, and is going to reside in his family this winter. . . . Mr. Alcott's going to Europe for the present seems to have blown over, he and H——— is building an arbour for Mr. Emerson, but H——— says, A——— pulls down as fast as he builds up, (quite characteristic) but it is rather expensive [and] somewhat tedious to poor Henry, to say nothing of endangering life and limbs for if here had not been a comfortable haystack near that he availed himself of by jumping into, when the top rafter was knock'd off, it might have been rather a serious affair. I do not know but I exaggerate a little, but at any rate jump he had to, and I believe it *was* in a hay mow. I hope they will find as soft a [p. 243] landing place, one and all, when they drop from the clouds.

—Aunt Maria Thoreau, Letter to Prudence Ward, September 25, 1847, in *ibid.*, pp. 243-244.

～ ～

Today Henry has gone to Salem to read another lecture they seem to be wonderfully taken with him there, and next month he is to go to Portland, to deliver the same, and George wants him to keep on to Bangor they want to have him there, and if their funds will hold out they intend to send for him, they give 25 dollars, and at Salem and Portland 20—he is preparing his Book for the press and the title is to be, Waldien (I don't know how to spell it) or life in the Woods. I think the title will take if the Book don't. I was quite amused with what Sophia told me her mother said about it the other day, she poor girl was lying in bed with a sick head ache when she heard Cynthia (who has grown rather nervous of late) telling over her troubles to Mrs. Dunbar, after speaking of her own and Helen's sickness, she says, and there's Sophia she's the greatest trial I've got, for she has complaints she *never will* get rid of, and Henry is putting things into his Book that never ought to be there, and Mr. Thoreau has faint turns and I don't know what ails him, and so she went on from one thing to another hardly knew where to stop, and tho it is pretty much so, I could not help smiling at Sophia's description of it. As for Henry's book, you know I have said, there were parts of it that sounded to me very much like blasphemy, and I did not believe they would publish it, on reading it to Helen the other day Sophia told me she [p. 248] made the same remark, and coming from her, Henry was much surprised, and said she did not understand it, but still I fear they will not persuade him to leave it out.

—Aunt Maria Thoreau, Letter to Prudence Ward, February 28, 1849, in *ibid.*, pp. 248-249.

‿ ∽

By the way have you heard what a strange story there was about Miss Ford, and Henry, Mrs. Brooks said at the convention, a lady came to her and inquired, if it was true, that Miss F_____ had committed, or was going to commit suicide on account of H_____ Thoreau, what a ridiculous story this is. When it was told to H_____ he made no remark at all, and we cannot find out from him any thing about it, for a while, they corresponded, and Sophia said that she recollected one day on the reception of a letter she heard H_____ say, he shouldn't answer it, or he must put a stop to this, some such thing she couldn't exactly tell what.

—Aunt Maria Thoreau, in *ibid.*, p. 258. [Miss Ford did not commit suicide, but lived for thirty years longer, admiring Thoreau to the very end of her life.]

‿ ∽

When I was in school Thoreau gave me some of his pencils w[h]ich he made. He stopped making pencils in 1845. One day I went up to Princeton on Wachusett Mountain with him. We spent one night at Wachusett. We found some old boards and he said they would answer just as well for a quilt as a roof. He said Watatick Mountain was as perfect as a pudding. We visited together every hill in this vicinity. When Thoreau wanted graphite for his pencils he went clear to Canada for it—he wasn't satisfied with what there was here.

When Thoreau died, Emerson said about him, "He always said he wouldn't go in a church but he's a-going in this time!"

Thoreau used to take runaway slaves up to South Acton and put them on the train there. He knew there were too many southern sympathizers here.

Alcott and Channing and all the rest of them used to go down to Walden to see Thoreau at a place at Walden Pond, but he only kept two chairs there.

One time Emerson and Thoreau agreed not to pay their taxes because they were so high. Well Thoreau didn't pay and they put him in the lock-up. When Emerson came to see him I guess he'd gone ahead and paid his because he said to Thoreau, "Henry! Henry! Why do I find you here?" Then Thoreau said, "Ralph! Ralph! Why aren't you here?"

—Howard Melvin, from "Howard Melvin Passes Away in 85th Year," *Concord Journal*, December 14, 1939.

∽ ∾

Our household is now enlarged by the presence of Henry Thoreau who may stay with me a year, I do not remember if I have told you about him: but he is to have his board &c. for what labor he chooses to do: and he is thus far a great benefactor & physician to me for he is an indefatigable & a very skilful laborer & I work with him as I should not without him and expect now to be suddenly well & strong though I have been a skeleton all the spring until I am ashamed. Thoreau is a scholar & a poet & as full of buds of promise as a young apple tree.

—Ralph Waldo Emerson, Letter to William Emerson, June 1, 1841, in Ralph L. Rusk, *The Letters of Ralph Waldo Emerson* (New York: Columbia, 1939), II, 402.

∽ ∾

H.T. is full of noble madness lately, and I hope more highly of him than ever. I know that nearly all the fine souls have a flaw which defeats every expectation they excite but I must trust these large frames as of less fragility—than the others. Besides to have awakened a great hope in another, is already some fruit is it not?

—Ralph Waldo Emerson, Letter to Margaret Fuller, September 13, 1841, in *ibid.*, II, 447.

ᔓ ᔕ

My pleasure at getting home on Saturday night at the end of my task was somewhat checked by finding that Henry Thoreau who has been at his father's since the death of his brother was ill & threatened with *lockjaw!* his brother's disease. It is strange—unaccountable—yet the symptoms seemed precise & on the increase. You may judge we were all alarmed & I not the least who have the highest hopes of this youth. This morning his affection be it what it may, is relieved essentially, & what is best, his own feeling of better health established.

—Ralph Waldo Emerson, Letter to William Emerson, January 24, 1842, in *ibid.*, III, 4.

ᔓ ᔕ

I am sorry that you, & the world after you, do not like my brave Henry any better. . . . I admire this perennial threatening attitude, just as we like to go under an overhanging precipice. It is wholly his natural relation & no assumption at all.

—Ralph Waldo Emerson, Letter to Margaret Fuller, July 19, 1842, in *ibid.*, III, 75.

ᔓ ᔕ

And now goes our brave youth into the new house, the new connexion, the new City. I am sure no truer & no purer person lives in wide New York; and he is a bold & a profound thinker though he may easily chance to pester you with some accidental crotchets and perhaps a village exaggeration of the value of facts. Yet I confide, if you should content each other, in Willie's soon coming to value him for his real power to serve & instruct him.

—Ralph Waldo Emerson, Letter to William Emerson, May 6, 1843, in *ibid.*, III, 172. [This letter was written when Thoreau left for William Emerson's home on Staten Island to become a tutor for Willie Emerson.]

ᔓ ᔕ

Mrs. Ripley & other members of the opposition came down the other night to hear Henry's Account of his housekeeping at Walden [p. 377] Pond, which he read as a lecture, and were charmed with the witty wisdom which ran through it all.

—Ralph Waldo Emerson, Letter to Margaret Fuller, February 28, 1847, in *ibid.*, III, 377-378.

Ꮬ Ꮾ

Mr. Alcott & Henry are laboring at the summer house, which, in spite of their joint activity, has not yet fallen. A few more spikes driven would to all appearance shatter the supporters. I think to call it Tumbledown-Hall.

—Ralph Waldo Emerson, Letter to Lidian Emerson, August 23, 1847, in *ibid.*, III, 411.

Ꮬ Ꮾ

My two plants the deerberry vaccinium stamineum and the golden flowers Chrysopsis ——, were eagerly greeted here. Henry Thoreau could hardly suppress his indignation that I should bring him a berry he had not seen.

—Ralph Waldo Emerson, Letter to William Emerson, September 28, 1853, in *ibid.*, IV, 388. [Rusk notes that Emerson had found the plants in Yarmouth, Mass.]

Ꮬ Ꮾ

All American kind are delighted with "Walden" as far as they have dared say, The little pond sinks in these very days as tremu- [p. 459]lous at its human fame. I do not know if the book has come to you yet;—but it is cheerful, sparkling, readable, with all kinds of merits, & rising sometimes to very great heights. We account Henry the undoubted King of all American lions. He is walking up & down Concord, firm-looking, but in a tremble of great expectation.

—Ralph Waldo Emerson, Letter to George Partridge Bradford, August 28, 1854, in *ibid.*, IV, 459-460.

Ꮬ Ꮾ

Mr[.] Thoreau met your New Bedford Rev. Mr[.] Thomas, at my house, last evening. The naturalist was in the perfect spirits habitual to him, and the minister courteous as ever, &, as it happened, cognisant of the Cape, & of Henry's travels thereon. I am bound to be specially sensible of Henry T['] merits, as he has just now by better surveying quite innocently made 60 rods of woodland for me, & left the adjacent lot, which he was measuring, larger than the deed gave it. There[']s a surveyor for you!

—Ralph Waldo Emerson, Letter to Daniel Ricketson, January 10, 1858, in *ibid.*, V, 95.

I am sure he [Thoreau] is entitled to stand quite alone on his proper merits. There might easily have been a little influence from his neighbors on his first writings. He was not quite out of college, I believe, when I first saw him; but it is long since I, and I think all who knew him, felt that he was the most independent of men in thought & in action.

—Ralph Waldo Emerson, Letter to James Bradley Thayer, August 25, 1865, in *ibid.*, V, 424. [Written in reply to an article by Thayer dismissing Thoreau as an imitator of Emerson.]

The Monday before Commencement [1837], then the last Wednesday in August, was the appointed time. To reach Cambridge in season involved then going down Sunday night, and my arrangements to spend the nights with David Henry Thoreau, as we all called him then, had all been comfortably agreed upon. . . . Nothing memorable can I remember happened on that momentous ride bearing a green boy to the first of his decisive trials in real life, and I was dropped at the yard gate where Thoreau met me and took me to his room in Stoughton. I was anxious of the morrow's fate, overawed by the dull old college walls, and not a little inclined to be over-thoughtful at the sudden change it all implied. But these fancies were soon dispelled, a burst of Thoreau's classmates into his room, headed by Charles Theodore Russell, Trask and others who chaffed Thoreau and his Freshman in all sorts of amusing ways, and took down some of our local pride and Concord self-conceit for which I soon found out that my host was as distinguished in college as afterwards. These roaring seniors fresh from vacation's fun and with no more college duties to worry about made a sharp contrast to a Sunday evening at home. It was seeing something of the end before even the beginning. There had been some kind of a row with the faculty and the trouble was carried into the Criminal Court and I had heard the county side of it at home and now was told the students' side by some of the actors or sympathizers and got some ideas of college discipline that varied essentially from the home notion. It was startling and novel to hear "Old Prex" and other nicknames familiarly applied to such dignitaries as Concord had almost worshipped, and I fear that the introduction wasn't of the most useful sort to just such a boy as I was.

—John Shepard Keyes, in Raymond Adams, "Thoreau at Harvard: Some Unpublished Records," *New England Quarterly*, XIII (March, 1940), 32.

When six years old I began to attend the Academy then kept by Phineas Allen, the poorest teacher and worst school I ever knew anything about personally. . . . Here for schoolmates I had among the older boys . . . Henry Thoreau. [p. 73] . . .

I had kept up my pleasant acquaintance with Thoreau, who was [a little later] living in his shanty at Walden, where I sometimes went to see him, and oftener met him in his walks or on the river. I had some of his naturalist instincts and tastes and used to compare notes with him of birds and beasts, though I was no botanist as he was. His life at Walden has been somewhat misrepresented, as it was by no means so much that of a hermit as is now thought. He was at Mr. Emerson's and the village nearly every day, often partaking of meals there and at his father's house, and though not intrusive was altogether too egotistic to be either shy or retiring. He loved the woods, the pond, and the river, and having met a disappointment in his other love sought their consolation in preference to that of society.

—John Shepard Keyes, in Amelia F. Emerson, "John Shepard Keyes," in *Memoirs of Members of the Social Circle in Concord: Fifth Series* (Cambridge: Riverside, 1940), pp. 73, 80.

We [William H. Brown and Richard Fay Barrett] once found a rare nest in the Cyrus Hosmer swamp, which we reported to Mr. Thoreau, who went with us to see it. Mr. Thoreau told us it was a Virginia rail's nest. He took an egg from the nest, blew it carefully, and deposited it in a bandanna handkerchief in the tall crown of his drab soft hat.

—William H. Brown, "Richard Fay Barrett," in *ibid.*, p. 103.

Happily for us boys [the Josiah Bartlett sons and Edward Emerson], there was then no law against collecting birds' eggs, which pursuit, as practiced by a few of us under the friendly interest of Mr. Thoreau, was harmless, for we always left the mother bird her share of the eggs. Mr. Thoreau gave us a knowledge of the beautiful spots in Concord, and the kinds of birds, their habits, and songs; and incidentally also of flowers, trees, animals, and reptiles—a delight at the time and through life. He did not often go with us, except when we were proud to show "Dave" (as he was irreverently called) some special find, but he was always ready to answer our questions and show us his collections, and when Ned and I were big enough to go to Wachusett or Monadnoc, took great interest, like an elder brother, in advising us about our camping.

—Edward W. Emerson, "Edward Jarvis Bartlett," in *ibid.*, p. 113.

He [Thoreau] despises the world, and all that it has to offer, and, like other humorists, is an intolerable bore. I shall cause it to be known to him that you sat up till two o'clock reading his book; and he will pretend that it is of no consequence, but will never forget it. . . . he is not an agreeable person, and in his presence one feels ashamed of having any money, or a house to live in, or so much as two coats to wear, or having written a book that the public will read —his own mode of life being so unsparing a criticism on all other modes, such as the world approves.

—Nathaniel Hawthorne, Letter to Monckton Miles, in Edward Mather, *Nathaniel Hawthorne: A Modest Man* (New York: Crowell, 1940), p. 334.

The late George Wheeler once told me that Thoreau had passed him when a boy many times without speaking or looking up, when he could have stopped a moment and given him some friendly advice.

—Percy W. Brown, *Middlesex Monographs* (Cleveland: Rowfant Club, 1941), p. 36.

As for Thoreau, there is one chance in a thousand that he might write a most excellent and readable book; but I should be sorry to take the responsibility, either towards you or him, of stirring him up to write anything. . . . He is the most unmalleable fellow alive—the most tedious, tiresome, and intolerable—the narrowest and most notional—and yet, true as all this is, he has great qualities of intellect and character. The only way, however, in which he could ever approach the popular mind, would be by writing a book of simple observation of nature, somewhat in the vein of White's *History of Selborne.*

—Nathaniel Hawthorne, Letter to Evert Duyckinck, 1845, in F. O. Matthiessen, *American Renaissance* (New York: Oxford, 1941), p. 196.

Under his seeming trustfulness and frankness . . . [Thoreau] conceals an immense amount of pride, pretention and infidelity.

—Isaac Hecker, Letter to Orestes Brownson, October 29, 1854, in Theodore Maynard, *Orestes Brownson* (New York: Macmillan, 1943), p. 278.

On Friday . . . Mr. Thoreau's funeral is to take place. He was Concord itself in one man—and his death makes a very large vacuum. I ought to be at his funeral for the sake of shewing [*sic*] my deep respect and value for him to others, though I could much better mourn him at home. . . .

I suppose he believed that beats and reptiles, birds and fishes fulfilled their ends, and that man generally came short. So he respected the one and avoided the other.

His Alpine purity, his diamond truth, his stainless sincerity, his closeness to nature and faithful rendering—these are immortal beauties in him. He has now stepped out of his French body—and his soul has taken up its fitting celestial manifestation. And he has doubtless found the Victoria Regia, which would not grow wild in Concord, even though it were the birthplace of Henry Thoreau! and though he declared he should one day find it here.

—Sophia Hawthorne, in two letters to the James Fieldses in 1862, in Randall Stewart, "The Hawthornes at the Wayside, 1860-1864," *More Books,* XIX (September, 1944), 273.

꙳ ꙳

When Thoreau was a young man, he visited Plymouth and Duxbury, and as enthusiastic pedestrians never tire of walking, he attempted to continue his stroll around Captain's Hill to the north shore of Clark's Island. When the tide is at its lowest ebb, this does not look so impossible! The sand flats even invite one to pace their shining surface! The channel looks narrow enough to be jumped across, and the three miles, which at high tide are a foaming sea, or a level blue sheet of water, look but a short stretch to traverse.

Mr. Thoreau gauged everything by his beloved Concord River—there an island could be waded to; here was evidently an island—let us wade over there! But there are islands and islands, channels and channels! And a rising tide on a flat in Plymouth Harbor is a swift river, full of danger.

Fortunately for our Concord guest, a small fishing boat was at hand just at the nick of time to save him for his task of writing many volumes for the future joy of all lovers of nature! The skipper landed him at the North End—the back door of the island, so to speak, and there he was greeted by the "lord of the isle," known to all his friends as "Uncle Ed," Edward Winslow Watson, and a worthy representative of the Pilgrims who spent their first Sunday on this island.

Bluff and hearty was his welcome, and his first question was, "Where d'ye hail from?" Mr. Thoreau, fresh from the rescue, must have been breathless from climbing the cliff and overcome with the mighty clap on his slender back that welcomed his answer, "From Concord, Sir, my name is Thoreau," with "You don't say so! I've read somewhere in one of your books [*Walden*] that you 'lost a hound, a horse, and a dove.' Now what do you mean by it?"

Mr. Thoreau looked up with shy, dark blue eyes, as someone said he looked like a wild woodchuck ready to run back to his hole, and he was very ruddy of complexion, with reddish brown hair and wore a green coat—he looked up then in shy astonishment at this breezy, broad-shouldered, white-haired sea farmer, reader of his books, "Well, Sir, I suppose we have all had our losses." "That's a pretty way to answer a fellow," replied the unsatisfied student of a fellow-poet and lover of nature.

Mr. Thoreau meekly followed him to the hospitable "Old House" where so many Concord philosophers have eaten the asparagus, turnips, clams and lobsters that are better there than in any other dining-room, even in New England where those fruits of the sea and the soil are always good.

After he had borne patiently the well-deserved reproofs for his great rashness—"Where would you have been now, if Sam Burgess hadn't happened to get belated hauling in his lobster pots, I'd like to know, eh?"—the talk turned to tales of Norsemen, of adventure by sea and land—the wood fire was blazing to dry the wet and weary traveler; the lamps were lighted; and from the depths of the big old-fashioned arm chair rose and fell the long arms of the teller of tales. Excited by his ever-increasing audience, who peered in at the open windows and stopped to listen until all the island flocked to hear what "that man that thought he could wade across from Duxbury" had to say for himself, and egged on by Uncle Ed's questions and unreserved criticism, he talked far into the night, a night never to be forgotten by those who were there to see and to hear.

The Watson boys, four in number, tall, stalwart followers of the sea, and all handsome, fresh and ready listeners, sat around in fascinated silence, their blue eyes getting bigger and bigger as Mr. Thoreau launched out into tales of ancient sea adventures of the times of the Vikings and of his own French ancestors.

The shy woodchuck, under the inspiration of such an audience, forgot how far he was from his hole, so to speak, and held them by his eloquence, breathless and spellbound.

And he returned by high tide, having gained, let us hope, a greater respect for Plymouth Harbour, with its ebb and flow of mighty waters,—as his hearers had gained an insight into a wider world of travel and adventure.

—Ellen Watson, "Thoreau Visits Plymouth," *Thoreau Society Bulletin*, XIX (October, 1947), 1.

⊱ ⊰

In passing I must recount to you an amusing circumstance. There was an unusual difficulty about ringing the bell of the Unitarian Meeting-house, and those who never hesitated before, now shrunk back, and did not dare attempt it. Five or six individuals who were asked declined for one or another reason. Your friend, David Henry Thoreau, (no foreigner, but one whom Concord should be proud to number among her sons,) seeing the timidity of one unfortunate youth, who dared not touch the bell rope, took hold of it with a strong arm; and the bell (though set in its own way), pealed forth its summons right merrily.—This reluctance among those timid gentlemen to ring the bell seems to me very amusing. One of them went to ask *leave* to ring it of one of the committee who take charge of the meeting-house, but not finding him at home, declined taking action on the subject.

—A. M. W., Letter to N. P. Rogers of August [?], 1844, in Wendell P. Glick, "Thoreau and the 'Herald of Freedom,' " *New England Quarterly*, XXII (June, 1949), 201. [The bell was to announce Emerson's address sponsored by the unpopular Abolitionists, to commemorate the abolition of slavery in the West Indies.]

⊱ ⊰

Mrs. Thoreau invited Mrs. Loomis and myself to spend the summer of 1854 with her at Concord, and when Rowse came, Mrs. Thoreau invited him to stay at her house while he was studying Henry's face.

I was very much interested in watching him while he was watching the Expression of Henry's face. For two or three weeks he did not put a pencil to paper; but one morning at breakfast, he suddenly jumped up from the table, asked to be excused and disappeared for the rest of the day. The next morning he brought down the crayon, almost exactly in its present form, scarcely another touch was put upon it.

It is for me, on the whole, the most satisfactory likeness, for it represents Henry just as he was in that summer, so memorable to me, memorable for my intimacy with Henry.

—Eben J. Loomis, Letter to Alfred W. Hosmer, June 13, 1896, in *Thoreau Society Bulletin*, XXX (January, 1950), 4. [This crayon portrait appears as the frontispiece of this book.]

‡‡‡

I cannot let another sun set without acknowledging your kind note of sympathy for us at this time. Although we have met with an irreparable loss, & great is the mystery of that Providence which has gathered this dark shadow about us, yet so much love & wisdom is manifest amidst it all, that I feel as if a beautiful miracle had been wrought in the life, sickness & death of my dear brother, & the memory of his sweet & virtuous soul must ever cheer & comfort me.

—Sophia Thoreau, Letter to Marianne Dunbar, May 22, 1862, in Walter Harding, "The Correspondence of Sophia Thoreau and Marianne Dunbar," *Thoreau Society Bulletin*, XXXIII (October, 1950), 1.

‡‡‡

I saw Thoreau last night, and it is exquisitely amusing to see how he imitates Emer[p. 18]son's tone and manner. With my eyes shut I shouldn't know them apart.

—James Russell Lowell, Letter to Loring, July 12, 1838, in Leon Howard, *Victorian Knight Errant* (Berkeley: University of California, 1952), pp. 18-19.

‡‡‡

Now about Thoreau—"My Henry" as his mother used to call him. I never imagined anything great could be said of him. Mr. Thoreau and his wife were devoted Christians, and intellectual; but when I first knew them they were poor. The four children all grown up, as I a schoolgirl remember them, were finely educated and in sympathy with reforms:—"comeouters," strong abolitionists, and Christian workers. John was a teacher in the Academy, and was one of those saintly minded, clean young men that are seldom seen. He was a bright spot everywhere; the life of every gathering, and when he died suddenly by poison from the barber's razor the sun seemed to have gone out and the family's support withdrawn.

"David Henry" after leaving college was eccentric and did not like to, and so would not, work. The opposite of John in every particular, he was thin, insignificant, poorly dressed, careless looking young man, with thin, straight, shaggy hair and pale blue, wattery [*sic*] looking eyes. After his brother's death the town demanded of him his own poll tax. He refused indignantly; "he was a free man and would not pay a tax in a state that endorsed slavery;" and he spent one night in jail. Some friend paid it that year and set him free but lost "David Henry's" friendship by the act. The next spring he was not to be found; he had gone to the woods near Walden Pond and had established himself in an unused charcoal burner's hut. Here in the solitude he became acquainted with himself and began to write.

Emerson was a lover of those woods and many hours they spent together. Once after a lecture by Thoreau someone remarked how much like Emerson he had spoken; his mother overhearing replied, "Yes, Mr. Emerson is a perfect counterpart of my 'David Henry.'" She almost worshipped him.

"David Henry" did not care whether he was decently clothed, or not. The ladies of the charitable society proposed to make him some cotton shirts, but thot it best, first to ask his mother if it would be agreeable to him. Dear Mrs. Thoreau at the next meeting said, "I told my David Henry that you would like to make him some unbleached cotton shirts; he said 'unbleached mother, unbleached. Yes, that strikes my ears pleasantly; I think they may make me some.'" A practical farmer's wife with no sentiment said in an aside, "Strike his ears pleasantly, indeed. I guess they will strike his back pleasantly when he gets them on."

—Priscilla Rice Edes, in Raymond Adams, "Thoreau and His Neighbors," *Thoreau Society Bulletin*, XLIV (Summer, 1953), 2. [Mrs. Edes is in error both about the dating of Thoreau's jail experience and about the source of his cabin.]

∽ ∾

One day . . . we children saw Mr. Thoreau standing right down there across the road near the Assabet. He stood very still, and we knew he was watching something in the water. But we knew we must not disturb him, and so we stayed up here in the dooryard. At noontime he was still there, watching something in the water. And he stayed there all afternoon.

At last, though, along about supper time, he came up here to the house. And then we children knew that we'd learn what it was he'd been watching. He'd found a duck that had just hatched out a nest of eggs. She had brought the little ducks down to the water. And Mr. Thoreau had watched all day to see her teach those little ducks about the river.

And while we ate our suppers there in the kitchen, he told us the most wonderful stories you ever heard about those ducks.

—Abby Hosmer, in *ibid.*, XLIV, 4.

≫ ⊂

To me Emerson once said, "There was no bow in Thoreau, he never sought to please his hearers or his friends."

—F. B. Sanborn, in Kenneth Cameron, *Emerson, Thoreau and Concord in Early Newspapers* (Hartford: Transcendental, 1958), p. 45.

≫ ⊂

A neighbor told us that he used to pass her door frequently, and she was always reminded of nothing else but an owl when she noticed him. He had a hooked nose, bushy, unkempt whiskers, and his eyes, big, round, sharp and piercing, looked out searchingly through his hair which hung over them. He was short and ungainly, and he had a stooping figure and a shuffling gait. And, she added, "I don't understand why his books should be so popular." Such is fame at home.

—[Alfred?] Munroe, in *ibid.*, p. 71.

≫ ⊂

Thoreau was very chary of taking life, and was once known to carry some canker worms he had found in his bed-room down into the yard rather than throw them out the window, saying in reply to a remark on the subject that we knew not of what value they might really be in some subtle processes of nature. His peculiarity in this respect, combined with his habitual diffidence, once made him the hero of a ludicrous incident. Desiring to catch a woodchuck alive, without permitting the animal to injure itself in its frantic efforts to escape, he applied to a veteran trapper, a dissipated Nimrod and village hanger on for instruction.

"Mr. W——," he began, "is there any way to get woodchucks without trapping them with—"

"Yes; shoot 'em, you —— fool," replied the disreputable mentor, without waiting for the naturalist to complete the sentence.

—Anonymous, in *ibid.*, p. 86.

∾ ∾

Colonel Higginson, who had personal knowledge of H. D. Thoreau, declares that both Channing and Lowell have done the quaint New Englander injustice in emphasizing his eccentricities and not placing sufficient stress on his vigor, good sense and clear perceptions. Colonel Higginson says that as a companion he was essentially sincere, wholesome and enjoyable. Though more or less a humorist, nursing his own whims, and capable of being tiresome when they came uppermost, he was easily led away from them to the vast domains of literature and nature, and then poured forth endless streams of the most interesting talk. His home life was thoroughly affectionate and faithful—he never made his whims an excuse for mere selfishness. His life-long celibacy, the colonel says, was due to the noblest unselfishness—an early act of lofty self-abnegation toward his own brother, whose love had taken the same direction with his own.

—Anonymous, in *ibid.*, p. 140.

∾ ∾

Mr. Hawthorne once wrote a pleasant letter introducing H. D. Thoreau to Mr. Epes Sargent, and Mr. Sargent has just communicated this letter to Harper's Weekly. "There is a gentleman in the town of the name of Thoreau," says Hawthorne, "a graduate of Cambridge, and a fine scholar, especially in old English literature, but withal a wild, irregular, Indian-like sort of fellow, who can find no occupation in life that suits him. He writes, and sometimes—often for aught I know—very well indeed. . . . In the Dial for July there is an article on the natural history of this part of the country, which will give you an idea of him as a genuine and exquisite observer of nature—a character almost as rare as that of a true poet. He writes poetry also—for instance, 'To the Maiden in the East,' 'The Summer Rain,' and other pieces in the Dial for October, which seem to be very careless and imperfect, but as true as bird notes."

—Anonymous, in *ibid.*, p. 148.

∽ ∾

The pure sweet books of Thoreau are a great addition to our literature. When I read them I always hear his own sweet sensitive voice and am conscious of the shyness that half regrets they should be printed. The first time I ever saw Thoreau I heard him read one of his "Autumn" papers in Harry Blake's parlor in Worcester. If it is good to read these things for one's self, it was still better to hear him read them. Never since have I been in the country at that season when his description of the royal ranks of the purple poke berries and the steady beaming of the yellow hank weed on the hillside has not risen in my mind. He fascinated every one of us, and yet he had been so hard to persuade! This may have been in 1858. In December, 1859, I went up to Concord to give a lecture before the Lyceum. I took tea with my friend Mr. Emerson, and as a literary lecture from a woman was at that time an almost untried experiment, there was a little question at table as to whom of the Concord people would come out to hear. "I suppose," said Mr. Sanborn, "that Thoreau will come?" "No," said Mr. Emerson. "I saw him this morning. He says women never have anything to say!" And at that Mrs. Emerson and I laughed merrily, for it was the last charge that we should have expected anyone to bring against us.

In due time we went to the hall. I think I was about a third through when I saw a person enter who looked like a working man. He had on a green baize jacket, and seated himself on the end of the very last bench by the door.

I am always in the habit of speaking to the remotest auditor, and so I began to talk to him, and as I talked he edged nearer and nearer till at last he was so close to the platform that I lost sight of him and forgot him altogether. At the close of the lecture I came down to grasp the hands of waiting friends and found myself directly behind the green jacket. Emerson was in the front and my ears caught the words: "Why, Thoreau, I thought you was not coming," and the reply: "But *this* woman had something to say!" He told me afterwards that he had been on the river all day and dropped in on his way home to see what I looked like and "had to stay." I thought it a pleasant victory then, for he waited to persuade me to remain over the next day and spend it at his home with himself, his mother and sister.

It was a day I shall never forget, filled to the brim with charming talk. We were good comrades all. Before I left he showed me a superb set of Hindu classics, fitted into a polished box, which had been sent him by an English gentleman, to whom he made Walden waters sweet. His eyes sparkled as they looked at his treasure, and I asked him if he could read them. "Oh, no!" he said. "And will you not learn," I asked. "For what good?" he answered. "Now this box holds everything; then I might find it very empty." It was that same week, I think, that I asked Emerson if he had read something new in German, and he said that he "did not care to read anything that was not written in English."

How glad I am now that I staid at Thoreau's request. It was the only whole day I was ever able to spend with the three whom death soon began to separate.

—Caroline H. Dall, in Joseph Slater, "Caroline Dall in Concord," *Thoreau Society Bulletin*, LXII (Winter, 1958), 1.

∾ ∾

My memory goes back a long way, but it does not quite reach that day in Cambridge when my mother invited Henry Thoreau to come to the house to see her wonderful new baby. He came in, boldly enough, and so remained until, with mistaken zeal, the nurse placed me in his arms, doubtless thinking it would be an especial treat to the shy recluse. Far from it—he did not know which end was which! My terrified mother caught sight of two wildly waving little pink feet sticking out at the top, poor little head quite lost in the lower invisible end of the bundle. After one agonized moment the bewildered man, with a groan of relief, relinquished me to the giver. Apparently babies bore no large part in Henry's scheme of life.

Henry Thoreau was an especial friend of my father and mother. They spent the first two or three summers after their marriage in 1853 at his mother's house in Concord. One afternoon the three were taking a quiet rowing trip on the placid Concord River, a diversion to which they were greatly devoted when, as they were approaching a fine old [p. 1] oak on the river bank, Henry ceased rowing, stood up suddenly in the tiny skiff, looked upon into the huge tree with sometime akin to adoration and said, as one inspired, "Why, there is enough in that tree alone to keep one man happily busy all his life!" His face was alight with fervour as he went on to tell of the rich reward awaiting him who would take the oak-tree for his lifework. "The whole story of creation and all of natural history is in that one tree! Why does anyone want to take long journeys to study anything? It is all here." My mother was deeply impressed by his shining face turned upward, and often spoke of that rare evening when she had caught an instant glimpse of all futurity. . . .

He and my father were both interested in Indian relics still to be found all over the country. My father once said to him as they walked along a country road, that it was unfortunate these reminders of the past were being gathered up by the general run [p. 2] of persons neither interested in them nor properly instructed.

"Oh, well, there are always plenty left," said Henry, stooping over at the moment to pick up a perfect stone arrow-head.

During one of their happy and prolific summers with him, my parents became acquainted with Rowse, who was also spending some weeks at the Thoreaus', drawing in crayon the portrait of Henry, although to "sit for a portrait" was as much outside his plan as holding a friend's baby right end up. Sometimes the artist would leave the table abruptly in the midst of a meal, excusing himself afterward

by explaining to his hostess—small, vivid, and alert Mrs. Thoreau—
that a sudden turn of Henry's head had given him new insight. He
had just seen an expression cross his face which must be recorded
else one aspect of his mind and changing thought would be lost.
Rowse would rush to his easel to put on paper at once the glimpse
into Henry's real personality. That portrait, many times reproduced,
was the only one which his intimate old friends cared to keep as the
permanent representation of the shy naturalist, and it became the one
most liked by his family, until all had died and there is no one left
to judge. [p. 3] ...

Mrs. Thoreau—a noteworthy housekeeper—used to tell us glee-
fully that Henry was by no means so utterly indifferent to the good
things of life as he liked to believe himself, and that regularly every
week of his self-enforced retirement he came home to eat a deliciously
prepared dinner which their old family cook took pains to have as
perfect as she knew how, and which he very evidently enjoyed to the
full after his abstemious days at Walden. My mother's humourous
account of Henry's intense satisfaction in coming home for those
wonderful dinners during the "hermitage" was a new angle of the
naturalist's life and likings.

—Mabel Loomis Todd, "The Thoreau Family Two Generations Ago,"
Thoreau Society Booklet, XIII (1958), 1-4.

Henry was the purest-looking man that ever lived.

—Mary A. Wilder Loomis, in *ibid.*, XIII, 19.

H. T. has been reading Aristotle and found that it is good, a
fact which Mr. E[merson] says, has been the property of every
schoolboy for two thousand years.—Henry you know thought he had
discovered Aristotle, the good creature (I mean H.).

—Ellery Channing, Letter to Mrs. Marston Watson, June 15, 1860, in
Kenneth Walter Cameron, "Thoreau and Emerson in Channing's Letters to
the Watsons," *Emerson Society Quarterly*, XIV (1959), 78.

Jan. 4 '93.

Thoreau's bro[ther] J[oh]n was of practical rather than literary bent. Singular, it is that there is so lit[t]l[e] of him in Henry's b[oo]k W[ee]k on Conc[ord] when he too was bred in our sch[oo]ls & had the same adv[enture]s Henry had. He was frightened to death. He cut his finger, lockjaw followed. Henry held him in his arms when he died. Henry told me for 2 or 3 d[ay]s after that he felt the lockjaw tightening on him too—so gr[ea]t was his sympathy.

Henry was very affectionate; he had a gr[ea]t deal of sympathy that p[eo]ple did not k[no]w; during his last illness he rec[ei]v[e]d a gr[ea]t deal of attent[io]n; p[eo]pl[e] w[e]r[e] const[an]tly com[in]g & send[in]g him fl[owe]rs &c. He c[a]m[e] to feel v[er]y diff[eren]tly tow[ar]d p[eo]pl[e], & s[ai]d if he had kn[own] he w[oul]dn't h[a]v[e] b[ee]n so offish. He had got into his h[ea]d bef[ore] that p[eo]pl[e] didn't mean what they said. . . .

Fr[om] Mr. E[dward] Hoar. Dec. 30, '92.

I have just fin[ished] r[ea]d[in]g Thoreau's "Winter." Th[e]r[e] is not so much nat[ura]l hist[ory] in it as in s[o]m[e] o[the]r w[or]ks, not so much as there is of matter addressed to man's moral nature.

I h[a]v[e] greatly regretted that I did not kn[ow] Thoreau better. Did you not often go out w[ith] him? Yes, I did; I was one of the few to whom he granted that favor. I was shown that side of his nature to the full, the nat[ural] hist[ory] side, the minute observer. But th[e]r[e] w[e]r[e] o[the]r sides to him, and I was wholly unaware then of the moral side that app[ea]rs so str[on]gly in his b[oo]ks. He did not show me that in our walks. Thoreau was intensely a moralist, to him everything was valuable acc[ording] as it appealed to the moral sentiment & he w[oul]d lose no oppor[tunity] to intone a moral sentiment. Nor would he lose any oppor[tunity] for observ[in]g nature, even if it was to get up in dark night and watch for hours the lightning and a rotten log in Maine. He was ready to open that side of himself to any one who w[oul]d pay the price. But that meant, to go w[ith] him in his walk; to walk long & far; to h[a]v[e] wet feet & go so for hours; to pull a boat all day & to come home late at night after many miles. If you w[oul]d do that w[ith] him, he w[oul]d take you w[ith] him. If you flinched at anyth[in]g, he had no more use for you.

Thoreau was of a very fine-grained family. He knew he had not long to live & he determined to m[a]k[e] the most of it. How to observe and acq[ui]r[e] knowl[e]dge & secure the [word?] aspects of life w[ithou]t much expenditure of money was his great study. He w[oul]d not wait as most men, to acq[ui]r[e] a competence before settling down to realize the ends of life. He w[oul]d show how they c[oul]d be secured w[ithou]t money; or w[ith] very little. This was the object of his Walden Pond.

Thoreau's fam[ily] had a scrofulous tendency; his s[iste]r Sophia, a very fine-grained nature, died of consumption and so did his bro[ther]; he died in Thoreau's arms & that n[ear]ly killed Henry. . . .

I could not becom[e] a g[oo]d ornithologist. When I was y[oun]g I was a g[oo]d shot, & c[oul]d hit a bird on the wing at 200 y[ar]ds. But when I bec[a]m[e] acq[uain]t[e]d w[ith] Henry Thoreau, he persuaded me out of it. He w[oul] nev[er] shoot a bird, & I th[in]k his method gr[ea]tly pref[era]ble to that of Mr. J[oh]n Burroughs. Thoreau w[oul]d lie & watch the movem[en]ts of a bird for h[ou]rs & also get the [word?] he wanted. He used to say that if you shot the bird, you got only a dead bird anyway; you c[oul]d make out a few p[ar]ts in anatomy or plumage just such as all Dr. Coues' work is; but you c[oul]dn't see how the bird lives & acts. Since then I h[a]v[e] never shot a bird. . . .

I th[in]k Thoreau has suf[fe]r[re]d in his editing. I th[in]k m[an]y th[in]gs h[a]v[e] b[ee]n publ[ished] w[hic]h sh[oul]d not h[a]v[e] b[ee]n, notes & hints in [word?] to guide himself in future observ[ations] wh[ich] are of no use to the public.

—Edward S. Burgess, "Notes on Concord People," Manuscript in Concord Free Public Library, Concord, Mass.

⤳ ⤶

The story that Thoreau made one pencil and then stopped takes on quite a different aspect in the light [of] investigation into the history of the business. As Henry and his father brought the lead used for the pencils to a high degree of perfection, it was wanted by a firm in Boston for the stereotype business, and selling it for that purpose was so much more profitable than making pencils that the latter was carried on only as a cover for the other, which it was desirable to keep secret. To keep it a secret, the lead was carried from the mill to the house, and then shipped to Boston from there.

—Anonymous, Manuscript in the Alfred Hosmer Collection, Concord Free Public Library, Concord, Mass.

[Mr. Samuel A. Chase is] a *dear* old gentleman. He *boarded with Thoreau* one winter, at Haverhill, with a Mrs. Webster; he thought it was 1852 or 3; Thoreau was surveying; he was embarrassed through the publication of his book, and trying to earn money. They used to walk together often.

Think of it! and if a bird appeared he showed how Thoreau's hand would go out to stop him from another step (*not* the *bird!* I am too excited to be lucid). . . . He said he did not believe he (Thoreau) ever in all his life did *one wrong thing*. He was "all *purity and goodness personified*." He said the moisture would come to his eyes whenever he spoke of his mother; he was a *loving* man. And I think what I was most glad to hear was that Thoreau said—"Fifty years from now the majority of people will believe as I do now." Aren't you glad that *he knew it?* It would take the keen edge from his loneliness. . . .

He said the lady with whom they boarded was a stiff old fashioned Methodist who tried *her best* to "convert" Thoreau; but he said "he was too hard a nut for her to crack."

—Henrietta M. Daniels, Letter to Alfred W. Hosmer, March 11, [1899], Manuscript in the Alfred Hosmer Collection, Concord Free Public Library, Concord, Mass.

It was Mr. Samuel Barrett of Barrett's Mill Road who used to experiment with the frogs. We would be at work in the hay field raking hay by hand rake . . . when he would show me how Thoreau made the frogs jump. He would take the rake and run it along in the grass t[o]ward a frog who would think a snake was after it and jump near twenty feet sometimes and yet neither Mr. Barrett or Thoreau would kill a snake, frog, or mouse.

—Horace Hosmer, Letter to Alfred W. Hosmer, undated, Manuscript in the Alfred Hosmer Collection, Concord Free Public Library, Concord, Mass.

Looking at the pictures [photographs of Maria and Henry Thoreau] brings back to me very vividly the pleasant days long ago, when Henry Thoreau and I tramped over the Concord hills and boated on the Concord river; picking up Indian relics, investigating the birds, flowers, fish and other things: and talking all the while on every subject in which either or both of us was interested.

I always found Henry very hospitable to a new idea. If I happened to suggest some new thought, he would think it over, not saying much at the time, but afterward, perhaps the next day, or week, he would refer to it, having made up his mind since whether to accept or reject it.

It was delightful to hear him talk; his opinions were well formed, clear and gave no uncertain sound.

I spent the summer at Mr. Thoreau's house at the time Mr. [Samuel] Rowse was in Concord, and Thoreau, Rowse and myself frequently sat up until twelve or one o'clock, talking on "fate, free-will, foreknowledge absolute," or other topics equally or more interesting.

—Eben J. Loomis, Letter to Alfred W. Hosmer, June, 1896, Manuscript in Alfred Hosmer Collection, Concord Free Public Library, Concord, Mass.

∽ ∾

The story of the meeting at the jail of Mr. Emerson and Mr. Thoreau was told me by Maria Thoreau in the following words:— "Henry, why are you here?" "Waldo, why are you *not* here?" So I think that may be considered authentic and accurate.

—Eben J. Loomis, Letter to Alfred W. Hosmer, May 21, 1894, Manuscript in Alfred Hosmer Collection, Concord Free Public Library, Concord, Mass.

∽ ∾

My friend Thoreau has a very pleasant acidulous drink, requiring only the addition of sugar. The sap of the birch, white, black and yellow. The former the most aromatic. It is drawn in March as soon as the sap begins to flow. Thoreau uses for spouts the upland sumach, makes the holes in the trees with augurs, filling the spout previously.

—Daniel Ricketson, Diary for December 10, 1858 (from copy in the possession of Mrs. Henry Wheelwright, Bangor, Maine.)

∽ ∾

Mr. Pierce said he remembered Thoreau well, though he himself was only a boy of twelve when he died. Apparently, he had not talked with him much, but says he was a familiar figure about town, and was much respected by the villagers for his upright character and general integrity. What surprised me was that he did not allude to the fact many of his townspeople regarded him as odd and eccentric. Mr. Pierce said that Thoreau was a close friend of young Edward Emerson, son of the philosopher, and that the two of them volunteered for service in the Union Army but were rejected for poor physical condition. He added that Thoreau was anxious to get into the army. It is hard to believe what Pierce could base this on, for there is no allusion to it in any of the biographies or the latest and most intensive studies of Thoreau.

An incident Mr. Pierce remembers more than any other one in connection with Thoreau was the latter's prominent part in the John Brown Commemoration Service held in Concord on a Sunday evening in December, 1859. Thoreau gave a stirring address on that occasion, while Emerson, Alcott, Channing, and others contributed to the program. Evidently Thoreau was chairman and arranged the ceremonies. Mr. Pierce recalls helping his father move a piano or an organ into the hall where the meeting took place.

Mr. Pierce said he always tried to account in his mind for the reason behind Thoreau's daily wanderings through the fields and woods about Concord. He came to the conclusion he did it to be out of doors, exercising for his health which was none too good, and which resulted in death by consumption in 1862. He also mentioned the many inquiries about Thoreau of late years and seemed a trifle amazed at the great interest in him, but thought that he certainly must have been a great man because of it.

—W. Stephen Thomas, "Notes of a Conversation of Frank Pierce of Concord with W. Stephen Thomas, October 22, 1932." Manuscript in the possession of W. Stephen Thomas, Director, Rochester Museum of Arts and Sciences, Rochester, New York.

∽ ∾

The lecture on Wednesday evening, was by H. D. Thoreau, Esq., of Concord, Mass. The subject was announced in the papers as "Home, or domestic economy," but the real topic was "Myself—I." The lecture was unique, original, comical, and high-falutin. It kept the audience wide awake, and most pleasantly excited for nearly two hours. . . . It was like the dashing out of a comet that had broken loose from its orbit—hitting here and there, a gentle rap at this folly, and a severe one at that—but all in good nature.

—Anonymous, "The Lyceum," *Eastern Argus Semi-Weekly* [Portland, Maine], March 23, 1849.

∽ ⌒

The "Walden Pond" philosopher, (Mr. Thoreau, of Concord,) delivered his second lecture at Brinley Hall Friday evening. It was a continuation of his history of two years of "life in the woods;" a mingled web of sage conclusions and puerility—wit and egotistical effusions—bright scintillations and narrow criticisms and low comparisons. He has a natural poetic temperament, with a more than ordinary sensibility to the myriad of nature's manifestations. But there is apparent a constant struggle for eccentricity. It is only when the lecturer seems to forget himself, that the listener forgets that there is in the neighborhood of "Walden Pond" another philosopher [Emerson] whose light Thoreau reflects; the same service which the moon performs for the sun. Yet the lecturer says many things that not only amuse the hour, but will not be easily forgotten. He is truly one of nature's oddities; and would make a very respectable Diogenes, if the world were going to live its life over again, and that distinguished citizen of antiquity should not care to appear again upon the stage.

—Anonymous, "Lake Philosophy," *Worcester* [Massachusetts] *Palladium*, May 2, 1849.

∽ ⌒

The third lecture of this course will be given at Brinley Hall, this evening. Being absent from town on the evening when the first lecture was given, we did not have the good fortune to hear it—a circumstance we regretted, because the commendations we heard of it assure us that it would have been a source of enjoyment to us. Those commendations had possibly led us to expect too much, and we are free to say, that in hearing the second lecture, we were disappointed. We had looked for a bold, original thinker, who would give us the results of his observations and reflections, with a vigor, freshness, and independence, which would win our respect and admiration, even though it might not convince us. We said that we were disappointed. This lecturer evidently is not deficient in ability, and might very probably attain to more than a respectable rank, if he were satisfied to be himself, Henry D. Thoreau, and not aim to be Ralph Waldo Emerson or any body else. But, so far as manner, at least was concerned, the lecture was a better *imitation* of Emerson than we should have thought possible, even with two year's [*sic*] seclusion to practice in. In the ideas, too, there was less of originality than we had looked for, and recollections of Carlyle as well as of Emerson, were repeatedly forced upon the mind. The style was mostly Emersonian, with occasional interludes, in which the lecturer gave us glimpses of himself beneath the panoply in which he was enshrouded, and we are perverse enough to confess ourself better pleased with him as Thoreau than as Emerson, so far as these opportunities afforded us the means of judging.

We are no admirers of the cynicism, whether real or affected, of the school to which we suppose the lecturer belongs. It strikes us that one who is capable of such high enjoyments, as they sometimes profess, from the contemplation of the works of creation in their *lower* manifestations, might, if his mind were rightly constituted, find increased pleasure in communion with the last, best, and highest subject of creative power, even though in most individual cases, it may fail to come up to the standard for which it was designed. . . .

We hope our readers will go to the lecture, this evening, and hear for themselves. We would not miss of going on any consideration of an ordinary character. We are to have, among other things, the lecturer's experience, during his two years' seclusion from the world, *in raising beans!* Farmers and horticulturists will probably be elevated upon the philosophical influence of that avocation.

—Anonymous, "Thoreau's Lectures," *Worcester* [Massachusetts] *Daily Spy*, May 3, 1849.

∾ ᴄ

The performance of this gentleman, before the Lyceum, was unique. All who heard him lecture here two years ago were doubtless prepared for something eccentric and original, and we are quite sure they were not disappointed! His subject might be termed A Ramble upon Cape Cod,—along its wreck strewn shores—across its desert sands, and among its amphibious inhabitants. All the minute peculiarities of these, were presented in the light of a peculiarly quaint and humorous fancy. Mr. Thoreau is a most acute observer, and he has a singularly graphic style of describing what he has seen. He is an observer of nature, animate and inanimate, but he sees everything from a peculiar point of view, all is bathed in the light of a strong imagination. He takes all things by the angles, and sets them before you in the most quaint phrase. He reaches out into the immensity of nature, and startles you by bringing dissimilarities together in which for the first time you perceive resemblances. Again he bewilders you in the mists of transcendentalism, delights you with brilliant imagery, shocks you by his apparent irreverence, and sets you in a roar by his sallies of wit, which springs from ambush upon you. He lies in wait for you, and dodges around about, ever and anon thrusting grotesque images before you. You cannot anticipate him. He is the most erratic of travelers. One moment he is in the clouds, and the next eating hen clams by the sea shore, or whittling kelp, that he "may become better acquainted with it." You have scarce ceased to smile at his last pun, before you are overwhelmed by a great thought or what, by the manner of its clothing, is cleverly made to appear such!

All this, you feel, is not the result of effort. It is the natural outpouring of the man. He could not speak otherwise if he would. His style is a part of himself, as much as his voice, manner, and the peculiar look which prepares you for something quaint, and adds its effect far more than words. And it is for this reason that we are now attempting to describe the man instead of reporting his lecture. His voice and manner, which are more than half of what he says, we cannot transfer to paper. He must be heard to be enjoyed. In short he is an original, who follows no beaten path, but has struck out one for himself, full of winding bouts and odd corners; perplexing labyrinths, and commanding prospects; now running over mountain summits, lost in the clouds, and anon descending into quiet vales of beauty, meandering in the deep recesses of nature, and leading—nowhither! To men with imagination enough to enjoy an occasional ramble through the domains of thought, wit and fancy, for the ramble's sake, he is a delightful companion, but to your slow plodder, who clings to the beaten track as his only salvation, he is incomprehensible—an ignis fatuus, luring honest men into forbidden paths.

This was well illustrated by the remarks of the audience at the close of the lecture. We were amused at the various comments made. One worthy man, who has more of the practical than the imaginative in his composition, was demanding with a smile forced from him by the tickling fancies of the lecturer, that the committee should "pay him for the time lost in listening to such trash!" A fair philosopher of sixteen thought he possessed "a vein of satire, but spoke of the clergy with too much levity." A sober young man declared it the "greatest piece of nonsense he ever listened to," while another thought it trivial, and even profane! But then, again, there were others who were infinitely amused with his quaint humor, delighted with his graphic descriptions, and his far-reaching flights of imagination. To them it was "a rich treat."— Then there were those, as there always are, who were ready to quarrel with the lecture because it did not square with their pre-conceived standard of what a lyceum lecture should be. It was very well as almost anything else than a lecture! "If they had come to listen to a story, they would have been delighted," but as it was given to them as a lecture, they could not enjoy it! We would advise all such, to rid their minds of rigid rules, and be prepared to receive whatever comes, judging it by what it is, rather than by what it is *not*.

—Anonymous, "Mr. Thoreau's Lecture," *Portland* [Maine] *Transcript*, January 25, 1851.

∾ ᘉ

The third lecture of this series was delivered on Tuesday evening, by HENRY THOREAU, better known, perhaps, as the "Concord Hermit." By the published programme of the course, Rev. T. Starr King was announced as the third lecturer, but circumstances preventing his appearance, Mr. Thoreau came as his substitute. As most of our readers know, Mr. Thoreau is an enthusiastic lover of nature—nature unadorned, unaided by art—nature in her wildest moods—in her own glorious, grand, sublime beauty, as she developes herself far away from the haunts of men, in the forest, the field, and the meadow, on the hillside and in the deep glen, by the still lake and the running stream. His theme, on this occasion, was of course his favorite one, for "out of the fullness of the heart the mouth speaketh." He took his hearers with him in an imaginary stroll through his favorite haunts, the fields and forests in the vicinity of Concord, where he himself has spent the best part of his life, less in communication with man than with the birds and the trees and the flowers that spring up for man's enjoyment without man's cultivation or consent.

We wish Mr. Thoreau had communicated some of the enthusiasm of his heart to his words, for then we think his lecture would have interested many more than it did. We feel compelled to say that we think he is a far better writer than reader or lecturer; and it is to us rather a mystery how a man with so much real fire, so much wholesome love of the beautiful in nature, can be so tame, so dull, even, in expressing the thoughts that fill his soul and pervade every part of his being. It is an anomaly in human nature undoubtedly designed for some good purpose, but wholly beyond our comprehension. . . .

Taken as a whole, we believe the lecture was enjoyed by a large proportion of the audience, and was listened to with deep attention by such, though we noticed that a few uneasy ones left the hall before it was finished. The manner, rather than the matter of a lecture is most liable to criticism from a promiscuous assembly, and in this instance we fear it was not so favorable for the lecturer as it should have been. But we certainly speak for ourselves, and we think, also, for a goodly number in the audience on Tuesday evening, when we return thanks to the committee who arranged the lectures, for the privilege afforded us of rambling for an hour with Mr. Thoreau through the fields and forests of the good old town of Concord.

—Anonymous, "Frazier Hall Lectures," *Lynn* [Massachusetts] *Weekly Reporter*, April 30, 1859, p. 2.

∽ ∾

The Second lecture of the course before the Young Men's Institute was delivered on Tuesday evening last, by H. D. Thoreau of Concord, Mass. Mr. Thoreau is the author of two or three very entertaining books, one of which at least, descriptive of "Life in the Woods" has passed through several editions, has acquired a deservedly high reputation but as a popular lecturer is evidently out of his element, in fact, as Artemus Ward would say, lecturing is not his "fort." The subject—"Autumnal Tints" is a suggestive one, and in some hands would have formed the basis of a very interesting lecture,—as it was, it was dull, common-place and unsatisfactory. There was nothing of the poetical discoverable in it. It is possible however, that the monotonous style in which it was delivered prevented the audience from duly appreciating whatever of real merit it contained as a composition. On the whole, probably no lecture[r] before the Institute has so thoroughly disappointed his auditory.

—Anonymous, "Institute Lecture," *Waterbury* [Connecticut] *American*, December 14, 1860.

I spent many happy moments with the eccentric Henry D. Thoreau before his remarkable works had gained him such a reputation. It was in the Summer of 1850 when I first saw this distinguished Naturalist. I met him accidentally, or rather found myself in his company one day at Provincetown. I was standing on the wharf waiting to take the stage for Truro. The driver, a small consequential sort of man, who had recently come upon the route, was bustling around, stowing away the baggage, and helping in the ladies and babies. Most of the passengers were already seated; I had secured a place on the top; the horses were restive; the driver was about to mount his box and take the reins, when a person stepped from among the bystanders and asked *Jehu* for a place alongside of him. He was a man of short stature, compactly built, and of florid complexion. His eyes were blue and singularly piercing, while everything about him betokened firmness and strength of character. As he took his seat I saluted him, and so did the other passengers, of whom there were several. I remarked casually upon the weather and the novelty of the scenery. I did not then know that I was speaking to one "whose opinions, conversation, studies, work and course of life," as Mr. Emerson says, "made him a searching judge of men." Had I known this,

I should not have entered into conversation; I should have sat still and studied him. But I was young. I knew nothing of Walden Pond or the manner of life he had been leading. Still less did I dream that the stranger before me was then on the Cape gathering the materials for one of the most interesting and instructive works I ever read. I presume he measured me at a glance. But as I did not realize the fact, it made no difference. I kept up a conversation with him, and ere long he charmed and delighted me as he had many men before. A day or two after I found out who this interesting person was. He told me then of his strange experience—his excursions—his insatiable love of nature. We took walks together—we botanized—sometimes around the little hamlet on the Highlands, with its white lighthouse and cottage attached, where the keeper lived, and sometimes miles away. Then we would make a perilous descent down the steep bank and enter the Clay Pounds, or on the beach, above the dashing waves, sit for hours, to gaze on the vast expanse of ocean, and see the ships pass and repass. To these scenes does my mind revert as I again revisit the place. . . .

While there he did not mingle much with the family except at meals. Most of the time when not on his excursions he spent in his own room. Yet the charm of his conversation was such that his society was highly prized. He always found something to talk about. In his walks around the lighthouse, simple objects, such as others had passed by a hundred times without notice, afforded him opportunisy [sic] to make the most interesting and suggestive remarks. . . . His conversation was what the inclination of my soul and the want of my heart demanded.

—Anonymous, "Home Correspondence: Cape Cod—Henry D. Thoreau," *New York Tribune*, July 24, 1869, p. 5.

∽ ∾

As a ladies' man and a dandy, Thoreau would not be deemed a success, but as a student of nature in its most subtle windings, he had few equals living or dead. He possessed a character and lived a life peculiar to himself, and when out of his sphere, was common-place enough, but in nature's undiscovered realm was the most interesting of men.

It was his delight to study the habits of and become intimately acquainted with the lower animals, and they in turn seemed to understand and appreciate him.

He would sit motionless for hours, and let the mice crawl over him and eat cheese out of his hand (and not scream; think of that girls).

The fish and the mud turtles were the subjects of his patient study. The mud turtles he told me were the largest wild animals in Massachusetts, he having discovered and secured one in Fair Haven Bay that weighed nearly one hundred pounds.

On one of his accustomed rambles he came where I was at work near the river, and hearing a well known sound that is heard in the low land along the banks of the Assabet, a sound as of a bird, yet somewhat like the notes of a tree-toad, only more bird-like, he entered into conversation about it.

The noise alluded to always excited wonder especially with the older people, they believing it to be some kind of bird, as nothing but a bird can sing so sweetly, yet on going where the sound came from, nothing could be discovered. It made its appearance in the last of summer and disappeared in the early autumn.

It was the received opinion of the people fifty years ago that the swallows dove into the water and burrowed in the mud during the winter, and as they were first and last seen over the ponds and streams, and hence the mysterious sounds were supposed to emanate from some kind of a bird.

Thoreau said it was a frog and he thought he could show it to me. He described it as apparently a green leaf, and when near it would point in the direction with the stick he held in his hand. After giving me minute directions how to proceed and to do in all things as he did, we started in the direction of the object we had in view, which was some eight or ten rods distant. When it sang we hastened on and just before the last note was uttered, we stopped till it began again and then on as before. When we were within a few rods of it, we dropped on our hands and knees, and worked up to it stealthily, but only when it sang. At last we were rewarded with a full view of it some twelve feet distant. It rose slowly, inflated itself and uttered its little song. It had planned a retreat in case of surprise, and directly under the leaf it had a hole running down to the water and when we approached it disappeared.

Thus was solved by the sagacity of Thoreau, what had been heretofore a wonder and a mystery.

—Joseph Hosmer, "An Hour with Thoreau," *Concord Freeman*, August 22, 1878.

∞ ∾

He [Henry James, Sr.] never heard any attempt to typify God as a soul, without thinking of Thoreau's remark to [Bronson] Alcott at a conversation when the Concord philosopher began by saying, "All souls are plural." "I'm sorry for that," said Thoreau; "one is more than I can take care of."

—Mrs. John T. Sargent, ed., *Sketches and Reminiscences of the Radical Club* (Boston: James R. Osgood and Co., 1880), p. 56.

∽ ∾

Of the many beautiful suburban towns that environ Boston, Concord stands in the front rank. Setting aside its local history, and the hallowed associations that came up from the eight generations of my blood and kin that lie buried beneath its green turf; the old spot, with its varied landscapes of forests, lake and river, its grand old elms and good clean streets, is a place that in all things is hard to equal.

The people, also, have a delightful ease and independence that you find nowhere else. There are no distressingly rich and no poor in the town, but all possess an abundance of wealth that ministers to their mental and bodily wants and comforts.

Individuality is the one characteristic of the place, and it seems to be cultivated there. What other place in this wide world would tolerate a company of learned and distinguished persons a month in discussing great and vital questions on the Talleyrand Plan, viz: that words were given not to convey, but to cover them up?

A person is loved, honored and respected here, and holds his or her social position whether they believe in Bob Ingersoll's "mistakes of Moses" or John Calvin's creed; in devils incarnate or no devils at all. All live on that high-up democratic table land of solid-mind-your-own-business that belongs to that grand old town.

Fair Haven Cliffs, one of the favorite resorts of the Thoreaus', must be seen to be known and appreciated. The Concord river, with its serpentine figure pushing its way to the ocean; the Monadnoc and Washusett in the distance, together with Lake Walden in full view on the east, presents the same appearance to us that they did in our boyhood, and to remind us that, while we are changing and passing, they are not! Nothing can surpass this sublime picture of beauty and loveliness.

I rode up the boiling spring (minus the boil) on Fair Haven Hill, recently, and then took the path that Thoreau had often trod, over the top, down the "devil's stairway," over rocks, down its craggy sides, now sliding, now hanging by a twig that was anchored firmly to its side on to the bottom of the cliffs. I then followed westwards through brush and bramble to the river. The descent is not difficult, but the ascent is quite another thing. It was the same old way that, in my boy days, in company with John and Henry Thoreau, we wandered one bright spring day in a year that has so long since past that it now seems dim and shadowy. Many recollections were pleasing, but I often found my eyes wet with tears.

The ramble gave me a vivid reminder of one of Henry's exploits in after years, when he covered himself with brush and leaves one autumn night and awaited developments. After he had snugly prepared himself for the night's watch, he remained quiet. In the course of a few hours he heard the tread of an animal about his couch or hiding place. It was dark and prevented him from seeing what it was. Presently it began to poke its way in, when he with one punch of his cane revealed the fact that a skunk had come to say good evening to him. (In the skunk's own way.) Foxes he often saw and heard.

The drives among its hills and valleys, and through the several villages after an absence of six years was very interesting and pleasing, and for which I am indebted to my old friend R. N. Rice, and others for their politeness and company on many occasions.

—Joseph Hosmer, "In Praise of Concord Town," *Concord Freeman*, November 24, 1881.

⚭ ⚭

Thoreau was an enigma to all of us. No one could place him. His reticence and shyness, together with his rambling over the fields, waters and woodlands, by night and day, was uncommon and mysterious to his townspeople, to say the least. His field of operations was unknown and hidden to all. He studied the mysteries of nature's laws, with an earnest pleasure if not with brilliant results.

When he trundled his wheelbarrow down to the river's bank just at dusk, freighted with pitch-pine knots for an all night float on the "bosom" of his Concord, one of his neighbors would sometimes say, "I wonder how many gold dollars Thoreau expects to find on the bottom of the river?" and another "thought he would eventually become insane."

Thoreau was no egotist and he did not tell us all he knew, but like a skillful general, kept his reserves well in hand. Many persons may have seen at about this season of the year (Sept. 1st), a yellowish colored water grass in the Concord and Assabet rivers. It is to be found on the sandy bottom at "Hubbard's," and "Uncle Ben Hosmer's" fishing places, (that were) on the Concord. It grows entirely under the water, and the current gives to it a serpentine motion. It had always been a fruitful theme and a study to us as to how it came there, and how it renewed itself from year to year. It had no flower and no seed that we could discover, but it annually came and disappeared from altogether unknown causes to us. One day as Thoreau was perambulating the intervals on the Assabet, I asked him concerning this grass, if it was not a spontaneous production of nature? He said that it had a flower of a very delicate pinkish white, not larger than a pea; that it blossomed in the night and closed before sunrise in a fair day, so sensitive are the petals to the light. The grass was (and is now probably), very plenty on the bottom of the Assabet, from the railroad bridge near Derby's, to the same bridge east of the prison.

It is nearly twenty years since we laid away in Sleepy Hollow the machine, or body, that represented the will power, or spirit of the person, that we called H. D. Thoreau. When shut up in jail for non-payment of taxes, he said that H. D. Thoreau was out on the street all the same attending to his business, only the body that had done nothing was confined in prison walls.

Whatever relates to him, or that tends to reveal him as he was, is eagerly caught up and read by the public. His fame increases as the years roll away and the body becomes dust. He has many peculiar and absurd ideas, viewed from our standpoint, but the following apostrophe to the Concord Lyceum will be read and admired by all men hundreds of years hence as today, for the philosophical truths enunciated, the poetic beauty of expression, and its pure naturalness.

"I had often stood on the banks of the Concord, watching the lapse of the current, an emblem of all progress, following the same law with the system, with time, and all that is made; the weeds at the bottom gently bending down the stream, shaken by the watery wind, still planted where their seeds had sunk, but ere long to die and go down likewise; the shining pebbles, not yet anxious to better their condition, the chips and weeds, and occasional logs and stems of trees, that floated past, fulfilling their fate, were objects of singular interest to me, and at last I resolved to launch myself on its bosom, and float whither it would bear me."

—Joseph Hosmer, "Reminiscences of Thoreau," *Concord Freeman*, September 1, 1882.

∞ ∞

Thoreau's figure seems to me as distinct as if I had seen him yesterday. He was during more than two years a diligent student [at Harvard], bright and cheerful. I consulted him more than once about the translations of some of Horace's odes. In his junior year, he went out to Canton to teach school. There he fell into the company of Orestes A. Brownson, then a transcendentalist. He came back a transformed man. He was no longer interested in the college course of study. The world did not move as he would have it. While walking to Mount Auburn with me one afternoon, he gave vent to his spleen. He picked up a spear of grass, saying: "Here is something worth studying; I would give more to understand the growth of this grass than all the Greek and Latin roots in creation." The sight of a squirrel running on the wall at that moment delighted him. "That," said he, "is worth studying." The change that he had undergone was thus evinced. At an earlier period he was interested in all our studies. Many people today are deeply interested in his writings. My own interest in them has never been so great as that of some of my friends. The fault is probably my own.

—Amos Perry, "Old Days at Harvard," *Boston Transcript*, June 21, 1899.

∞ ∞

That Thoreau, he lived in a hut out there by the pond, he wasn't much, besides that he was insulting; he was an insulting man. . . .

Why, do you know my grandfather and Henry Thoreau pounded lead together [pencil making], yessir, they pounded lead together. . . .

Do you know what he said to my grandfather, I'll tell you what he said.

My grandfather used to take Thoreau home to eat dinner. Henry

Thoreau ate dinner at my grandfather's house plenty of times, when they were poundin' lead together.

One time my grandfather took Henry Thoreau home with him to eat dinner. When they got to the house the pigs were loose. My grandfather said, "Henry, help me drive the pigs out of the yard; you stand in the barn door over there. . . .

"You stand there and don't let the pigs run into the barn," grandfather asked Thoreau to guard the door. Henry stood in the door. Just then one of the pigs made a run for the barn. Henry started to head him off but the pig ran right between his legs. Knocked Henry right off his feet. He got up, dusted himself off and he said to my grandfather, *"Mr. Flannery, only an Irish pig would do a thing like that."* . . .

Imagine that, imagine him saying a thing like that . . . an Irish pig . . . I tell you that man was insulting.

—Charles Flannery, in John E. Nickols, "Thoreau and the Pig," *Thoreau Society Bulletin,* LXXVII (Fall, 1961), 1.

∽ ∾

Went up to see Henry Thoreau who is about starting on his expedition to the White Mts[.] in his boat. He has all things arranged prime and will have a glorious time if he is fortunate enough to have good weather. He showed me all the minutiae of packing and invited me up there to eat some fine melons in the evening. . . .

I spent . . . the rest of the time getting the fellows ready to go to the Thoreaus['] melon spree. We went about 9 and saw a table spread in the very handsomest style with all kinds and qualities of [p. 89] melons and we attacked them furiously and I eat [sic] till what with the wine & all I had quite as much as I could carry home.

—John Shepard Keyes, Diary for August 29, 1839, in Walter Harding, *The Days of Henry Thoreau* (New York: Knopf, 1965), pp. 89-90.

∽ ∾

Thoreau was wholly a Concordian. He was not a remarkable boy in any way only a decent scholar in our lower schools, and fitted for college, Harvard then requiring but little, by a year or two in the

Academy here. His father a poor dull inefficient man, always in debt, his Mother a proud ambitious woman who insisted on having Henry Educated [*sic*], and worked hard to accomplish it. In college he had no particular prominence for anything, was rather clownish and a butt for the jokes of the livelier fellows. I remember spending the three days before his commencement in his room with him (while being examined for admission in 1837) and being greatly amused at the fun and chaff of his classmates, who came to see him. He came back to Concord & with his brother opened a private school, and the boys made much fun of him. A picture of a booby in an almanack that year, resembled him so much that it was cut out, and shown round among his scholars as a likeness! and it did resemble him more than most caricatures. His school was not a success after his brother's death, and he gave it up and became a follower of Mr. Emerson who procured him a situation as tutor in Judge Emerson's family in N.Y. and after that in his own family where he lived several years. During this time, he was much with Mr. E.[,] caught his tones, manner, accent and expression as well as ideas and opinions till all who knew both were amused and exasperated at the close imitation. Then he began his Walden life and eked out his scanty fair [*sic*] in the woods by many a good meal at Mr. Emerson's or his mother[']s or Aunt[']s in the village. He affected or became very odd in his ways and his views, resisted taxation, because of the pro-slavery constitution of the U.S.! gave up voting & refusing to pay his poll tax of $2.00 was committed to jail here [p. 2] by the collector, and released after a short detention by the payment of the tax by Mr. Sam Hoar the Judge's father, and of sympathy for the family who were neighbours. . . . Thoreau occasionally lectured before the Lyceum here, before he printed anything, and the queer mixture of sense & nonsense he got off in his Emersonian style created much more laughter than applause in his audience. His life outdoors in the woods or the river was mostly solitary, occasionally in the company of Channing, the poet, & rarely with Hawthorne or Emerson or some of the cranks Emerson's fame drew to Concord and in this way he lived on, sometimes doing a job of surveying and plotting the lands of the farmers, when he wanted money; and doing this work with great care and accuracy, till his books were published, and he began to be read and talked about. His later years were spent in his own family home, where by the aid of his Aunts, who had some property the circumstances were more prosperous. During his last years, his health failed and he became more of a recluse from outside than ever before. One of his last public appearances was at the meeting of the citizens of Concord to hold funeral exercises on the day of the Execution of John Brown and was characteristic. It had been arranged that all who took part should read suitable selections from books, not trust to their own expression of indignation lest in the intense excitement of the occasion language might be used that would make trouble; Mr. Emerson, Mr. Alcott, the minister & others all conformed to the agreement but Thoreau made a long speech of his own ideas and opinions! As to my impressions of him as a man, he has been called the poet naturalist without much claim to either title. He was Indian like in his observations, not scientific, and his poetry was more bookish than original, except in the metre. He was a very quiet shy reserved boy, and as a man showed the same traits in his intercourse with others, reserving his egotism and conceit for his journal and his books. . . . He was *not* a mere intellectual machine but in his young manhood had a love affair of which you will see many traces in his journal from 1840 to 42 or 3. It amounted to nothing, except that not being reciprocated it perhaps tended to make him more recluse and unsociable. In these years, he was very agreeable and interesting to the children of Mr. Emerson, who loved him dearly & to this day have great affection for his memory. Later on he ceased to show this affectionate side of his character, though he could always interest and amuse the boys of the village by his power of observation of natural objects, when they met him in his walks. "Nature" one good lady said to him "you always talk about Nature, as if she was your mother-in-law"!

In person he was about the average size rather above than below medium height, "active spare and wiry" never well dressed in his manhood, always suggesting in his looks something of the hermit, very light blue almost gray eyes, "swarthy complexion and an inscrutable expression." I agree with you that he "never gave a warm grasp of the hand," to any acquaintances nor perhaps to his friends in his later years for he was very undemonstrative, but he did have some tenderness in his eyes,"* and a warm smile to those he loved and liked, while he could be very cold and forbidding to those who did not he thought appreciate him and his opinions. Until his health began to fail, he was clean-shaved, after that he let his beard grow, a tawny [word] full one, that with the whim that possessed him, of never blacking his boots, gave him

*[Open quotation marks missing in the original source.—Ed.]

an uncouth uncivilized look. He had a rather full mouth and lips that retained a youthful almost lisping appearance, till hidden by his beard, and a pleasant agreeable voice in conversation, a dry wit, and many quips in his familiar talk. As said before he had few intimates. He could talk much with a good listener but was silent under any discussion or disagreement, and was never convinced by any argument. He had unbounded faith in himself, but was without ambition, and independent of all social or political considerations. His philosophy of life was that of an educated Indian; to read Plato in his wigwam, visit the college library when not hunting and fishing, and have all the learning and civilization of the past ages, ready at hand when he cared to seek them, to pay no taxes, walk where he chose without regard to fences or paths, but carefully survey and accurately measure each man's land who would pay him for it, attend no church or school, but preach himself when invited and secured listeners— . . .

You may think my view of him "Philistine," for I confess to something of that in me,—but as you have the other side in the 'life' and 'cult' of him, your picture may be truer for the shadows.

—John Shepard Keyes, Letter to Francis H. Underwood, November 15, 1886, in *Thoreau Society Bulletin*, CIII (Spring, 1968), 2-3.

☞ ☜

Mr. Thoreau was always unkempt. His clothes were ill fitting, his coat had a big wrinkle in the back; vest too short, giving glimpses of buckles and suspenders; and pants too short, showing unpolished bootlegs.

Every hair of his head seemed to have an individuality of its own, and at war with every other hair creating a painful discord. I think his laundry work must have been his own personal care. No washerwoman would have risked her laundry reputation and turned off such work.

It seems almost cruel to criticise him so unmercifully; but he did the same to others and this was only a schoolgirl's opinion. Now, I might not notice such things.

His cynicism—his sneering at others, knew no bounds. People who were rich were thieves and did not use their money right. If they were poor, they were worthless and idle. He thought there should be no money—that people should exchange labor when they wanted anything. Perhaps he was a Socialist; I have never been able to know exactly what they believe.

There was one redeeming trait in his character; he loved nature and all animals and birds as much as he disliked people, and all society. He rarely smiled but when he did, it transfigured him; what was homely became beautiful; but the smile soon died and there was not much in life to bring it back.

He was a vegetarian; believed it was wrong to murder anything. He was of medium height, very thin, with rather stooping shoulders and angular features.

Thoreau had written one book then. He gave me a copy. I have forgotten the title.

—Celia P. R. Frease, in "She Helped Open Cincinnati Medical Colleges to Women," *Cincinnati Post & Times-Star,* April 12, 1969.

∞ ∞

[*1842.*]
Henry Thoreau had been one of the family for the last year, & charmed Waldo [Emerson's young son] by the variety of toys whistles boats popguns & all kinds of instruments which he could make & mend; & possessed his love & respect by the gentle firmness with which he always treated him.

—Ralph Waldo Emerson, *The Journals and Miscellaneous Notebooks* (Cambridge: Harvard University Press, 1970), VIII, 165.

∞ ∞

B. W. Lee of Newport, New York, said, "The year I was sixteen, I went to the Thoreau school in the Old Academy for two months. Henry Thoreau had a very small class of boys in Greek and Latin and maybe had young ladies in French. He used to come in just before recess both morning and afternoon. He came in at a rapid pace, commenced work at once in his peculiar odd way and the boy that had not got his lesson did not receive much mercy or taffy. He was very strict in that matter. As well [p. 80] as I can remember, he was a thin, spare man, thin-faced, light complexion[ed], and weighed perhaps 140 pounds, rather on his dignity, and so far as I can remember not inclined to joking and fun, with his scholars outside of the school house." . . .

William Ellery Channing says that the work that Henry did in the family pencil factory was just in proportion to the needs of the family. When they were straitened in means because of any special needs, like building the house, then he would go to work and do more; but, for himself, he would never have done any of the mechanical work. [p. 81]

Benjamin Tolman told me, "Once or twice Thoreau came to my printing office to look over the proof of something of his that I was printing—his Cattle Show address and some other things, and I went to his home, too, about proof. He was agreeable and pleasant, but I didn't see much of him or talk with him because he knew so much more and was so superior a man to me that I didn't feel like it." But when I asked, "But you don't mean that he put on airs of superiority; he was companionable and friendly, wasn't he?" He replied, "Always! Oh, yes, he was a very pleasant person."

Warren Miles, who worked in the Thoreau pencil factory, when asked if he knew Thoreau, replied, "Yes, I knew him very well." "What should you say of him?" "He was a good mechanic—rather inclined to improvements of arts as well as mechanical matters. He was better educated on Nature than any man I ever saw. I remember a long talk we had about mud turtles and about wildflowers. He would almost always get up some argument so as to get one interested. He liked creatures. He told me that he rather tamed a squirrel that lived close by him, and that he was about as much company as a person after he got him used to him."

George Keyes told me that he attended the Academy when it was taught by the Thoreau brothers. "How were they as schoolmasters?" "Very pleasant indeed. Yes, I have a very pleasant impression left in my mind of that school. I remember how interesting his stories were. One evening shortly after his return from Cape Cod, he told us about that expedition and about the old worn copper coin he found on the beach. Another time he was delighted because, being out very early in the morning, he had found the track of some very rare wild animal in the snow leading right up the meadow. He was light-haired, better looking than his portraits, had a healthy complexion with a bright color, though rather pale for an out-of-doors man. He had a strong [p. 82] prominent nose and good eyes; a face that you would long remember."

Talked with James Garty about H.D.T. I asked, "Suppose I did not know of him and asked you what kind of man he was, what would you say of him?" "*Well, it wouldn't do to have everybody like him,* of his way of thinking. Oh, he was a good sort of man and was straight and I think would pay every cent he owed to any man—I don't know whether he had any debts—but what I mean when I say it would be bad if everybody thought as he did that he didn't believe in government."

Frank C. Brown remembers Thoreau's singing "Tom Bowline" and "that he put his heart into it." He knew that he used to entertain his mother (Mrs. Lucy C. Brown) by singing and by dancing (*pas seul*). Thoreau used to give Frank natural history information, especially about the forest trees, and found him always willing, even eager, to impart. He doesn't clearly recollect his personal appearance, except his prominent nose and that his skin seemed dark, probably from out-of-door exposure, tan. (Mrs. Frank Brown said that his look and complexion and eye reminded one of a longshoreman.) Frank said that the principal impression left by Thoreau was his universal knowledge—that he went to him with every question as to birds, trees, etc., and he could tell him about them. He recalls him as good-humored and talkative and as habitually in good spirits.

Mrs. Edwin Bigelow knew the Thoreau family well for years, when they lived opposite in the Parkman House. Her first recollection of Henry is seeing him a youth with fair hair and erect, a serious face with mouth drawn together in a characteristic curve, come out of the yard and walk towards the Academy where he then taught. She knew at once by his gait and bearing that he was a gentleman. As a neighbor, Henry was pleasant and helpful, but by no means aggressive or vain or egotistical, drop[p. 83]ping in and out and lending a hand naturally as it came his way to do so. He was friendly to his Irish neighbors and good to stray cats and dogs and always humane to animals, and more than this, *respected* them.

Mrs. Bigelow tells how at the "Little Woods" picnics, Henry would tell all to sit absolutely quiet and close together—then he would go forward cautiously, sprinkle crumbs before them, and then, retreating, seat himself a little before the others and begin a sort of rolling or humming sound and would draw squirrels to come and eat at last out of his hands. He would open his hands in the river and let the fish swim into them.

One Sunday as the congregations were coming home from church, Henry Thoreau came up the street with a tree in his hand which he had dug up to plant. His old aunt, the Orthodox Miss Dunbar, hastened out to reprove him and abate this scandal in the family, but he answered her pleasantly, "Aunt Louisa, I have been worshipping in my way, and I don't trouble you in your way."

I asked Mrs. Bigelow about Thoreau's connection with the Underground Railroad. While Henry Thoreau was in the woods, the slaves sometimes were brought to him there, but obviously there was no possible concealment in his house, so he would look after them by day, and at nightfall, get them to his mother's or another house of hiding. He was always ready to help with service and didn't count risk, and also, although he had little money, always gave or advanced money to a slave who needed it. Sometimes this was repaid from the fund. It was no part of his plan in making the Walden hermitage to make there a refuge for fugitives, that was only incidental.

Dr. Thomas Hosmer of Bedford . . . went with the Thoreaus in search of Indian relics. Once he found a sort of hollow, scooped like a small amphitheatre, on the side of the bluff over the Great Meadows and showed it to Thoreau who said, "This is artificial, made by the Indians, and we ought to find evidences [p. 84] of their fires here." They accordingly dug at the center and found charcoal and Indian relics, a mortar and pestle, etc. Hosmer also found a large block of the dark-grey flint with white specks such as most of the arrow and spearheads found in the neighborhood were made of, the mass weighing nearly fifty pounds. He showed it to the Thoreaus who told him that the nearest place where that stone was native to the soil, geographically, was Norwich, Connecticut.

[Reminiscing further of his days as a student in the Thoreau school] Hosmer said Thoreau spoke of the certainty we must feel of a wise and friendly power over us. He bade the boys and girls think, if any of them should go into a shop and see all the nicely finished wheels, pinions, springs and frame pieces of a watch lying spread out on a bench and again came to find them exactly put together and working in unison to move the hands on a dial and show the passage of time—whether they could believe that this had come by chance or rather should know that somebody with thought and plan and power had been there. This, I believe, used to be a familiar argument and example in philosophical and religious treatises, but its use in the Grammar School by the young schoolmaster showed that he knew himself there to teach broadly and awaken thought and not merely his lessons in the rudiments of letters.

There was a class in Natural Philosophy. If any pupil seemed to care for the study and took pains with [his] drawings on the blackboard illustrating the principles, Henry would take much interest and pains to help him along. The brothers would sometimes come out into the school yard at recess and join the children in their amusements; John more than Henry who was not so familiar with all the children as his elder brother but was interested in individual children.

Sometimes in winter the Bedford boys came swiftly and smoothly up the frozen river on skates. One day three Concord boys derided their old-fashioned skates and strapping which the Bedford boys defended by appealing to the test of best performance. Henry, hearing this, said, "Come boys, that's a good [p. 85] challenge. I move we accept it and go down to the river in the afternoon. If they find fault with the skates they must show that they can do better on theirs." It was agreed on and as they went to the river, Hosmer argued with Henry Thoreau that the race ought to begin from the moment they knelt on the ice to buckle on the skates, saying that in the quality of the skates should properly be included the care and speed with which they could be put on. But Henry said, "No, I shall overrule that: the question is now of speed in skating." Afterward he visited Thoreau [who was] living at Walden [and] who talked with him, inquiring of him of what use he found his school studies in life.

Edward Neally told me that when he was a boy he carried the chain for Thoreau on a survey near Fairhaven. Later he did so often, and his interest in natural history (birds, beasts and fishes; he never took to botany) was first awakened by him and afterwards he cared greatly for it and collected for the Natural History Society and sometimes for the Smithsonian Institute at Washington.

Thoreau seemed a careful manager, and he found him very different from what some people think; he always seemed jolly and

social, liked a joke. The difference between him and other scientific men
that he had seen, like Agassiz and Horace Mann, was they liked to have
the creature killed and dissect and examine it carefully in every way to
see how it was made, "but Thoreau liked to study 'em living. He didn't
like to have 'em killed (oh, he didn't mind if I'd shoot a duck when we
were out together), but he would rather know what they'd do. He had
more patience than any man I ever knew. He would keep still and watch
what they would do for more than an hour and a half. I would get tired
waiting, but he wouldn't. He was a very strong man for his size, thick-set
though he wasn't very large. He always walked with easy long steps; it
would tire me well to keep up with him."

"How did people in general like him; what did the folks on the
Milldam [Concord's main street] think of him?" "They rather liked him
as a rule. Some of them couldn't understand him. He [p. 86] had a few
who were his enemies. One of them was a farmer, a good man, too, but
he thought ill of Thoreau and always spoke badly of him. But the trouble
began years ago when the Thoreaus set his woods afire by accident and
they was burned over. Another thing he never liked was that Thoreau
said to him one day when he met him on his farm that he got all the hard
work and trouble out of it and Thoreau got all the beauty out of it. You
see, he didn't know how to take it. Thoreau didn't mean any harm.
There was another man that was always down on Thoreau, but then for
that matter, he lost wood by that same fire. Most people rather liked
him, but many didn't understand him." Neally said (in answer to my
inquiry as to whether he thought Thoreau a helpful, friendly man to his
kind), "Yes, if I had been in trouble and needed assistance I don't know
but I'd have turned to him as quick as to any man."

Sam Staples told me, "I used to go surveying with Thoreau a great
deal. We've run a great many lines together. He was a good surveyor and
very careful. Albert Wood'll tell you that he never in his surveying finds
any better work done than that that Henry Thoreau did.

"When I bought that farm next to your father's, I had him run the
lines for me. I guess 'twas about the last work he did. Well, the line
against your father's pear orchard and meadow running down to the
brook I'd always supposed was right, as his hedge ran, and so I dug that
ditch between his meadow and mine, right in the line of the hedge. Well,
when we come to run the line, the corner of the hedge on the Turnpike
was right, but when we got to the other end of the hedge, 'twas several

feet over on to what I'd bought. And at the brook, the ditch which I'd dug to it from the hedge-corner, supposing that was the line, came much as a rod into my meadow by the deed. That tickled Thoreau mightily. 'We'll call Emerson down and show it to him,' says he. 'Oh, never mind,' says I, 'he don't know about it; let it be as it is.' 'No,' says he, 'I'll get Emerson down.' So he went up to the house and told him we got something to show him down [p. 87] at the meadow, and he put on his hat and came down along with Henry. Well, when we got him down there, Thoreau, says he, 'I didn't think this of you, Mr. Emerson, stealing so much land of Staples here.' Well, your father was troubled when he saw where the ditch was over in my land. 'I'll pay you for the land,' says he, 'what's it worth?' 'Oh, no,' says I, 'I dug the ditch there supposing the hedge was the line. 'Twan't your fault. 'Twas the man you bought of showed you where to put the hedge. Let it be as the ditch is now.' It pleased Thoreau to get that joke on him."

Elizabeth J. Weir went to school (1843) to Miss Sophia Thoreau in the Parkman House. She saw John and Henry as not alike: John had less pronounced features and was plumper. Henry had *fair* hair, large eyes—with outer parts of lids drooping, and large pupils—very blue. She listened eagerly for stories of birds and squirrels. He had a pleasing appearance to young people and children. So much life! She can see him with the children around him standing on the door-steps with one foot on the upper step telling stories and a circle of children about him. People misunderstood him—on the street he didn't always stop "to pass the time of day," but sometimes passed on his business without noticing people—thinking. At his mother's house with Sophia, all the little everyday things were made funny and agreeable. Henry would give such pleasant turns to conversation, make things spicy and interesting. He saw the ludicrous side; enjoyed the unusual. Like twins—he and Sophia; he opened his thought to her.

[Miss Weir worked much at Mr. Emerson's.] Henry would come in and offer to mend things. He saw what was waiting, as an odd job, and mended it. If Mrs. Emerson were there, they would have pleasant little conversations; get on deep subjects. Henry was a help to Mrs. Emerson in all ways, being younger—he appreciated her fine mind and beautiful thought, and she thus helped educate him. He loved her elder sister Mrs. Brown, and was as a son to her. She depended on him; she would say, "Run [p.88] over to Mr. Emerson's and see if Henry is there. Get him to

come over and see if anything can be done about my stove's smoking."
He would look at the damper or latch and mend and fit. While at work at
these jobs, he would prolong the conversation. It seemed a favour to
him to ask him to do something. He burned out the chimneys on rainy
days, the excited children watching the process.

I met Daniel F. Potter this morning, November 17, 1904, and said
to him, "Mr. Potter, I understand that Henry Thoreau once give you a
thrashing." He was passing me to go into the post office, but turned
instantly and said, "Yes, he did, and it smarts still." He spoke with
energy, and I thought with a little feeling. "Then it wasn't justly
given?" I asked. "No, sir, it wasn't," he replied. "I can tell you all about
it if you want to know." And standing in the doorway to the post office,
with a particularly sharp wind doing no good, I am sure, to his inflamed
right eye, he told me the following, which I give in words as near to his as
I can. He spoke as if he remembered the incident perfectly.

"I was a little fellow of ten, and was going to school in the brick
school house that is now the Masonic Hall. There were men teachers
there, but I'd just come from the district school, where I had a woman
teacher. Now the women teachers taught, when we'd finished with a
lesson, to put away our books and fold our arms." And the little old man
illustrated, blinking through his spectacles. "Well, the rule at the
Academy was that a boy should always have a book before him. First
thing I knew, Henry Thoreau called me up and thrashed me. He
thrashed twelve other boys that day, thirteen in all, and resigned the day
after.

"I didn't understand the reason for this then, but I found out later.
It seems he'd been taken to task by someone—I think 'twas Deacon
Ball—for not using the rod enough. So Thoreau thought he'd give the
other way a thorough trial, and he did, for one day. The next day he said
he wouldn't keep school any longer, if that was the way he had to do it.
[p. 89]

"When I went to my seat, I was so mad that I said to myself, 'When
I'm grown up, I'll whip you for this, old feller.' But," and Mr. Potter
chuckled, "I never saw the day I wanted to do it.—Why, Henry
Thoreau was the kindest hearted of men. He only kept school in
Concord for two weeks."

Horace Hosmer, another student in the school, states, "Henry told his mother to buy gold and plumbago at the commencement of the war; Louis F. Ball told me that he should have made twice as much as he did had he followed Henry's advice."

—Edward Waldo Emerson, "A Different Drummer," in Walter Harding, ed., *Henry David Thoreau: A Profile* (New York: Hill & Wang, 1971), pp. 80-90.

∽ ∾

When teaching in Concord, I knew Thoreau rather intimately. I look back on him as striding with duck-like legs across the common towards his weather beaten home. He had a long body low to the ground. His face was a long oval & it wore an air of solemnity. I fancy that he was consciously, a priest of nature. His life was ideal and independent of the artificialities of society. When I knew him he lived with his father who was a pencil maker. The son showed me the process, one day, of rounding and grooving the cedar for the lead. His soul was stainless as glass. . . . In the course of his contemplative life, he became as independent of Mr. Emerson's views as Mr. Emerson was of the views of the multitude.

—Isaac Newton Goodhue, Diary for May 19, 1900, in Roger W. Cummins, "Thoreau and Isaac Newton Goodhue," *Thoreau Society Bulletin*, CXXIII (Spring, 1973), 2.

∽ ∾

At the time of the first World's Fair in London [1851] Thoreau met one morning the richest man in Concord and asked him when he would leave for the Great Fair. The man said, "Why I am not going. I have just paid five hundred dollars for a pair of oxen." While the man was talking about something else Thoreau stared at him so hard, the man asked, "Are you sick? You look so strange." "No wonder," said Thoreau. "You are the first man I have ever seen with a pair of oxen hung around his neck."

—Susan Beeson, Letter to Charles Perry, November 13, 1929, in Thomas Blanding, "Beans, Baked and Half-Baked," *Concord Saunterer*, XI (Fall, 1976), 13.

∽ ∾

As a teacher Henry was "merciless" i.e. the thing to be done must *be* done *correctly.* He was rigidly exacting—a *faithful* teacher to the parent whose child he had & to the child. He never mixed with the schoolboys; he was hated. The bell tolled instead of rang, when he taught alone during John's illness. Did not answer the boys['] questions by the River. "He had no enemies." He did not have the "love-idea" in him: i.e. he did not appear to feel the *sex*-attraction.

—Horace R. Hosmer in conversation with Samuel Arthur Jones, in George Hendrick, ed., *Remembrances of Concord and the Thoreaus* (Urbana: University of Illinois Press, 1977), p. 131.

∽ ᗡ

David [Henry Thoreau] had a party of gentlemen, Thursday evening, to eat melons. I went in to see the table, which was adorned with sunflowers, cornstalks, beet leaves & squash-blossoms. There were forty-six melons, fifteen different kinds; & apples, all the production of his own garden. This is the only thing of interest that has happened in town this week. When we went in to see the tables, Mrs. Thoreau felt called upon to apologize for Henry having a party, it having been spread abroad by her that such customs met with his contempt & entire disapprobation.

—Elizabeth Hoar, Letter to the Bowles family of Springfield, undated, in *Thoreau Society Bulletin*, CXXXVIII (Winter, 1977), 5.

∽ ᗡ

I have often heard my old uncle, who lived to be ninety-three, tell of how he, as a boy, often went to Thoreau's cove at Walden Pond, and once ventured to the door of the Hermit's cabin and asked for a drink of water, to which Thoreau replied: "My son, I drink the waters of the pond. If it is good enough for me, it is good enough for you."

—Maud Appleton McDowell, in *Thoreau Society Bulletin*, CXLI (Fall, 1977), 8.

∽ ᗡ

Mr. Thoreau's services as a land surveyor were in constant demand, and whenever we met him as we roamed the woods and fields, he was very cordial and never failed to direct us to the ripest blueberries and to the trees which bore the best chestnuts. His familiarity with animals was an ever present wonder to us. He pulled the woodchuck out of his hole by the tail, the hunted fox came to him for protection, and we once saw two wild striped squirrels run into his open waistcoat, and he had only to put his hand in the water to bring out the much coveted trout.

But no entreaties ever induced him to show us where his rare floral friends made their homes. He had no secrets, however, from Mr. Minot Pratt, and only a couple years before his death I had an amusing interview with him. Mr. Pratt had promised to take me to the only place in Concord where the climbing fern could be found. I had given my word of honor that I would not tell, and in due season we were on the ground. In the midst of our enjoyment we heard a snapping of twigs, a brisk step, in the bordering thicket, and in a second Mr. Thoreau's spare figure and amazed face confronted us. Mr. Pratt answered for my trustworthiness, and so won over Mr. Thoreau by representing what a deed of charity it was to enlighten my ignorance that he climbed with us into our clumsy vehicle and by circuitous ways took us to the haunt of a much rarer plant which he said nobody else in Concord had ever found. I was sincerely grateful and not backward in telling him so. But noticing an odd twinkle in Mr. Pratt's eye, I asked him later what it meant. He told me he [p. 100] had known of the plant years before Mr. Thoreau found it, and that the spot was not half a mile from where Mr. Thoreau discovered us. He had doubled and redoubled upon his track [simply] to puzzle and prevent my ever finding the place again. [November 10, 1891.]

—Annie Sawyer Downs, "Mr. Hawthorne, Mr. Thoreau, Miss Alcott, Mr. Emerson, and Me,"*American Heritage*, XXX, no. 1 (December, 1978), 100-101. Used by permission. Copyright 1978 by American Heritage.

∽ ∾

I was in one of the stores the other day, when a gentleman said, "Well, you are having quite a little to say about Henry Thoreau, did you know him?" "No" I replied, "I never even saw him, that I know of."

"Well, I have, I used to work, when a boy at Sam Barrett's mill," (grist mill, near North branch on Spencer brook) "and Thoreau used to come in there quite often. He was in one day when some boys were there, and they asked me if I was going in swimming, I said, no, I was afraid of the water snakes. Thoreau said they would not hurt me, and asked if there was any chance of one being out, so I shut off the water, and we went up the brook, found one about three feet long, when Thoreau went up carefully, picked up the snake, and showed us that it had no sting in its tail, and no bones in its head, that would give it power to bite, & that it was perfectly harmless, and since that time," he added, "I lost all my fear of the snakes."

—Alfred W. Hosmer, Letter to S. A. Jones, November 20, 1895, in Fritz Oehlschlaeger and George Hendrick, eds., *Towards the Making of Thoreau's Modern Reputation* (Urbana: University of Illinois Press, 1979), p. 247.

∽ ∾

George Bartlett used to visit Thoreau at Walden & remembers how the house was arranged. He recalls his pausing to hear distant birds, telling what bird it was, whether male or female that sung or chirped; also calling attention to insect sounds & his inferring the insect's state of mind.

[Walton Ricketson remembers that his mother] used to play on the piano and once asked Thoreau if he cared for music and sung himself. "Yes," he said, "I am fond of music and, when I am in the woods, I sometimes like to sing,["] and when she asked him if he would sing to the family he said, "Oh, I fear, if I do, I shall take the roof of the house off!" His hostess urged him, and sat down to play his accompaniment, and he sang "Tom Bowline." He sang with spirit and expression giving the full sentiment of the verses. [This I (Edward Emerson), well remember as a child. I used to think how much he used to care for this mythical or representative Tom Bowline, and it seems as if he stood in his mind for his lost brother, for there was sympathy & admiration and a tear in his voice.] Ricketson remembers also his singing "Row brothers Row."

[Warren Miles told me:] "I think that the reason that he went down to Walden to live was to pry into the arts of Nature to get something that wasn't open to the public[.] He liked the creatures. He told me that he rather tamed a squirrel that lived close by him and that he was about as much company as a person after he got him used to him. He seemed to think that its Nature could be improved."

[According to Horace Hosmer], one day Henry T. said to old Joseph Hosmer, "Do you know a white grape that bears every year on high land?" "Yes, only one, up near [the] Sudbury line near Deacon Dakin's rye field. If you go to leeward of it you'll smell it." Henry laughed and said he didn't believe another man knew of that vine. . . .

Once I [Horace Hosmer] was with the school boys on the banks of the river and one asked, "What makes those heaps of stones in the river? We knock 'em down with our boat and the next week they are built up." Just then H. D. T. came along and I was deputed to ask him. His answer was "I asked an old Crow Indian and he said that muskrats made 'em. I told him that he was mistaken and I knew more than he[,"] and I asked and he said[,] "Lamprey eels made 'em."

Edward Neally says that Henry Thoreau told him that he believed the Indians about Concord would have been more likely to bury their dead on Nashawtuc [Hill], where the Assabet comes to the high bank, than elsewhere and gave as a reason that they could bring their dead in canoes conveniently from their settlements which were mainly along the higher banks of the two branches and [the] main river. This spot would be easily accessible from all their places by canoes. Later when the Lowell R. R. cut was made his prophecy was fulfilled by the finding of two Indian skeletons on the hillside within a few rods of the river just above the Hemlocks.

Mrs. Deacon White . . . used to visit the Thoreaus. She liked Miss Sophia much. They were a very pleasant kindly family among themselves. Henry she did not get so well acquainted with in those days[,] he seemed rather silent, perhaps depressed (it was soon after John's death).

When he went to Walden the family worried about him a good deal at first. It seemed a dangerous and uncomfortable adventure. The first night that he slept there she and Miss Sophia were so filled with anxiety about him that they got little sleep.

She went down with Miss Sophia one of the first days that he lived there and carried him some food that his Mother wanted him to have. She thought he didn't like to receive it very well. The house seemed very bare of everything.

—Edward Waldo Emerson, "Notes on Thoreau." Manuscript in the possession of the late Raymond Emerson, Concord, Massachusetts.

Appendixes

I. A Thoreau Chronology

1817 Born in Concord, Massachusetts, July 12, third child of John and Cynthia Dunbar Thoreau.

1829–1833 Educated at Concord Academy.

1833–1837 Educated at Harvard College, graduating with a B.A. in 1837.

1837 Taught for a few days in Concord public schools but resigned when he was required to administer corporal punishment.

1838–1841 Conducted a private school in Concord with his brother John.

1839 Made excursion on the Concord and Merrimack Rivers with his brother John.

1840 First essays and poems published in the *Dial*.

1841–1843 Lived with Ralph Waldo Emerson and his family.

1842 His brother John died.

1843 From May to December tutored William Emerson's children on Staten Island.

1844 With Edward Hoar, accidentally set fire to Concord woods.

1845–1847 Lived in a cabin at Walden Pond.

1846 Was arrested and imprisoned for one night for nonpayment of taxes.
Made a trip to the Maine woods.

1847–1848 Lived with the Emerson family while Ralph Waldo Emerson was in England on a lecture tour.

1848 Delivered a lecture on "Civil Disobedience" in Concord and for the first time began to lecture outside Concord.

1848   Published his first book, *A Week on the Concord and Merrimack Rivers.*
       Made his first trip to Cape Cod.
1850   Made another trip to Cape Cod and an excursion to Canada with Ellery Channing.
1853   Made a second trip to the Maine woods.
1854   Published *Walden.* Lectured on "Slavery in Massachusetts" in Framingham.
1855   Again visited Cape Cod.
1856   Surveyed the Eagleswood community in Perth Amboy, New Jersey, and visited Walt Whitman in Brooklyn.
1857   Visited Cape Cod and the Maine woods. Met Captain John Brown in Concord.
1858   Visited the White Mountains and Monadnock.
1859   Father died. Lectured on "A Plea for Captain John Brown."
1860   Camped out on Mount Monadnock. Contracted the cold that led to his fatal illness.
1861   Visited Minnesota with Horace Mann, Jr., in a vain search for health.
1862   Died, May 6, in Concord.

II. Biographical Notes
on the Authors

John Albee (1833). Poet; literary critic; and disciple of Emerson. He visited Emerson in Concord in May, 1852.

Amos Bronson Alcott (1799). Educator; author; father of Louisa May Alcott; close associate of Ralph Waldo Emerson; resident of Concord from 1840; superintendent of Concord schools from 1859 to 1865.

Louisa May Alcott (1832). Daughter of Bronson Alcott; author of *Little Women* and other children's classics; resident of Concord from 1840 on.

William Rounseville Alger (1822). Unitarian clergyman in Boston; denounced Thoreau's philosophy in *The Solitudes of Nature and of Man* (1867).

George Bartlett (1832). Lifetime resident of Concord and later author of the standard guidebook *Concord: Historic, Literary, and Picturesque* (Boston: Lothrop, 1885).

Susan Beeson. Has not been identified.

Mrs. Edwin Bigelow. A close friend of the Thoreaus, she was active in the Underground Railroad in Concord, helping to smuggle escaped slaves to freedom in Canada.

Harrison Gray Otis Blake (1816). Ex-clergyman; teacher; resident of Worcester; perhaps Thoreau's most devoted disciple; from 1848 on the two men corresponded and visited with each other regularly; inheritor from Sophia Thoreau of Thoreau's manuscript journals.

Frank C. Brown (1829). A nephew of Mrs. Ralph Waldo Emerson, he grew up in Concord and became one of Thoreau's closest young friends.

Mary Hosmer Brown (1856). Granddaughter of Thoreau's friend Edmund Hosmer. She was born in Detroit, Michigan, in 1856, but visited Concord frequently.

Theo[philus] Brown (1811). Worcester tailor; close friend of H. G. O. Blake; frequent visitor to Thoreau at Concord.

William H. Brown (1849). Son of a Concord dry-goods merchant; later for many years deacon of the Concord First Parish Church.

Edward S. Burgess (1855). Biologist and educator; lived in Washington, D.C., and New York City; a friend of Edward Sherman Hoar; interviewed Hoar in 1892 and compiled from the interview an extensive manuscript entitled "Notes on Concord People" (now in the Concord Free Public Library), which is filled with cryptic abbreviations that I have expanded within brackets. Mrs. Marcia Moss, curator of collections at the Concord Free Public Library, has recently identified Burgess, who had been a mystery to Thoreau scholars for many years.

John Burroughs (1837). New York State nature writer and disciple of Emerson; visited Concord only after Thoreau's death.

Mr. Carr. Sanborn identifies Mr. Carr simply as a friend from Concord, New Hampshire, "who came down . . . to work in the mills and on the farm of the Barretts" of Concord, Massachusetts.

[William] Ellery Channing (1818). Poet, biographer of Thoreau and his closest companion for many years; resident of Concord from 1842 on; nephew of the Unitarian clergyman of the same name.

Samuel A. Chase. Apparently a resident of Haverhill, Massachusetts, where Thoreau occasionally did some surveying for his Dunbar cousins.

Ednah Littlehale Cheney (1824). Author; reformer; biographer of Louisa May Alcott; frequent visitor in Concord.

Robert Collyer (1823). Unitarian clergyman whom Thoreau visited in Chicago in May of 1861.

Moncure Daniel Conway (1832). Unitarian clergyman; biographer of Emerson; a native of Virginia, he became an ardent Abolitionist. While a student at Harvard Divinity School in the early 1850's, he frequently visited Thoreau and Emerson in Concord.

George Willis Cooke (1848). Unitarian clergyman; lecturer; biographer of several minor Transcendentalists; resident of nearby Lexington.

George William Curtis (1824). Author; Brook Farmer; resident of Concord in the mid-1840's when he helped Thoreau raise the frame of his Walden cabin; later an editor of *Harper's Magazine.*

Caroline H. Dall (1822). Reformer; writer; lecturer; wife of Thoreau's Harvard classmate Charles H. A. Dall, a Unitarian missionary to India.

Henrietta M. Daniels. Resident of West Newton, Massachusetts, and friend of Thoreau's disciple, H. G. O. Blake.

Annie Sawyer Downs (c. 1836). She grew up in Concord, the daughter of a homeopathic physician. In later years she became known as both a poet and a botanist.

Mary Brown Dunton (1842). Daughter of Reverend Addison Brown, an amateur botanist whom Thoreau visited in Brattleboro, Vermont, in 1856. She later sent Thoreau boxes of mayflowers in 1858 and 1859.

Priscilla Rice Edes (1831). Born in neighboring Littleton, she moved to Concord in 1850 when she married Robert B. Edes, Jr.

Edward Waldo Emerson (1844). Son of Ralph Waldo Emerson; later a medical doctor in his native Concord. In 1917, to commemorate the centennial of Thoreau's birth and to defend his childhood friend from charges of coldness and inhumanity, he published *Henry Thoreau as Remembered by a Young Friend.*

Lidian Jackson Emerson (1802). Wife of Ralph Waldo Emerson.

Ralph Waldo Emerson (1803). Essayist; lecturer; former Unitarian clergyman; moved to Concord in 1835 and shortly thereafter became acquainted with Thoreau; Thoreau lived in the Emerson household from 1841 to 1843 and from 1847 to 1848.

James T. Fields (1817). Author; senior member of Ticknor & Fields, publishers of *Walden;* editor of *Atlantic Monthly* (1861–1870).

Charles Flannery. The grandson of Michael Flannery, an Irish resident of Concord whom Thoreau befriended.

Pat Flannery. C. T. Ramsey, who reports this interview, says simply that Flannery was a Concord Irishman.

Celia P. R. Frease (1830). A resident of southern Ohio, she was one of the early woman graduates of the medical school in Geneva, New York. Where or how she got to know Thoreau is unknown, though it was possibly through Horace Greeley, who was a close friend.

Mrs. Daniel Chester French (1861). Born in Washington, D.C.; married the famous Concord sculptor; did not come to Concord until 1878, sixteen years after Thoreau's death.

Margaret Fuller (1810). Journalist; critic; coeditor with Emerson of the *Dial*; frequent visitor in Emerson's home; married Count D'Ossoli in Rome in 1849; drowned in shipwreck off Fire Island in 1850.

Richard Frederick Fuller (1821). Brother of Margaret Fuller; Thoreau tutored him in Concord in 1842 when he was preparing to enter Harvard College; later a Boston lawyer and poet.

William Henry Furness (1802). Unitarian clergyman in Philadelphia; close friend and correspondent of Ralph Waldo Emerson; author of many books on theology.

James Garty [Garrety ?]. An Irish resident of Concord.

Issac Newton Goodhue (183?). A schoolteacher in Concord, later a lawyer in Boston and Minneapolis.

John Goodwin (1803). A Concord hunter and fisherman, thought by some of his neighbors to be a ne'er-do-well.

Horace Greeley (1811). Editor of the *New York Tribune* and for many years literary agent for Thoreau.

William Hague (1808). Clergyman in New York and Boston; friend of Ralph Waldo Emerson.

David Greene Haskins (1818). Episcopal clergyman; classmate of Thoreau at Harvard; cousin and friend of Ralph Waldo Emerson.

Julian Hawthorne (1846). Son of Nathaniel Hawthorne; novelist; resident of Concord from 1860 on.

Nathaniel Hawthorne (1804). Novelist and short story writer; resident of Concord from 1842 to 1845 and from 1860 to 1864; curator of the Salem Lyceum in the late 1840's.

Sophia Peabody Hawthorne (1809). Wife of Nathaniel Hawthorne; sister of Elizabeth Peabody and Mary Peabody Mann; resident of Concord from 1842 to 1845 and from 1860 on.

Isaac Hecker (1819). Brook Farmer; member of Bronson Alcott's Fruitlands community; boarder in the Thoreau household in 1844; later a Roman Catholic priest, editor of the *Catholic World*, and founder of the Paulist Fathers.

Samuel Storrow Higginson (183?). A student in F. B. Sanborn's private school in Concord in the late 1850's; graduated from Harvard in 1863.

Thomas Wentworth Higginson (1823). Reformer, Unitarian clergyman in Worcester, Newburyport, and Boston; abolitionist; colonel of a Negro regiment in the Civil War; later discoverer and editor of Emily Dickinson's poems.

Edward Sherman Hoar (1823). Son of Concord's leading citizen, Samuel Hoar; brother of Senator George Hoar and Judge Ebenezer Rockwood Hoar; companion of Thoreau on many of his excursions both in Concord and to the White Mountains and the Maine woods.

Elizabeth Hoar (1814). A daughter of Samuel Hoar and a close friend of Emerson.

George F. Hoar (1826). Native and resident of Concord; lawyer; representative and later senator from Massachusetts.

Mrs. Samuel Hoar (1783). Daughter of Roger Sherman, signer of the Declaration of Independence; wife of Concord's leading citizen; mother of Edward and George Hoar.

Sallie Holley (1818). Active throughout the North in the antislavery movement; heard Thoreau deliver a lecture in Worcester, Massachusetts.

Abigail Hosmer (1839). Daughter of Thoreau's Concord friend and neighbor Edmund Hosmer.

Alfred W. Hosmer (1851). Concord dry goods store proprietor and early Thoreau enthusiast.

Edmund Hosmer (1798). A Concord farmer and close friend of Thoreau; the "long-headed farmer" whom Thoreau describes in *Walden* as often visiting him at his cabin.

Horace R. Hosmer (1830). A pupil in Thoreau's private school and resident of Concord; brother of Joseph Hosmer.

James Kendall Hosmer (1834). Author; librarian; frequent visitor in Concord as a child.

Jane Hosmer (1835). Daughter of Thoreau's Concord friend and neighbor Edmund Hosmer.

Joseph Hosmer (1814). A close friend and companion of Thoreau's brother John; he later lived in Chicago.

Thomas Hosmer (1822). A resident of nearby Bedford; student in Thoreau's school; later a dentist in Boston.

William Dean Howells (1837). Novelist; editor; visitor to Concord in 1860.

Charles T. Jackson (1805). Chemist; geologist; codiscoverer of surgical anesthesia; brother-in-law of Ralph Waldo Emerson; secretary of Boston Society of Natural History.

Henry James, Sr. (1811). Lecturer and writer on Swedenborgianism; father of William James, the psychologist, and Henry James, the novelist; frequent visitor to the home of Ralph Waldo Emerson. Thoreau visited him in New York City in 1843.

Samuel Arthur Jones. Michigan physician and early disciple of Thoreau; did not visit Concord until after Thoreau's death.

George Keyes (1832). Resident of Concord and pupil in the Thoreau private school.

John Shepard Keyes (1821). Resident of Concord; later a state senator and district court judge.

Rose Hawthorne Lathrop (1851). Daughter of Nathaniel Hawthorne; resident of Concord from 1860 on; later married George Parsons Lathrop; eventually became a Roman Catholic nun, Mother Alphonsa, and founder of the Servants of Relief for Incurable Cancer.

B. W. Lee. A pupil in Thoreau's school.

Eben J. Loomis (1828). Mathematician; astronomer; editor of *American Ephemeris and Nautical Almanac,* 1850–1900; father of Mabel Loomis Todd; frequent summer boarder with the Thoreau family.

Mary A. Wilder Loomis. Daughter of Concord's Trinitarian minister; wife of Eben Loomis; mother of Mabel Loomis Todd.

James Russell Lowell (1819). Author; professor of modern languages at Harvard; editor of *Atlantic Monthly,* 1857–1861; he quarreled with Thoreau in 1857 over the editing of an essay Thoreau had submitted to the *Atlantic Monthly.*

Emily Lyman. Friend of Alfred Hosmer; probably a resident of Concord.

Mary Peabody Mann (1806). Wife of Horace Mann, the educator; sister of Elizabeth Peabody and Sophia Hawthorne; resident of Concord from 1860 on.

Maud Appleton McDowell. Nothing is known of her (nor of her uncle) other than that she told this little anecdote in her *Joy of Memories* (Dorset, Vt., 1937, p. 10).

Howard Melvin (1855). A lifelong resident of Concord; in his later years he sold souvenirs to tourists visiting Concord and spun long reminiscences for them; since he was only seven when Thoreau died, his memories of Thoreau are not necessarily precise.

Warren Miles (1822). He assisted the Thoreaus in their pencil business, particularly with the grinding of the graphite.

Barney Mullins. A one-time resident of Concord who later settled in Freedom Center, Outagamie County, Wisconsin; David Starr Jordan describes him as "the most illiterate man I know who had ever heard of Thoreau."

Alfred Munroe (1817). Resident of Concord and schoolmate of Thoreau; later the author of numerous books and articles on Concord.

Edward Neally. A young Irish resident of Concord who through Thoreau's encouragement later became an amateur authority on Concord fauna and Indian relics.

Amos Perry (1812). A classmate of Thoreau at Harvard, later a teacher, postmaster, and United States Consul in Tunis.

Frank Pierce (1849). Like his father before him, he ran a shoe store in Concord for many years.

Parker Pillsbury (1809). Reformer and abolitionist; frequent visitor to Concord; friend of the Thoreau family.

Daniel F. Potter (1830). A lifelong resident of Concord, he had been a pupil in Thoreau's school.

Minot Pratt (1805). One of the mainstays of the Brook Farm experiment; for many years a resident of Concord; author of a flora of Concord (unpublished).

Mrs. Minot Pratt (180?). For many years a resident of Concord; her son John married Anna Alcott, one of the "Little Women."

Josiah Quincy (1772). President of Harvard University, 1829–1845.

John Witt Randall (1813). Poet; zoologist; resident of nearby Stowe, Massachusetts.

S. E. Rena. Except for the obvious fact that she must have been a friend of Thoreau, there is no further clue to her identity. It is quite possible that the name is a pseudonym.

Grindall Reynolds (1822). Born in Franconia, New Hampshire; in 1858 he became minister of the First Parish in Concord, the church with which Thoreau's family was most closely associated.

Daniel Ricketson (1813). New Bedford Quaker; historian; poet; he read *Walden* within a few days of its publication in 1854 and started a correspondence with Thoreau that blossomed into a friendship marked by frequent visits back and forth between New Bedford and Concord.

Walton Ricketson. Son of Daniel, he later sculpted several busts and bas-reliefs of Thoreau.

Ezra Ripley (1751). Unitarian clergyman for many years in

Concord; pastor to the Thoreau family; step-grandfather of Ralph Waldo Emerson.

Mrs. William S. Robinson. Married one of Thoreau's schoolmates in 1848 and thereafter lived in Concord off and on for some years. Mr. Robinson was an active writer for the anti-slavery cause.

E[lias] Harlow Russell (1836). Worcester friend of H. G. O. Blake; later principal of Worcester Normal School; inheritor from Blake of Thoreau's manuscript journals.

Franklin Benjamin Sanborn (1831). Author, journalist, reformer, biographer of Thoreau; in 1855 he established residence in Concord, opening a private school and boarding with the Thoreau family.

Mrs. John T. Sargent (1827). A Boston bluestocking.

Edward Simmons (1852). Born in Concord; he later became a well-known mural painter.

Charles M. Skinner (1852). Associate editor of the *Brooklyn Eagle* and nature essayist.

Elizabeth Oakes Smith (1806). Author, lecturer, reformer; occasional visitor to Concord.

Samuel Staples (1813). Born in Mendon, Massachusetts; came to Concord in 1833; worked as a carpenter and bartender; in 1843 became town jailer; in 1846 he arrested Thoreau for nonpayment of taxes.

Frank Preston Stearns (1846). Author, critic; occasional visitor to Concord.

"The Taverner." Pseudonym of a columnist in a small Boston weekly magazine of the 1890's.

Mrs. Cynthia Thoreau (1787). Mother of Thoreau.

Maria Thoreau (179?). Maiden aunt of Thoreau; she often boarded with the Thoreau family.

Sophia Thoreau (1819). Younger sister of Thoreau.

Mabel Loomis Todd (1856). Daughter of Thoreau's friend Eben Loomis; frequent visitor to Concord and the Thoreau family; later famous as the editor of Emily Dickinson's poetry.

Benjamin Tolman (1822). A printer in Concord.

A. M. W. Apparently a woman resident of Concord who was active in the anti-slavery cause.

George Ward. Brother of Prudence Ward and frequent visitor in the Thoreau household.

Prudence Ward. Frequent boarder in the Thoreau household.

Henry Warren. A pupil in the Thoreau private school.

Benjamin Marston Watson. Fellow student with Thoreau at Harvard; minor Transcendentalist; farmer; resident of Plymouth, Massachusetts.

Ed Watson. Farmer resident of Plymouth, Massachusetts.

Ellen Watson. Resident of Plymouth, Massachusetts; daughter of Benjamin Marston Watson.

Hector Waylen. English vegetarian who made a "pilgrimage" to Thoreau's Concord in the 1890's.

Elizabeth J. Weir (1830). A Concord native, she worked as a governess for the Emerson children and became a close friend of Sophia Thoreau.

John Weiss (1818). Classmate of Thoreau at Harvard; friend of Emerson; Unitarian clergyman and writer.

George Wheeler (1842). A lifelong resident of Concord; was a pupil in the school of Thoreau's friend F. B. Sanborn.

Charles King Whipple (1808). An assistant editor of William Lloyd Garrison's antislavery *Liberator*.

Edwin Percy Whipple (1819). Author, lecturer, book critic, essayist; friend of Emerson and occasional visitor to Concord.

Mrs. Deacon White. Widow of John White, who for many years ran a store in Concord, a store in which Thoreau's father clerked for a time as a young man.

Walt Whitman (1819). Poet, author of *Leaves of Grass;* Thoreau visited him briefly in Brooklyn, New York, in 1856.

Frederick L. H. Willis (1830). Friend, visitor and frequent boarder with the Alcott family; he claimed to be the original of Laurie in Louisa May Alcott's *Little Women;* later a Unitarian clergyman, medical doctor, and lecturer.

James B. Wood (1824). A native of Concord; in later years he established his residence in Vermont but continued to visit frequently in Concord.

Charles J. Woodbury. Williams College student who interviewed Emerson on a visit to Williamstown, Massachusetts, in 1865.

III. Bibliography

Thoreau's Writings

The standard edition of Thoreau's writings has been the Walden or Manuscript Edition, published by Houghton Mifflin in 1906, supplemented by *Collected Poems of Henry Thoreau*, edited by Carl Bode (Johns Hopkins Press, 1964), and *The Correspondence of Henry David Thoreau*, edited by Walter Harding and Carl Bode (New York University Press, 1958). It is gradually being replaced by *The Writings of Henry D. Thoreau*, edited by Walter Harding *et al.* (Princeton University Press, 1971–   ), of which, to date, nine of a proposed twenty-five volumes have appeared. The best one-volume collection is *A Week on the Concord and Merrimack Rivers / Walden / The Maine Woods / Cape Cod*, edited by Robert Sayre (Library of America, 1985). The 1906 fourteen-volume edition of Thoreau's Journal has been reprinted in two volumes by Dover Publications: *The Journal of Henry D. Thoreau*, edited by Bradford Torrey and Francis H. Allen (ISBN 0-486-20312-3 and 0-486-20313-1).

Writings about Thoreau

The most comprehensive biography of Thoreau is *The Days of Henry Thoreau*, by Walter Harding (Knopf, 1965; Dover, 1982). *A New Thoreau Handbook*, by Walter Harding and Michael Meyer (New York University Press, 1980), surveys and evaluates the entire field of Thoreau literature. *The Recognition of Henry David Thoreau*, edited by Wendell Glick (University of Michigan Press, 1969), is the most comprehensive collection of criticism of Thoreau. *The Thoreau Society Bulletin*, issued quarterly since 1941 (current address: State University College, Geneseo, NY 14454), is devoted entirely to the study of Thoreau.

Index

Index

A CATALOG OF SELECTED
DOVER BOOKS
IN ALL FIELDS OF INTEREST

A CATALOG OF SELECTED DOVER
BOOKS IN ALL FIELDS OF INTEREST

DRAWINGS OF REMBRANDT, edited by Seymour Slive. Updated Lippmann, Hofstede de Groot edition, with definitive scholarly apparatus. All portraits, biblical sketches, landscapes, nudes. Oriental figures, classical studies, together with selection of work by followers. 550 illustrations. Total of 630pp. 9⅛ × 12¼.
21485-0, 21486-9 Pa., Two-vol. set $25.00

GHOST AND HORROR STORIES OF AMBROSE BIERCE, Ambrose Bierce. 24 tales vividly imagined, strangely prophetic, and decades ahead of their time in technical skill: "The Damned Thing," "An Inhabitant of Carcosa," "The Eyes of the Panther," "Moxon's Master," and 20 more. 199pp. 5⅜ × 8½. 20767-6 Pa. $3.95

ETHICAL WRITINGS OF MAIMONIDES, Maimonides. Most significant ethical works of great medieval sage, newly translated for utmost precision, readability. Laws Concerning Character Traits, Eight Chapters, more. 192pp. 5⅜ × 8½.
24522-5 Pa. $4.50

THE EXPLORATION OF THE COLORADO RIVER AND ITS CANYONS, J. W. Powell. Full text of Powell's 1,000-mile expedition down the fabled Colorado in 1869. Superb account of terrain, geology, vegetation, Indians, famine, mutiny, treacherous rapids, mighty canyons, during exploration of last unknown part of continental U.S. 400pp. 5⅜ × 8½. 20094-9 Pa. $6.95

HISTORY OF PHILOSOPHY, Julián Marías. Clearest one-volume history on the market. Every major philosopher and dozens of others, to Existentialism and later. 505pp. 5⅜ × 8½. 21739-6 Pa. $8.50

ALL ABOUT LIGHTNING, Martin A. Uman. Highly readable non-technical survey of nature and causes of lightning, thunderstorms, ball lightning, St. Elmo's Fire, much more. Illustrated. 192pp. 5⅜ × 8½. 25237-X Pa. $5.95

SAILING ALONE AROUND THE WORLD, Captain Joshua Slocum. First man to sail around the world, alone, in small boat. One of great feats of seamanship told in delightful manner. 67 illustrations. 294pp. 5⅜ × 8½. 20326-3 Pa. $4.95

LETTERS AND NOTES ON THE MANNERS, CUSTOMS AND CONDITIONS OF THE NORTH AMERICAN INDIANS, George Catlin. Classic account of life among Plains Indians: ceremonies, hunt, warfare, etc. 312 plates. 572pp. of text. 6⅛ × 9¼. 22118-0, 22119-9 Pa. Two-vol. set $15.90

ALASKA: The Harriman Expedition, 1899, John Burroughs, John Muir, et al. Informative, engrossing accounts of two-month, 9,000-mile expedition. Native peoples, wildlife, forests, geography, salmon industry, glaciers, more. Profusely illustrated. 240 black-and-white line drawings. 124 black-and-white photographs. 3 maps. Index. 576pp. 5⅜ × 8½. 25109-8 Pa. $11.95

THE BOOK OF BEASTS: Being a Translation from a Latin Bestiary of the Twelfth Century, T. H. White. Wonderful catalog real and fanciful beasts: manticore, griffin, phoenix, amphivius, jaculus, many more. White's witty erudite commentary on scientific, historical aspects. Fascinating glimpse of medieval mind. Illustrated. 296pp. 5⅜ × 8¼. (Available in U.S. only)   24609-4 Pa. $5.95

FRANK LLOYD WRIGHT: ARCHITECTURE AND NATURE With 160 Illustrations, Donald Hoffmann. Profusely illustrated study of influence of nature—especially prairie—on Wright's designs for Fallingwater, Robie House, Guggenheim Museum, other masterpieces. 96pp. 9¼ × 10¾.   25098-9 Pa. $7.95

FRANK LLOYD WRIGHT'S FALLINGWATER, Donald Hoffmann. Wright's famous waterfall house: planning and construction of organic idea. History of site, owners, Wright's personal involvement. Photographs of various stages of building. Preface by Edgar Kaufmann, Jr. 100 illustrations. 112pp. 9¼ × 10.
23671-4 Pa. $7.95

YEARS WITH FRANK LLOYD WRIGHT: Apprentice to Genius, Edgar Tafel. Insightful memoir by a former apprentice presents a revealing portrait of Wright the man, the inspired teacher, the greatest American architect. 372 black-and-white illustrations. Preface. Index. vi + 228pp. 8¼ × 11.   24801-1 Pa. $9.95

THE STORY OF KING ARTHUR AND HIS KNIGHTS, Howard Pyle. Enchanting version of King Arthur fable has delighted generations with imaginative narratives of exciting adventures and unforgettable illustrations by the author. 41 illustrations. xviii + 313pp. 6⅛ × 9¼.   21445-1 Pa. $5.95

THE GODS OF THE EGYPTIANS, E. A. Wallis Budge. Thorough coverage of numerous gods of ancient Egypt by foremost Egyptologist. Information on evolution of cults, rites and gods; the cult of Osiris; the Book of the Dead and its rites; the sacred animals and birds; Heaven and Hell; and more. 956pp. 6⅛ × 9¼.
22055-9, 22056-7 Pa., Two-vol. set $21.90

A THEOLOGICO-POLITICAL TREATISE, Benedict Spinoza. Also contains unfinished *Political Treatise*. Great classic on religious liberty, theory of government on common consent. R. Elwes translation. Total of 421pp. 5⅜ × 8½.
20249-6 Pa. $6.95

INCIDENTS OF TRAVEL IN CENTRAL AMERICA, CHIAPAS, AND YUCATAN, John L. Stephens. Almost single-handed discovery of Maya culture; exploration of ruined cities, monuments, temples; customs of Indians. 115 drawings. 892pp. 5⅜ × 8½.   22404-X, 22405-8 Pa., Two-vol. set $15.90

LOS CAPRICHOS, Francisco Goya. 80 plates of wild, grotesque monsters and caricatures. Prado manuscript included. 183pp. 6⅜ × 9⅜.   22384-1 Pa. $4.95

AUTOBIOGRAPHY: The Story of My Experiments with Truth, Mohandas K. Gandhi. Not hagiography, but Gandhi in his own words. Boyhood, legal studies, purification, the growth of the Satyagraha (nonviolent protest) movement. Critical, inspiring work of the man who freed India. 480pp. 5⅜ × 8½. (Available in U.S. only)
24593-4 Pa. $6.95

ILLUSTRATED DICTIONARY OF HISTORIC ARCHITECTURE, edited by Cyril M. Harris. Extraordinary compendium of clear, concise definitions for over 5,000 important architectural terms complemented by over 2,000 line drawings. Covers full spectrum of architecture from ancient ruins to 20th-century Modernism. Preface. 592pp. 7½ × 9⅝. 24444-X Pa. $14.95

THE NIGHT BEFORE CHRISTMAS, Clement Moore. Full text, and woodcuts from original 1848 book. Also critical, historical material. 19 illustrations. 40pp. 4⅝ × 6. 22797-9 Pa. $2.50

THE LESSON OF JAPANESE ARCHITECTURE: 165 Photographs, Jiro Harada. Memorable gallery of 165 photographs taken in the 1930's of exquisite Japanese homes of the well-to-do and historic buildings. 13 line diagrams. 192pp. 8⅝ × 11¼. 24778-3 Pa. $8.95

THE AUTOBIOGRAPHY OF CHARLES DARWIN AND SELECTED LETTERS, edited by Francis Darwin. The fascinating life of eccentric genius composed of an intimate memoir by Darwin (intended for his children); commentary by his son, Francis; hundreds of fragments from notebooks, journals, papers; and letters to and from Lyell, Hooker, Huxley, Wallace and Henslow. xi + 365pp. 5⅜ × 8. 20479-0 Pa. $5.95

WONDERS OF THE SKY: Observing Rainbows, Comets, Eclipses, the Stars and Other Phenomena, Fred Schaaf. Charming, easy-to-read poetic guide to all manner of celestial events visible to the naked eye. Mock suns, glories, Belt of Venus, more. Illustrated. 299pp. 5¼ × 8¼. 24402-4 Pa. $7.95

BURNHAM'S CELESTIAL HANDBOOK, Robert Burnham, Jr. Thorough guide to the stars beyond our solar system. Exhaustive treatment. Alphabetical by constellation: Andromeda to Cetus in Vol. 1; Chamaeleon to Orion in Vol. 2; and Pavo to Vulpecula in Vol. 3. Hundreds of illustrations. Index in Vol. 3. 2,000pp. 6⅛ × 9¼. 23567-X, 23568-8, 23673-0 Pa., Three-vol. set $37.85

STAR NAMES: Their Lore and Meaning, Richard Hinckley Allen. Fascinating history of names various cultures have given to constellations and literary and folkloristic uses that have been made of stars. Indexes to subjects. Arabic and Greek names. Biblical references. Bibliography. 563pp. 5⅜ × 8½. 21079-0 Pa. $7.95

THIRTY YEARS THAT SHOOK PHYSICS: The Story of Quantum Theory, George Gamow. Lucid, accessible introduction to influential theory of energy and matter. Careful explanations of Dirac's anti-particles, Bohr's model of the atom, much more. 12 plates. Numerous drawings. 240pp. 5⅜ × 8½. 24895-X Pa. $4.95

CHINESE DOMESTIC FURNITURE IN PHOTOGRAPHS AND MEASURED DRAWINGS, Gustav Ecke. A rare volume, now affordably priced for antique collectors, furniture buffs and art historians. Detailed review of styles ranging from early Shang to late Ming. Unabridged republication. 161 black-and-white drawings, photos. Total of 224pp. 8⅜ × 11¼. (Available in U.S. only) 25171-3 Pa. $12.95

VINCENT VAN GOGH: A Biography, Julius Meier-Graefe. Dynamic, penetrating study of artist's life, relationship with brother, Theo, painting techniques, travels, more. Readable, engrossing. 160pp. 5⅜ × 8½. (Available in U.S. only) 25253-1 Pa. $3.95

HOW TO WRITE, Gertrude Stein. Gertrude Stein claimed anyone could understand her unconventional writing—here are clues to help. Fascinating improvisations, language experiments, explanations illuminate Stein's craft and the art of writing. Total of 414pp. 4⅜ × 6⅜. 23144-5 Pa. $5.95

ADVENTURES AT SEA IN THE GREAT AGE OF SAIL: Five Firsthand Narratives, edited by Elliot Snow. Rare true accounts of exploration, whaling, shipwreck, fierce natives, trade, shipboard life, more. 33 illustrations. Introduction. 353pp. 5⅜ × 8½. 25177-2 Pa. $7.95

THE HERBAL OR GENERAL HISTORY OF PLANTS, John Gerard. Classic descriptions of about 2,850 plants—with over 2,700 illustrations—includes Latin and English names, physical descriptions, varieties, time and place of growth, more. 2,706 illustrations. xlv + 1,678pp. 8½ × 12¼. 23147-X Cloth. $75.00

DOROTHY AND THE WIZARD IN OZ, L. Frank Baum. Dorothy and the Wizard visit the center of the Earth, where people are vegetables, glass houses grow and Oz characters reappear. Classic sequel to *Wizard of Oz*. 256pp. 5⅜ × 8. 24714-7 Pa. $4.95

SONGS OF EXPERIENCE: Facsimile Reproduction with 26 Plates in Full Color, William Blake. This facsimile of Blake's original "Illuminated Book" reproduces 26 full-color plates from a rare 1826 edition. Includes "The Tyger," "London," "Holy Thursday," and other immortal poems. 26 color plates. Printed text of poems. 48pp. 5¼ × 7. 24636-1 Pa. $3.50

SONGS OF INNOCENCE, William Blake. The first and most popular of Blake's famous "Illuminated Books," in a facsimile edition reproducing all 31 brightly colored plates. Additional printed text of each poem. 64pp. 5¼ × 7. 22764-2 Pa. $3.50

PRECIOUS STONES, Max Bauer. Classic, thorough study of diamonds, rubies, emeralds, garnets, etc.: physical character, occurrence, properties, use, similar topics. 20 plates, 8 in color. 94 figures. 659pp. 6⅛ × 9¼. 21910-0, 21911-9 Pa., Two-vol. set $15.90

ENCYCLOPEDIA OF VICTORIAN NEEDLEWORK, S. F. A. Caulfeild and Blanche Saward. Full, precise descriptions of stitches, techniques for dozens of needlecrafts—most exhaustive reference of its kind. Over 800 figures. Total of 679pp. 8⅛ × 11. Two volumes. Vol. 1 22800-2 Pa. $11.95
Vol. 2 22801-0 Pa. $11.95

THE MARVELOUS LAND OF OZ, L. Frank Baum. Second Oz book, the Scarecrow and Tin Woodman are back with hero named Tip, Oz magic. 136 illustrations. 287pp. 5⅜ × 8½. 20692-0 Pa. $5.95

WILD FOWL DECOYS, Joel Barber. Basic book on the subject, by foremost authority and collector. Reveals history of decoy making and rigging, place in American culture, different kinds of decoys, how to make them, and how to use them. 140 plates. 156pp. 7⅞ × 10¾. 20011-6 Pa. $8.95

HISTORY OF LACE, Mrs. Bury Palliser. Definitive, profusely illustrated chronicle of lace from earliest times to late 19th century. Laces of Italy, Greece, England, France, Belgium, etc. Landmark of needlework scholarship. 266 illustrations. 672pp. 6⅛ × 9¼. 24742-2 Pa. $14.95

ILLUSTRATED GUIDE TO SHAKER FURNITURE, Robert Meader. All furniture and appurtenances, with much on unknown local styles. 235 photos. 146pp. 9 × 12. 22819-3 Pa. $7.95

WHALE SHIPS AND WHALING: A Pictorial Survey, George Francis Dow. Over 200 vintage engravings, drawings, photographs of barks, brigs, cutters, other vessels. Also harpoons, lances, whaling guns, many other artifacts. Comprehensive text by foremost authority. 207 black-and-white illustrations. 288pp. 6 × 9. 24808-9 Pa. $8.95

THE BERTRAMS, Anthony Trollope. Powerful portrayal of blind self-will and thwarted ambition includes one of Trollope's most heartrending love stories. 497pp. 5⅜ × 8½. 25119-5 Pa. $8.95

ADVENTURES WITH A HAND LENS, Richard Headstrom. Clearly written guide to observing and studying flowers and grasses, fish scales, moth and insect wings, egg cases, buds, feathers, seeds, leaf scars, moss, molds, ferns, common crystals, etc.—all with an ordinary, inexpensive magnifying glass. 209 exact line drawings aid in your discoveries. 220pp. 5⅜ × 8½. 23330-8 Pa. $4.50

RODIN ON ART AND ARTISTS, Auguste Rodin. Great sculptor's candid, wide-ranging comments on meaning of art; great artists; relation of sculpture to poetry, painting, music; philosophy of life, more. 76 superb black-and-white illustrations of Rodin's sculpture, drawings and prints. 119pp. 8⅜ × 11¼. 24487-3 Pa. $6.95

FIFTY CLASSIC FRENCH FILMS, 1912–1982: A Pictorial Record, Anthony Slide. Memorable stills from Grand Illusion, Beauty and the Beast, Hiroshima, Mon Amour, many more. Credits, plot synopses, reviews, etc. 160pp. 8¼ × 11. 25256-6 Pa. $11.95

THE PRINCIPLES OF PSYCHOLOGY, William James. Famous long course complete, unabridged. Stream of thought, time perception, memory, experimental methods; great work decades ahead of its time. 94 figures. 1,391pp. 5⅜ × 8½. 20381-6, 20382-4 Pa., Two-vol. set $19.90

BODIES IN A BOOKSHOP, R. T. Campbell. Challenging mystery of blackmail and murder with ingenious plot and superbly drawn characters. In the best tradition of British suspense fiction. 192pp. 5⅜ × 8½. 24720-1 Pa. $3.95

CALLAS: PORTRAIT OF A PRIMA DONNA, George Jellinek. Renowned commentator on the musical scene chronicles incredible career and life of the most controversial, fascinating, influential operatic personality of our time. 64 black-and-white photographs. 416pp. 5⅜ × 8¼. 25047-4 Pa. $7.95

GEOMETRY, RELATIVITY AND THE FOURTH DIMENSION, Rudolph Rucker. Exposition of fourth dimension, concepts of relativity as Flatland characters continue adventures. Popular, easily followed yet accurate, profound. 141 illustrations. 133pp. 5⅜ × 8½. 23400-2 Pa. $3.50

HOUSEHOLD STORIES BY THE BROTHERS GRIMM, with pictures by Walter Crane. 53 classic stories—Rumpelstiltskin, Rapunzel, Hansel and Gretel, the Fisherman and his Wife, Snow White, Tom Thumb, Sleeping Beauty, Cinderella, and so much more—lavishly illustrated with original 19th century drawings. 114 illustrations. x + 269pp. 5⅜ × 8½. 21080-4 Pa. $4.50

SUNDIALS, Albert Waugh. Far and away the best, most thorough coverage of ideas, mathematics concerned, types, construction, adjusting anywhere. Over 100 illustrations. 230pp. 5⅜ × 8½. 22947-5 Pa. $4.50

PICTURE HISTORY OF THE NORMANDIE: With 190 Illustrations, Frank O. Braynard. Full story of legendary French ocean liner: Art Deco interiors, design innovations, furnishings, celebrities, maiden voyage, tragic fire, much more. Extensive text. 144pp. 8⅜ × 11¾. 25257-4 Pa. $9.95

THE FIRST AMERICAN COOKBOOK: A Facsimile of "American Cookery," 1796, Amelia Simmons. Facsimile of the first American-written cookbook published in the United States contains authentic recipes for colonial favorites—pumpkin pudding, winter squash pudding, spruce beer, Indian slapjacks, and more. Introductory Essay and Glossary of colonial cooking terms. 80pp. 5⅜ × 8½. 24710-4 Pa. $3.50

101 PUZZLES IN THOUGHT AND LOGIC, C. R. Wylie, Jr. Solve murders and robberies, find out which fishermen are liars, how a blind man could possibly identify a color—purely by your own reasoning! 107pp. 5⅜ × 8½. 20367-0 Pa. $2.50

THE BOOK OF WORLD-FAMOUS MUSIC—CLASSICAL, POPULAR AND FOLK, James J. Fuld. Revised and enlarged republication of landmark work in musico-bibliography. Full information about nearly 1,000 songs and compositions including first lines of music and lyrics. New supplement. Index. 800pp. 5⅜ × 8¼. 24857-7 Pa. $14.95

ANTHROPOLOGY AND MODERN LIFE, Franz Boas. Great anthropologist's classic treatise on race and culture. Introduction by Ruth Bunzel. Only inexpensive paperback edition. 255pp. 5⅜ × 8½. 25245-0 Pa. $5.95

THE TALE OF PETER RABBIT, Beatrix Potter. The inimitable Peter's terrifying adventure in Mr. McGregor's garden, with all 27 wonderful, full-color Potter illustrations. 55pp. 4¼ × 5½. (Available in U.S. only) 22827-4 Pa. $1.75

THREE PROPHETIC SCIENCE FICTION NOVELS, H. G. Wells. *When the Sleeper Wakes, A Story of the Days to Come* and *The Time Machine* (full version). 335pp. 5⅜ × 8½. (Available in U.S. only) 20605-X Pa. $5.95

APICIUS COOKERY AND DINING IN IMPERIAL ROME, edited and translated by Joseph Dommers Vehling. Oldest known cookbook in existence offers readers a clear picture of what foods Romans ate, how they prepared them, etc. 49 illustrations. 301pp. 6⅛ × 9¼. 23563-7 Pa. $6.50

SHAKESPEARE LEXICON AND QUOTATION DICTIONARY, Alexander Schmidt. Full definitions, locations, shades of meaning of every word in plays and poems. More than 50,000 exact quotations. 1,485pp. 6½ × 9¼. 22726-X, 22727-8 Pa., Two-vol. set $27.90

THE WORLD'S GREAT SPEECHES, edited by Lewis Copeland and Lawrence W. Lamm. Vast collection of 278 speeches from Greeks to 1970. Powerful and effective models; unique look at history. 842pp. 5⅜ × 8½. 20468-5 Pa. $11.95

CATALOG OF DOVER BOOKS

THE BLUE FAIRY BOOK, Andrew Lang. The first, most famous collection, with many familiar tales: Little Red Riding Hood, Aladdin and the Wonderful Lamp, Puss in Boots, Sleeping Beauty, Hansel and Gretel, Rumpelstiltskin; 37 in all. 138 illustrations. 390pp. 5⅜ × 8½. 21437-0 Pa. $5.95

THE STORY OF THE CHAMPIONS OF THE ROUND TABLE, Howard Pyle. Sir Launcelot, Sir Tristram and Sir Percival in spirited adventures of love and triumph retold in Pyle's inimitable style. 50 drawings, 31 full-page. xviii + 329pp. 6½ × 9¼. 21883-X Pa. $6.95

AUDUBON AND HIS JOURNALS, Maria Audubon. Unmatched two-volume portrait of the great artist, naturalist and author contains his journals, an excellent biography by his granddaughter, expert annotations by the noted ornithologist, Dr. Elliott Coues, and 37 superb illustrations. Total of 1,200pp. 5⅜ × 8.
Vol. I 25143-8 Pa. $8.95
Vol. II 25144-6 Pa. $8.95

GREAT DINOSAUR HUNTERS AND THEIR DISCOVERIES, Edwin H. Colbert. Fascinating, lavishly illustrated chronicle of dinosaur research, 1820's to 1960. Achievements of Cope, Marsh, Brown, Buckland, Mantell, Huxley, many others. 384pp. 5¼ × 8¼. 24701-5 Pa. $6.95

THE TASTEMAKERS, Russell Lynes. Informal, illustrated social history of American taste 1850's–1950's. First popularized categories Highbrow, Lowbrow, Middlebrow. 129 illustrations. New (1979) afterword. 384pp. 6 × 9.
23993-4 Pa. $6.95

DOUBLE CROSS PURPOSES, Ronald A. Knox. A treasure hunt in the Scottish Highlands, an old map, unidentified corpse, surprise discoveries keep reader guessing in this cleverly intricate tale of financial skullduggery. 2 black-and-white maps. 320pp. 5⅜ × 8½. (Available in U.S. only) 25032-6 Pa. $5.95

AUTHENTIC VICTORIAN DECORATION AND ORNAMENTATION IN FULL COLOR: 46 Plates from "Studies in Design," Christopher Dresser. Superb full-color lithographs reproduced from rare original portfolio of a major Victorian designer. 48pp. 9¼ × 12¼. 25083-0 Pa. $7.95

PRIMITIVE ART, Franz Boas. Remains the best text ever prepared on subject, thoroughly discussing Indian, African, Asian, Australian, and, especially, Northern American primitive art. Over 950 illustrations show ceramics, masks, totem poles, weapons, textiles, paintings, much more. 376pp. 5⅜ × 8. 20025-6 Pa. $6.95

SIDELIGHTS ON RELATIVITY, Albert Einstein. Unabridged republication of two lectures delivered by the great physicist in 1920–21. *Ether and Relativity* and *Geometry and Experience*. Elegant ideas in non-mathematical form, accessible to intelligent layman. vi + 56pp. 5⅜ × 8½. 24511-X Pa. $2.95

THE WIT AND HUMOR OF OSCAR WILDE, edited by Alvin Redman. More than 1,000 ripostes, paradoxes, wisecracks: Work is the curse of the drinking classes, I can resist everything except temptation, etc. 258pp. 5⅜ × 8½. 20602-5 Pa. $4.50

ADVENTURES WITH A MICROSCOPE, Richard Headstrom. 59 adventures with clothing fibers, protozoa, ferns and lichens, roots and leaves, much more. 142 illustrations. 232pp. 5⅜ × 8½. 23471-1 Pa. $3.95

PLANTS OF THE BIBLE, Harold N. Moldenke and Alma L. Moldenke. Standard reference to all 230 plants mentioned in Scriptures. Latin name, biblical reference, uses, modern identity, much more. Unsurpassed encyclopedic resource for scholars, botanists, nature lovers, students of Bible. Bibliography. Indexes. 123 black-and-white illustrations. 384pp. 6 × 9. 25069-5 Pa. $8.95

FAMOUS AMERICAN WOMEN: A Biographical Dictionary from Colonial Times to the Present, Robert McHenry, ed. From Pocahontas to Rosa Parks, 1,035 distinguished American women documented in separate biographical entries. Accurate, up-to-date data, numerous categories, spans 400 years. Indices. 493pp. 6½ × 9¼. 24523-3 Pa. $9.95

THE FABULOUS INTERIORS OF THE GREAT OCEAN LINERS IN HISTORIC PHOTOGRAPHS, William H. Miller, Jr. Some 200 superb photographs capture exquisite interiors of world's great "floating palaces"—1890's to 1980's: Titanic, Ile de France, Queen Elizabeth, United States, Europa, more. Approx. 200 black-and-white photographs. Captions. Text. Introduction. 160pp. 8⅜ × 11¼. 24756-2 Pa. $9.95

THE GREAT LUXURY LINERS, 1927–1954: A Photographic Record, William H. Miller, Jr. Nostalgic tribute to heyday of ocean liners. 186 photos of Ile de France, Normandie, Leviathan, Queen Elizabeth, United States, many others. Interior and exterior views. Introduction. Captions. 160pp. 9 × 12. 24056-8 Pa. $9.95

A NATURAL HISTORY OF THE DUCKS, John Charles Phillips. Great landmark of ornithology offers complete detailed coverage of nearly 200 species and subspecies of ducks: gadwall, sheldrake, merganser, pintail, many more. 74 full-color plates, 102 black-and-white. Bibliography. Total of 1,920pp. 8⅜ × 11¼. 25141-1, 25142-X Cloth. Two-vol. set $100.00

THE SEAWEED HANDBOOK: An Illustrated Guide to Seaweeds from North Carolina to Canada, Thomas F. Lee. Concise reference covers 78 species. Scientific and common names, habitat, distribution, more. Finding keys for easy identification. 224pp. 5⅜ × 8½. 25215-9 Pa. $5.95

THE TEN BOOKS OF ARCHITECTURE: The 1755 Leoni Edition, Leon Battista Alberti. Rare classic helped introduce the glories of ancient architecture to the Renaissance. 68 black-and-white plates. 336pp. 8⅜ × 11¼. 25239-6 Pa. $14.95

MISS MACKENZIE, Anthony Trollope. Minor masterpieces by Victorian master unmasks many truths about life in 19th-century England. First inexpensive edition in years. 392pp. 5⅜ × 8½. 25201-9 Pa. $7.95

THE RIME OF THE ANCIENT MARINER, Gustave Doré, Samuel Taylor Coleridge. Dramatic engravings considered by many to be his greatest work. The terrifying space of the open sea, the storms and whirlpools of an unknown ocean, the ice of Antarctica, more—all rendered in a powerful, chilling manner. Full text. 38 plates. 77pp. 9¼ × 12. 22305-1 Pa. $4.95

THE EXPEDITIONS OF ZEBULON MONTGOMERY PIKE, Zebulon Montgomery Pike. Fascinating first-hand accounts (1805–6) of exploration of Mississippi River, Indian wars, capture by Spanish dragoons, much more. 1,088pp. 5⅜ × 8½. 25254-X, 25255-8 Pa. Two-vol. set $23.90

A CONCISE HISTORY OF PHOTOGRAPHY: Third Revised Edition, Helmut Gernsheim. Best one-volume history—camera obscura, photochemistry, daguerreotypes, evolution of cameras, film, more. Also artistic aspects—landscape, portraits, fine art, etc. 281 black-and-white photographs. 26 in color. 176pp. 8⅜ × 11¼. 25128-4 Pa. $12.95

THE DORÉ BIBLE ILLUSTRATIONS, Gustave Doré. 241 detailed plates from the Bible: the Creation scenes, Adam and Eve, Flood, Babylon, battle sequences, life of Jesus, etc. Each plate is accompanied by the verses from the King James version of the Bible. 241pp. 9 × 12. 23004-X Pa. $8.95

HUGGER-MUGGER IN THE LOUVRE, Elliot Paul. Second Homer Evans mystery-comedy. Theft at the Louvre involves sleuth in hilarious, madcap caper. "A knockout."—Books. 336pp. 5⅜ × 8½. 25185-3 Pa. $5.95

FLATLAND, E. A. Abbott. Intriguing and enormously popular science-fiction classic explores the complexities of trying to survive as a two-dimensional being in a three-dimensional world. Amusingly illustrated by the author. 16 illustrations. 103pp. 5⅜ × 8½. 20001-9 Pa. $2.25

THE HISTORY OF THE LEWIS AND CLARK EXPEDITION, Meriwether Lewis and William Clark, edited by Elliott Coues. Classic edition of Lewis and Clark's day-by-day journals that later became the basis for U.S. claims to Oregon and the West. Accurate and invaluable geographical, botanical, biological, meteorological and anthropological material. Total of 1,508pp. 5⅜ × 8½.
21268-8, 21269-6, 21270-X Pa. Three-vol. set $25.50

LANGUAGE, TRUTH AND LOGIC, Alfred J. Ayer. Famous, clear introduction to Vienna, Cambridge schools of Logical Positivism. Role of philosophy, elimination of metaphysics, nature of analysis, etc. 160pp. 5⅜ × 8½. (Available in U.S. and Canada only) 20010-8 Pa. $2.95

MATHEMATICS FOR THE NONMATHEMATICIAN, Morris Kline. Detailed, college-level treatment of mathematics in cultural and historical context, with numerous exercises. For liberal arts students. Preface. Recommended Reading Lists. Tables. Index. Numerous black-and-white figures. xvi + 641pp. 5⅜ × 8½.
24823-2 Pa. $11.95

28 SCIENCE FICTION STORIES, H. G. Wells. Novels, *Star Begotten* and *Men Like Gods,* plus 26 short stories: "Empire of the Ants," "A Story of the Stone Age," "The Stolen Bacillus," "In the Abyss," etc. 915pp. 5⅜ × 8½. (Available in U.S. only)
20265-8 Cloth. $10.95

HANDBOOK OF PICTORIAL SYMBOLS, Rudolph Modley. 3,250 signs and symbols, many systems in full; official or heavy commercial use. Arranged by subject. Most in Pictorial Archive series. 143pp. 8⅛ × 11. 23357-X Pa. $5.95

INCIDENTS OF TRAVEL IN YUCATAN, John L. Stephens. Classic (1843) exploration of jungles of Yucatan, looking for evidences of Maya civilization. Travel adventures, Mexican and Indian culture, etc. Total of 669pp. 5⅜ × 8½.
20926-1, 20927-X Pa., Two-vol. set $9.90

DEGAS: An Intimate Portrait, Ambroise Vollard. Charming, anecdotal memoir by famous art dealer of one of the greatest 19th-century French painters. 14 black-and-white illustrations. Introduction by Harold L. Van Doren. 96pp. 5⅜ × 8½.
25131-4 Pa. $3.95

PERSONAL NARRATIVE OF A PILGRIMAGE TO ALMANDINAH AND MECCAH, Richard Burton. Great travel classic by remarkably colorful personality. Burton, disguised as a Moroccan, visited sacred shrines of Islam, narrowly escaping death. 47 illustrations. 959pp. 5⅜ × 8½. 21217-3, 21218-1 Pa., Two-vol. set $17.90

PHRASE AND WORD ORIGINS, A. H. Holt. Entertaining, reliable, modern study of more than 1,200 colorful words, phrases, origins and histories. Much unexpected information. 254pp. 5⅜ × 8½. 20758-7 Pa. $5.95

THE RED THUMB MARK, R. Austin Freeman. In this first Dr. Thorndyke case, the great scientific detective draws fascinating conclusions from the nature of a single fingerprint. Exciting story, authentic science. 320pp. 5⅜ × 8½. (Available in U.S. only) 25210-8 Pa. $5.95

AN EGYPTIAN HIEROGLYPHIC DICTIONARY, E. A. Wallis Budge. Monumental work containing about 25,000 words or terms that occur in texts ranging from 3000 B.C. to 600 A.D. Each entry consists of a transliteration of the word, the word in hieroglyphs, and the meaning in English. 1,314pp. 6⅜ × 10.
23615-3, 23616-1 Pa., Two-vol. set $27.90

THE COMPLEAT STRATEGYST: Being a Primer on the Theory of Games of Strategy, J. D. Williams. Highly entertaining classic describes, with many illustrated examples, how to select best strategies in conflict situations. Prefaces. Appendices. xvi + 268pp. 5⅜ × 8½. 25101-2 Pa. $5.95

THE ROAD TO OZ, L. Frank Baum. Dorothy meets the Shaggy Man, little Button-Bright and the Rainbow's beautiful daughter in this delightful trip to the magical Land of Oz. 272pp. 5⅜ × 8. 25208-6 Pa. $4.95

POINT AND LINE TO PLANE, Wassily Kandinsky. Seminal exposition of role of point, line, other elements in non-objective painting. Essential to understanding 20th-century art. 127 illustrations. 192pp. 6½ × 9¼. 23808-3 Pa. $4.50

LADY ANNA, Anthony Trollope. Moving chronicle of Countess Lovel's bitter struggle to win for herself and daughter Anna their rightful rank and fortune—perhaps at cost of sanity itself. 384pp. 5⅜ × 8½. 24669-8 Pa. $6.95

EGYPTIAN MAGIC, E. A. Wallis Budge. Sums up all that is known about magic in Ancient Egypt: the role of magic in controlling the gods, powerful amulets that warded off evil spirits, scarabs of immortality, use of wax images, formulas and spells, the secret name, much more. 253pp. 5⅜ × 8½. 22681-6 Pa. $4.50

THE DANCE OF SIVA, Ananda Coomaraswamy. Preeminent authority unfolds the vast metaphysic of India: the revelation of her art, conception of the universe, social organization, etc. 27 reproductions of art masterpieces. 192pp. 5⅜ × 8½.
24817-8 Pa. $5.95

CATALOG OF DOVER BOOKS

THE ART NOUVEAU STYLE BOOK OF ALPHONSE MUCHA: All 72 Plates from "Documents Decoratifs" in Original Color, Alphonse Mucha. Rare copyright-free design portfolio by high priest of Art Nouveau. Jewelry, wallpaper, stained glass, furniture, figure studies, plant and animal motifs, etc. Only complete one-volume edition. 80pp. 9⅜ × 12¼. 24044-4 Pa. $8.95

ANIMALS: 1,419 COPYRIGHT-FREE ILLUSTRATIONS OF MAMMALS, BIRDS, FISH, INSECTS, ETC., edited by Jim Harter. Clear wood engravings present, in extremely lifelike poses, over 1,000 species of animals. One of the most extensive pictorial sourcebooks of its kind. Captions. Index. 284pp. 9 × 12. 23766-4 Pa. $9.95

OBELISTS FLY HIGH, C. Daly King. Masterpiece of American detective fiction, long out of print, involves murder on a 1935 transcontinental flight—"a very thrilling story"—NY Times. Unabridged and unaltered republication of the edition published by William Collins Sons & Co. Ltd., London, 1935. 288pp. 5⅜ × 8½. (Available in U.S. only) 25036-9 Pa. $4.95

VICTORIAN AND EDWARDIAN FASHION: A Photographic Survey, Alison Gernsheim. First fashion history completely illustrated by contemporary photographs. Full text plus 235 photos, 1840–1914, in which many celebrities appear. 240pp. 6½ × 9¼. 24205-6 Pa. $6.00

THE ART OF THE FRENCH ILLUSTRATED BOOK, 1700–1914, Gordon N. Ray. Over 630 superb book illustrations by Fragonard, Delacroix, Daumier, Doré, Grandville, Manet, Mucha, Steinlen, Toulouse-Lautrec and many others. Preface. Introduction. 633 halftones. Indices of artists, authors & titles, binders and provenances. Appendices. Bibliography. 608pp. 8⅜ × 11¼. 25086-5 Pa. $24.95

THE WONDERFUL WIZARD OF OZ, L. Frank Baum. Facsimile in full color of America's finest children's classic. 143 illustrations by W. W. Denslow. 267pp. 5⅜ × 8½. 20691-2 Pa. $5.95

FRONTIERS OF MODERN PHYSICS: New Perspectives on Cosmology, Relativity, Black Holes and Extraterrestrial Intelligence, Tony Rothman, et al. For the intelligent layman. Subjects include: cosmological models of the universe; black holes; the neutrino; the search for extraterrestrial intelligence. Introduction. 46 black-and-white illustrations. 192pp. 5⅜ × 8½. 24587-X Pa. $6.95

THE FRIENDLY STARS, Martha Evans Martin & Donald Howard Menzel. Classic text marshalls the stars together in an engaging, non-technical survey, presenting them as sources of beauty in night sky. 23 illustrations. Foreword. 2 star charts. Index. 147pp. 5⅜ × 8½. 21099-5 Pa. $3.50

FADS AND FALLACIES IN THE NAME OF SCIENCE, Martin Gardner. Fair, witty appraisal of cranks, quacks, and quackeries of science and pseudoscience: hollow earth, Velikovsky, orgone energy, Dianetics, flying saucers, Bridey Murphy, food and medical fads, etc. Revised, expanded In the Name of Science. "A very able and even-tempered presentation."—The New Yorker. 363pp. 5⅜ × 8. 20394-8 Pa. $6.50

ANCIENT EGYPT: ITS CULTURE AND HISTORY, J. E Manchip White. From pre-dynastics through Ptolemies: society, history, political structure, religion, daily life, literature, cultural heritage. 48 plates. 217pp. 5⅜ × 8½. 22548-8 Pa. $4.95

SIR HARRY HOTSPUR OF HUMBLETHWAITE, Anthony Trollope. Incisive, unconventional psychological study of a conflict between a wealthy baronet, his idealistic daughter, and their scapegrace cousin. The 1870 novel in its first inexpensive edition in years. 250pp. 5⅜ × 8½. 24953-0 Pa. $5.95

LASERS AND HOLOGRAPHY, Winston E. Kock. Sound introduction to burgeoning field, expanded (1981) for second edition. Wave patterns, coherence, lasers, diffraction, zone plates, properties of holograms, recent advances. 84 illustrations. 160pp. 5⅜ × 8¼. (Except in United Kingdom) 24041-X Pa. $3.50

INTRODUCTION TO ARTIFICIAL INTELLIGENCE: SECOND, EN-LARGED EDITION, Philip C. Jackson, Jr. Comprehensive survey of artificial intelligence—the study of how machines (computers) can be made to act intelligently. Includes introductory and advanced material. Extensive notes updating the main text. 132 black-and-white illustrations. 512pp. 5⅜ × 8½. 24864-X Pa. $8.95

HISTORY OF INDIAN AND INDONESIAN ART, Ananda K. Coomaraswamy. Over 400 illustrations illuminate classic study of Indian art from earliest Harappa finds to early 20th century. Provides philosophical, religious and social insights. 304pp. 6⅛ × 9⅜. 25005-9 Pa. $8.95

THE GOLEM, Gustav Meyrink. Most famous supernatural novel in modern European literature, set in Ghetto of Old Prague around 1890. Compelling story of mystical experiences, strange transformations, profound terror. 13 black-and-white illustrations. 224pp. 5⅜ × 8½. (Available in U.S. only) 25025-3 Pa. $5.95

ARMADALE, Wilkie Collins. Third great mystery novel by the author of *The Woman in White* and *The Moonstone*. Original magazine version with 40 illustrations. 597pp. 5⅜ × 8½. 23429-0 Pa. $9.95

PICTORIAL ENCYCLOPEDIA OF HISTORIC ARCHITECTURAL PLANS, DETAILS AND ELEMENTS: With 1,880 Line Drawings of Arches, Domes, Doorways, Facades, Gables, Windows, etc., John Theodore Haneman. Sourcebook of inspiration for architects, designers, others. Bibliography. Captions. 141pp. 9 × 12. 24605-1 Pa. $6.95

BENCHLEY LOST AND FOUND, Robert Benchley. Finest humor from early 30's, about pet peeves, child psychologists, post office and others. Mostly unavailable elsewhere. 73 illustrations by Peter Arno and others. 183pp. 5⅜ × 8½. 22410-4 Pa. $3.95

ERTÉ GRAPHICS, Erté. Collection of striking color graphics: *Seasons, Alphabet, Numerals, Aces* and *Precious Stones*. 50 plates, including 4 on covers. 48pp. 9⅜ × 12¼. 23580-7 Pa. $6.95

THE JOURNAL OF HENRY D. THOREAU, edited by Bradford Torrey, F. H. Allen. Complete reprinting of 14 volumes, 1837–61, over two million words; the sourcebooks for *Walden*, etc. Definitive. All original sketches, plus 75 photographs. 1,804pp. 8½ × 12¼. 20312-3, 20313-1 Cloth., Two-vol. set $80.00

CASTLES: THEIR CONSTRUCTION AND HISTORY, Sidney Toy. Traces castle development from ancient roots. Nearly 200 photographs and drawings illustrate moats, keeps, baileys, many other features. Caernarvon, Dover Castles, Hadrian's Wall, Tower of London, dozens more. 256pp. 5⅜ × 8¼. 24898-4 Pa. $5.95

CHRISTMAS CUSTOMS AND TRADITIONS, Clement A. Miles. Origin, evolution, significance of religious, secular practices. Caroling, gifts, yule logs, much more. Full, scholarly yet fascinating; non-sectarian. 400pp. 5⅜ × 8½.
23354-5 Pa. $6.50

THE HUMAN FIGURE IN MOTION, Eadweard Muybridge. More than 4,500 stopped-action photos, in action series, showing undraped men, women, children jumping, lying down, throwing, sitting, wrestling, carrying, etc. 390pp. 7⅞ × 10⅝.
20204-6 Cloth. $19.95

THE MAN WHO WAS THURSDAY, Gilbert Keith Chesterton. Witty, fast-paced novel about a club of anarchists in turn-of-the-century London. Brilliant social, religious, philosophical speculations. 128pp. 5⅜ × 8½. 25121-7 Pa. $3.95

A CEZANNE SKETCHBOOK: Figures, Portraits, Landscapes and Still Lifes, Paul Cezanne. Great artist experiments with tonal effects, light, mass, other qualities in over 100 drawings. A revealing view of developing master painter, precursor of Cubism. 102 black-and-white illustrations. 144pp. 8¾ × 6⅜. 24790-2 Pa. $5.95

AN ENCYCLOPEDIA OF BATTLES: Accounts of Over 1,560 Battles from 1479 B.C. to the Present, David Eggenberger. Presents essential details of every major battle in recorded history, from the first battle of Megiddo in 1479 B.C. to Grenada in 1984. List of Battle Maps. New Appendix covering the years 1967–1984. Index. 99 illustrations. 544pp. 6½ × 9¼. 24913-1 Pa. $14.95

AN ETYMOLOGICAL DICTIONARY OF MODERN ENGLISH, Ernest Weekley. Richest, fullest work, by foremost British lexicographer. Detailed word histories. Inexhaustible. Total of 856pp. 6½ × 9¼.
21873-2, 21874-0 Pa., Two-vol. set $17.00

WEBSTER'S AMERICAN MILITARY BIOGRAPHIES, edited by Robert McHenry. Over 1,000 figures who shaped 3 centuries of American military history. Detailed biographies of Nathan Hale, Douglas MacArthur, Mary Hallaren, others. Chronologies of engagements, more. Introduction. Addenda. 1,033 entries in alphabetical order. xi + 548pp. 6½ × 9¼. (Available in U.S. only)
24758-9 Pa. $11.95

LIFE IN ANCIENT EGYPT, Adolf Erman. Detailed older account, with much not in more recent books: domestic life, religion, magic, medicine, commerce, and whatever else needed for complete picture. Many illustrations. 597pp. 5⅜ × 8½.
22632-8 Pa. $8.95

HISTORIC COSTUME IN PICTURES, Braun & Schneider. Over 1,450 costumed figures shown, covering a wide variety of peoples: kings, emperors, nobles, priests, servants, soldiers, scholars, townsfolk, peasants, merchants, courtiers, cavaliers, and more. 256pp. 8⅜ × 11¼. 23150-X Pa. $7.95

THE NOTEBOOKS OF LEONARDO DA VINCI, edited by J. P. Richter. Extracts from manuscripts reveal great genius; on painting, sculpture, anatomy, sciences, geography, etc. Both Italian and English. 186 ms. pages reproduced, plus 500 additional drawings, including studies for *Last Supper, Sforza* monument, etc. 860pp. 7⅞ × 10¾. (Available in U.S. only) 22572-0, 22573-9 Pa., Two-vol. set $25.90

AMERICAN CLIPPER SHIPS: 1833–1858, Octavius T. Howe & Frederick C. Matthews. Fully-illustrated, encyclopedic review of 352 clipper ships from the period of America's greatest maritime supremacy. Introduction. 109 halftones. 5 black-and-white line illustrations. Index. Total of 928pp. 5⅜ × 8½.
25115-2, 25116-0 Pa., Two-vol. set $17.90

TOWARDS A NEW ARCHITECTURE, Le Corbusier. Pioneering manifesto by great architect, near legendary founder of "International School." Technical and aesthetic theories, views on industry, economics, relation of form to function, "mass-production spirit," much more. Profusely illustrated. Unabridged translation of 13th French edition. Introduction by Frederick Etchells. 320pp. 6⅛ × 9¼. (Available in U.S. only)
25023-7 Pa. $8.95

THE BOOK OF KELLS, edited by Blanche Cirker. Inexpensive collection of 32 full-color, full-page plates from the greatest illuminated manuscript of the Middle Ages, painstakingly reproduced from rare facsimile edition. Publisher's Note. Captions. 32pp. 9⅜ × 12¼.
24345-1 Pa. $4.95

BEST SCIENCE FICTION STORIES OF H. G. WELLS, H. G. Wells. Full novel The Invisible Man, plus 17 short stories: "The Crystal Egg," "Aepyornis Island," "The Strange Orchid," etc. 303pp. 5⅜ × 8½. (Available in U.S. only)
21531-8 Pa. $4.95

AMERICAN SAILING SHIPS: Their Plans and History, Charles G. Davis. Photos, construction details of schooners, frigates, clippers, other sailcraft of 18th to early 20th centuries—plus entertaining discourse on design, rigging, nautical lore, much more. 137 black-and-white illustrations. 240pp. 6⅛ × 9¼.
24658-2 Pa. $5.95

ENTERTAINING MATHEMATICAL PUZZLES, Martin Gardner. Selection of author's favorite conundrums involving arithmetic, money, speed, etc., with lively commentary. Complete solutions. 112pp. 5⅜ × 8½.
25211-6 Pa. $2.95

THE WILL TO BELIEVE, HUMAN IMMORTALITY, William James. Two books bound together. Effect of irrational on logical, and arguments for human immortality. 402pp. 5⅜ × 8½.
20291-7 Pa. $7.50

THE HAUNTED MONASTERY and THE CHINESE MAZE MURDERS, Robert Van Gulik. 2 full novels by Van Gulik continue adventures of Judge Dee and his companions. An evil Taoist monastery, seemingly supernatural events; overgrown topiary maze that hides strange crimes. Set in 7th-century China. 27 illustrations. 328pp. 5⅜ × 8½.
23502-5 Pa. $5.95

CELEBRATED CASES OF JUDGE DEE (DEE GOONG AN), translated by Robert Van Gulik. Authentic 18th-century Chinese detective novel; Dee and associates solve three interlocked cases. Led to Van Gulik's own stories with same characters. Extensive introduction. 9 illustrations. 237pp. 5⅜ × 8½.
23337-5 Pa. $4.95

Prices subject to change without notice.

Available at your book dealer or write for free catalog to Dept. GI, Dover Publications, Inc., 31 East 2nd St., Mineola, N.Y. 11501. Dover publishes more than 175 books each year on science, elementary and advanced mathematics, biology, music, art, literary history, social sciences and other areas.